Appalachian Trail Guide
to New Hampshire-Vermont

Appalachian Trail Guide
to New Hampshire-Vermont

David Hooke
Field Editor

Ninth Edition

Appalachian Trail Conference
Harpers Ferry

Cover photo: Lost Pond, New Hampshire,
© 1998, Ann Gerckens

Published by the Appalachian Trail Conference
P.O. Box 807
Harpers Ferry, West Virginia 25425

Ninth edition
Printed in the United States of America on recycled paper.

ISBN 1-889386-02-2

Contents

Notice To All Trail Users

The information contained in this publication is the result of the best effort of the publisher, using information available to it at the time of printing. Changes resulting from maintenance work and relocations are constantly occurring, and, therefore, no published route can be regarded as precisely accurate at the time you read this notice.

Notices of pending relocations are indicated. Maintenance of the Trail is conducted by volunteers in maintaining clubs listed on pages 4 and 5, and questions about the exact route of the Trail should be addressed to the maintaining clubs or to the Appalachian Trail Conference, 799 Washington Street, P.O. Box 807, Harpers Ferry, W.Va. 25425-0807; telephone, (304) 535-6331. On the Trail, please pay close attention to—and follow—the white blazes and any directional signs.

Responsibility for Safety

It is extremely important to plan your hike, especially in places where water is scarce. Purify water drawn from any source. Water purity cannot be guaranteed. The Appalachian Trail Conference and the various maintaining clubs attempt to locate good sources of water along the Trail but have no control over these sources and cannot, in any sense, be responsible for the quality of the water at any given time. You must determine the safety of all water you use.

Certain risks are inherent in any Appalachian Trail hike. Each A.T. user must accept personal responsibility for his or her safety while on the Trail. The Appalachian Trail Conference and its member maintaining clubs cannot ensure the safety of any hiker on the Trail, and, when undertaking a hike on the Trail, each user thereby assumes the risk for any accident, illness, or injury that might occur on the Trail.

Enjoy your hike, but please take all appropriate precautions for your safety and well-being.

Although criminal acts are probably less common on the Appalachian Trail than in most other human environments, they do occur. Crimes of violence, including murder and rape, have taken place over the years. It should be noted that such serious crimes on the A.T. have a frequency rate on the order of fewer than one per year on a trail that enjoys three to four million visits in the same time. Even if such events are less common on the Trail than elsewhere, criminals can be more difficult to deal with because of the remoteness of most of the Trail. When hiking, you must assume the need for at least the same level of prudence as you would exercise if walking the streets of a strange city or an unknown neighborhood.

A few elementary suggestions can be noted. It is best not to hike alone, but do not assume safety just because you are hiking with a partner. Be cautious of strangers. Be sure that family and/or friends know your planned itinerary and timetable. If you customarily use a "Trail name," your home contacts should know what it is. Although telephones are rarely handy along the Trail, if you can reach one, dial 911, or ask the operator to connect you to the state police if you are the victim of, or a witness to, a crime.

The carrying of firearms is **not** recommended. The risks of accidental injury or death far outweigh any self-defense value that might result from arming oneself. In any case, guns are illegal on national parklands and in certain other jurisdictions as well.

Be prudent and cautious. Trust your gut.

How to Use This Guide

The Trail data in this guide have been divided into 18 New Hampshire-Vermont sections separated by highway crossings or other geographical features. The chapters for each Trail section are divided into three parts. The first part includes general information needed primarily for planning. This material is arranged under individual headings in the following order:

Brief Description of Section
Road Approaches
Maps
Shelters and Campsites
Regulations
Supplies and Services
Public Accommodations

The detailed "Trail Description," the actual guide to the footpath, follows in two parts. Data are given first for walking south on the Trail and then for walking north. Trail data are presented in both directions of travel so hikers do not have to mentally reverse Trail descriptions. A column of distances on the left gives the mileage from the start of the section to important points along the Trail. Each point (such as stream crossings, shelters, summits, or important turns) is briefly described, followed by directions to the next point.

The Appalachian Trail

The Appalachian Trail (A.T.) is a continuous, marked footpath extending more than 2,160 miles from Katahdin, a granite monolith in the central Maine wilderness, south to Springer Mountain in Georgia, mostly along the crest of the Appalachian Mountains.

The Trail traverses mostly public land in 14 states. Virginia has the longest section, with 547 miles, while West Virginia has the shortest, almost 25 miles along the Virginia-West Virginia boundary and a short swing into Harpers Ferry at the Maryland border. The highest elevation along the Trail is 6,643 feet at Clingmans Dome in the Great Smoky Mountains. The Trail is only 126 feet above sea level near its crossing of the Hudson River in New York.

Trail History

Credit for establishing the Trail belongs to three leaders and countless volunteers. The first proposal for the Trail to appear in print was an article by regional planner Benton MacKaye (rhymes with sky) of Shirley, Massachusetts, entitled, "An Appalachian Trail, a Project in Regional Planning," in the October 1921 issue of the *Journal of the American Institute of Architects*. He envisioned a footpath along the Appalachian ridge line where urban people could retreat to nature.

MacKaye's challenge kindled considerable interest, but, at the time, most of the outdoors/organizations that could participate in constructing such a trail were east of the Hudson River. Four existing trail systems could be incorporated into an A.T. The Appalachian Mountain Club (AMC) maintained an excellent series of trails in New England, but most ran north-south; the Trail could not cross New Hampshire until the chain of huts built and operated by the AMC permitted an east-west alignment. In Vermont, the southern 103 miles of the Long Trail, then being developed in the Green Mountains, were connected to the White Mountains by the trails of the Dartmouth Outing Club.

In 1923, a number of area hiking clubs that had formed the New York-New Jersey Trail Conference opened the first new section of the A.T., in the Harriman-Bear Mountain section of Palisades Interstate Park.

The Appalachian Trail Conference (ATC) was formed in 1925 to stimulate greater interest in MacKaye's idea and coordinate the clubs' work in choosing and building the route. The Conference remains a nonprofit educational organization of individuals and clubs of volunteers dedicated to maintaining, managing, and protecting the Appalachian Trail and its adjacent lands.

Although interest in the Trail spread to Pennsylvania and New England, little further work was done until 1926, when retired Judge Arthur Perkins of Hartford, Connecticut, began persuading groups to locate and cut the footpath through the wilderness. His enthusiasm provided the momentum that carried the Trail idea forward.

The southern states had few trails and even fewer clubs. The "skyline" route followed by the A.T. in the South was developed largely within the new national forests. A number of clubs were formed in various parts of the southern Appalachians to take responsibility for the Trail there.

Perkins interested Myron H. Avery in the Trail. Avery, chairman of the Conference from 1931 to 1952, enlisted the aid and coordinated the work of scores of volunteers who completed the Trail by August 14, 1937, when a Civilian Conservation Corps crew opened the last section (on the ridge between Spaulding and Sugarloaf mountains in Maine).

At the eighth meeting of the ATC, in June 1937, Conference member Edward B. Ballard successfully proposed a plan for an "Appalachian Trailway" that would set apart an area on each side of the Trail, dedicated to the interests of those who travel on foot.

Steps taken to effect this long-range protection program culminated first in an October 15, 1938, agreement between the National Park Service and the U.S. Forest Service for the promotion of an Appalachian Trailway through the relevant national parks and forests, extending one mile on each side of the Trail. Within this zone, no new parallel roads would be built or any other incompatible development allowed. Timber cutting would not be permitted within 200 feet of the Trail. Similar agreements, creating a zone one-quarter mile in width, were signed with most states through which the Trail passes.

After World War II, the encroachments of highways, housing developments, and summer resorts caused many relocations, and the problem of maintaining the Trail's wilderness character became more severe.

In 1968, Congress established a national system of trails and designated the Appalachian Trail and the incomplete Pacific Crest Trail as the initial scenic trails. The National Trails System Act directs the secretary of the interior, in consultation with the secretary of agriculture, to administer the Appalachian Trail primarily as a footpath and protect the Trail against incompatible activities and the use of motorized vehicles. Provision was also made for acquiring rights-of-way for the Trail, both inside and outside the boundaries of other federally administered areas.

In 1970, supplemental agreements under the act—among the National Park Service, the U.S. Forest Service, and the Appalachian Trail Conference—established the specific responsibilities of these organizations for initial mapping, selection of rights-of-way, relocations, maintenance, development, acquisition of land, and protection of a permanent Trail. Agreements also were signed between the park service and the various states, encouraging them to acquire and protect a right-of-way for the Trail outside federal land.

Slow progress of federal efforts and lack of initiative by some states led Congress to strengthen the National Trails System Act. President Jimmy Carter signed the amendment known as the Appalachian Trail Bill on March 21, 1978.

The new legislation emphasized the need for protecting the Trail, including acquiring a corridor, and authorized $90 million for that purpose. With less than 32 miles unprotected by mid-1998, this project is expected to be completed by the end of the decade.

In 1984, the Interior Department delegated the responsibility of managing the A.T. corridor lands outside established parks and forests to the Appalachian Trail Conference. The Conference and its clubs retain primary responsibility for maintaining the footpath.

The Conference is governed by a volunteer Board of Managers, consisting of a chair, three vice chairs, a treasurer, a secretary, an assistant secretary, 18 regional members, and two at-large members.

The Conference membership consists of organizations that maintain the Trail or contribute to the Trail project and individuals. ATC membership provides a subscription to *Appalachian Trailway News*, published five times a year, and 15 to 20 percent discounts on publications. The Conference also issues three newsletters, *The Register*, for Trail maintainers; *Trail Lands*, for contributors to its land-trust program; and *Inside ATC*, for principal donors.

The Conference publishes books on constructing and maintaining hiking trails, official A.T. guides, general information on hiking and Trail use, and other Trail-related books. Annual membership dues range from $18 to $30, with life memberships available for $500 (individual) or $750 (couple).

Membership forms and a complete list of publications are available from the Appalachian Trail Conference, P.O. Box 807, Harpers Ferry, W.Va. 25425; (304) 535-6331; (888) AT STORE (287-8673); or <www.atconf.org> on the Internet. The visitors center at ATC's central office (799 Washington Street) is open from nine a.m. to five p.m. (Eastern time) Monday through Friday and nine to four on weekends from mid-May through the last Sunday in October.

Maintaining Clubs

Three member clubs of the Appalachian Trail Conference maintain the Trail in New Hampshire and Vermont: The Appalachian Mountain Club (AMC) and the U.S. Forest Service maintain from Grafton Notch, Maine, south to Kinsman Notch; the Dartmouth Outing Club (DOC) maintains from Kinsman Notch south to Vt. 12; the Green Mountain Club (GMC) maintains from Vt. 12 south to the Massachusetts-Vermont state line. Each club has volunteers, summer crews, and caretakers who maintain the shelters and campsites.

AMC is a nonprofit volunteer organization of more than 46,000 members, established in Boston in 1876. The club publishes maps, guidebooks, and the periodical *Appalachia* and supports preservation efforts in the northeastern United States. It has an extensive system of shelters, trails, and mountain huts and maintains about 300 miles of trails, 120 miles of which are part of the A.T. in these states. For more information on the club, contact the Appalachian Mountain Club, Pinkham Notch Visitor Center, P.O. Box 298, Gorham, NH 03581, (603) 466-2721, or 5 Joy Street, Boston, MA 02108 (617) 523-0636.

DOC, the oldest college outing club in the United States, was formed in 1909. DOC maintains about 100 miles of trails, 75 of which are part of the A.T., and publishes several hiking maps and guidebooks. For more information on the club, contact Dartmouth Outing Club, P.O. Box 9, Hanover, NH 03755, (603) 646-2428.

GMC was formed in 1910 to establish and sponsor the Long Trail, one of the oldest long-distance hiking trails in the United States, predating the A.T. The Long Trail extends some 265 miles from Massachusetts to Canada and has 70 shelters and campsites. The Long

Trail and its nearly 175 miles of side trails compose a 440-mile system. (The southern 103 miles of the A.T. in Vermont coincide with the Long Trail.) GMC publishes several guidebooks and the *Long Trail News*. For additional information, write or call Green Mountain Club, Rural Route 1, Box 650, Waterbury Center, VT 05677, (802) 244-7037.

General Information

Hikers who use the Appalachian Trail for more than day-hiking need a thorough understanding of the Trail and should study the introductory parts of this guide carefully. Hikers planning an extended trip should write or call the Appalachian Trail Conference (ATC), P.O. Box 807, Harpers Ferry, W.Va. 25425-0807, (304) 535-6331, for advice and suggestions on long-distance hiking.

Except in the White Mountains, the Appalachian Trail in New Hampshire and Vermont is not in wilderness. From most elevations, towns or roads can be seen. If the route is lost, steady travel and persistence will probably bring the traveler to a highway. However, a poorly planned or ill-advised trip can result in unpleasant experiences and a night unintentionally spent in the woods.

The ruggedness of the terrain and the exertion required to walk the Appalachian Trail in New Hampshire and Vermont should not be underestimated. Do not travel here without adequate preparation, equipment, and physical conditioning.

All travelers in the New England woods should exercise extreme care with campfires or smoking.

Trail Marking

The Appalachian Trail is marked for travel in both directions. The marks are white-paint blazes about two inches wide and six inches high on trees, posts, and rocks. Occasionally, on open ledges, stone cairns identify the route. In some areas, diamond-shaped A.T. metal markers or other signs mark the Trail. Two blazes, one above the other, signal an obscure turn, a change in route, or a warning to check blazes carefully.

When the route is not obvious, normal marking procedure is to position the blazes so that anyone standing at one blaze will always be able to see the next. When the footway is unmistakable, blazes frequently are farther apart. If you have gone a quarter-mile without seeing a blaze, retrace your steps until you locate one and then check to ensure that you did not miss a turn. Since the Trail is marked for both directions, a glance back may locate blazes for travel in the opposite direction.

Side trails from the A.T. to water, viewpoints, and shelters usually are blazed in blue paint. Intersecting trails not part of the A.T. system are blazed in a variety of colors.

At trail junctions or near important features, the Trail route is often marked by signs. Some list mileages and other information.

Trail Relocations

Always follow the marked Trail. If it differs from the guidebook's Trail description, it is because the Trail was recently relocated in the area, probably to avoid a hazard or undesirable feature or to remove it from private property. If you use the old Trail, you may be trespassing and generating ill-will toward the Trail community.

Information on Trail relocations between guidebook revisions often is available from the ATC information department. Every effort has been made in this guide to alert you to relocations that may occur. Do not follow new trails that are not blazed, because they may not be open to the public yet.

Water

Although the A.T. may have sources of clean, potable water, any water source can become polluted. Most water sources along the Trail are unprotected and consequently very susceptible to contamination. All water should be purified by boiling, chemical treatment, and/or filtering before using. Take particular care to protect the purity of all water sources. Never wash dishes, clothes, or hands in the water source. Make sure food and human wastes are buried well away from any water source.

Weather

New England weather changes rapidly, especially in the mountains. During summer months, hikers can expect both hot and humid and cold and rainy days. Rain should be expected on all trips, and several rainy days in a row are common. If adequately equipped for wet conditions, hikers can travel all parts of the Trail, except perhaps sections above treeline, at any time of the summer in any weather.

(Occasionally, fords and stream crossings become hazardous due to high water. Waiting for the water level to lower is advisable.)

In addition to the generally damp soil in New England's hardwood and coniferous forests, many old roads used for the Trail have a growth of swale grass. Heavy dew, a frequent occurrence, makes for wet travel in the morning, and hikers should wear waterproof footgear.

Above timberline, bad weather often makes travel unsafe. Conditions of arctic severity can be encountered at higher elevations, even in summer. Publicized incidents of lost and injured travelers on the Presidential Range illustrate the serious dangers that can be encountered. Travelers here should be prepared physically and plan their hikes carefully. Adequate clothing and equipment are essential. No one should continue hiking in the Presidentials if storm warnings have been issued. About one hiker dies in the Whites each year.

The season for travel on the Appalachian Trail in New Hampshire and Vermont extends from May to November. The cooler, clearer weather and more satisfactory footway conditions during August, September, and October make those months preferable for travel.

At high elevations, snow is common in October and may occur earlier. When walking in late fall along alpine ridges, such as in the Presidential Range, be prepared for winter conditions.

Those hiking the entire Trail from Georgia to Maine late in the season may want to go directly to Katahdin from Vermont and hike back south to complete the Trail. That would prevent getting caught in an early Maine winter and arriving at Katahdin after Baxter State Park has closed for the season.

Snow and winter conditions are to be expected from November through April in New Hampshire and Vermont. The potential winter hiker should plan on encountering extended periods of severe cold (temperatures below zero Fahrenheit), extremely high winds, deep snow (requiring skis or snowshoes), shelters filled with snow, and cabins and huts closed for the winter. Deep and drifting snow also makes the Trail and its blazes exceedingly difficult to find. Any hiker planning winter travel on the Trail should first travel the route during summer.

Special equipment and training are needed for winter hiking and camping in New England. The rewards are great, but the hardships many. Do not underestimate the preparations necessary for a winter trip.

Equipment

The basic equipment rule is, never carry more than you need. Some items should be with you on every hike: the *A.T. Data Book*; guidebook and maps; canteen; flashlight, even on day trips; whistle; emergency food; tissues; matches and fire starter; multipurpose knife; compass; rain gear; proper shoes and socks; warm, dry spare clothes; and a first-aid kit (see page 24).

Take the time to consult periodicals, books, employees of outfitter stores, and other hikers before choosing the equipment that is best for you.

Getting Lost

Stop, if you have walked more than a quarter-mile (1,320 feet or roughly five minutes of hiking) without noticing a blaze or other Trail indicator (see page 6). If you find no indication of the Trail, retrace your course until one appears. The cardinal mistake behind unfortunate experiences is insisting on continuing when the route seems obscure or dubious. Haste, even in a desire to reach camp before dark, only complicates the difficulty. When in doubt, remain where you are to avoid straying farther from the route.

Hiking long distances alone should be avoided. If undertaken, it requires extra precautions. A lone hiker who suffers a serious accident or illness might be risking death if he has not planned for the remote chance of isolation. Your destinations and estimated times of arrival should be known to someone who will initiate inquiries or a search if you do not appear when expected. On long trips, reporting your plans and progress every few days is a wise precaution.

A lone hiker who loses his way and chooses to bushwhack toward town runs considerable risks if an accident occurs. If he falls helpless away from a little-used trail, he might not be discovered for days or even weeks. Lone hikers are advised to stay on the Trail (or at least on a trail), even if it means spending an unplanned night in the woods in sight of a distant electric light. Your pack should always contain enough food and water to sustain you until daylight, when a careful retracing of your steps might lead you back to a safe route.

Navigation

The compass variation, or declination, in New Hampshire and Vermont varies from 17 degrees at the Maine line to 14 degrees at the Massachusetts line. Therefore, true north varies from 14 to 17 degrees to the right of the compass pointer, depending upon the hiker's location. This considerable variation should be taken into account when the hiker orients himself or his map. The exact compass declination at different sections along the Trail is shown on each guide map.

Distress Signals

An emergency call for distress consists of three short calls, audible or visible, repeated at regular intervals. A whistle is particularly good for audible signals. Visible signals may include, in daytime, light flashed with a mirror or smoke puffs; at night, a flashlight or three small bright fires.

Anyone recognizing such a signal should acknowledge it with two responses—if possible, by the same method—then go to the distressed person and determine the nature of the emergency. Arrange for more aid, if necessary.

Most of the A.T. is used enough that, if you are injured, you can expect to be found. However, if an area is remote and the weather bad, fewer hikers will be on the Trail. In this case, it might be best to study the guide for the nearest place people are likely to be and attempt to move in that direction. If it is necessary to leave a heavy pack behind, be sure to take essentials, in case rescue is delayed. In bad weather, a night in the open without proper covering could be dangerous.

Pests

Black flies, mosquitoes, and "no-see-ums" (midges) are prevalent in New Hampshire and Vermont from May through August.

Hikers who have never experienced the dense clouds of black flies common in June are forewarned: They make life in the outdoors miserable. Wet or rainy weather will prolong the black-fly season. Fly-proof tents are essential for a good night's sleep. Even then, the tiny no-see-ums sometimes slip through mosquito netting. Several good insect repellents are on the market, but, in periods of heavy fly hatches, they are not very effective.

In the mountains, most insects disappear with the cooler evening temperatures. Black flies usually disappear by the middle of September but can continue into October.

Poisonous snakes are rare along this section of the Trail.

Poison ivy grows here but is rare at the Trail's higher elevations.

Parking

Park in designated areas. If you leave your car parked overnight unattended, you may be risking theft or vandalism—*do not leave valuables in your car*. Please do not ask Trail neighbors for permission to park your car near their homes.

Hunting

Hunting is prohibited in many state parks and on National Park Service lands—whether acquired specifically for protection of the Appalachian Trail or as part of another unit of the national park system. However, most of the boundary lines that identify these lands have yet to be surveyed. It may be very difficult for hunters to know where they are on NPS Trail lands. Hunters who approach the A.T. from the side, and who do not know that they are on Trail lands, may also have no idea that the Trail is nearby. The Trail traverses several other types of landownership, including national forest lands and state gamelands, on which hunting is allowed as part of a multiple-use management plan (national forests) or specifically for game (state gamelands).

Some hunting areas are marked by permanent or temporary signs, but any sign is subject to vandalism and removal. The prudent hiker, especially in the fall, makes himself aware of local hunting seasons and wears blaze orange during them.

Trail Ethics

In New Hampshire and Vermont, the Appalachian Trail crosses very little private property, but in all cases, treat the land with care to preserve the beauty of the Trail environment and ensure the Trail's integrity.

Improper use can endanger the continuity of the Trail. Private landowners may order hikers off their property and close the route. Vandalism, camping and fires where prohibited, and other abuse can result in Trail closure. Please follow a few basic guidelines:

Do not cut, deface, or destroy trees, flowers, or any other natural or constructed feature.

Do not damage fences or leave gates open.

Do not litter. Carry out all trash. Do not bury it for animals or others to uncover.

Do not carry firearms.

Be careful with fire. Extinguish all burning material; a forest fire can start more easily than many realize.

In short: Take nothing but pictures, leave nothing but footprints, kill nothing but time.

Dogs are often a nuisance to other hikers and to property owners. Landowners complain of dogs running loose and soiling yards. The territorial instincts of dogs often result in fights with other dogs. Dogs also frighten some hikers and chase wildlife. If a pet cannot be controlled, it should be left at home; otherwise, it will generate ill-will toward the Appalachian Trail and its users. Also, many at-home pets' muscles, foot pads, and sleeping habits are not adaptable to the rigors of A.T. hiking.

Ask for water and seek directions and information from homes along the Trail only in an emergency. Some residents receive more hiker visitors than they enjoy. Respect the privacy of people living near the Trail.

Keep to the defined Trail. Cutting across switchbacks, particularly on graded trails, disfigures the Trail, complicates route-finding, and causes erosion. The savings in time or distance are minimal; the damage is great. In areas where log walkways, steps, or rock treadway indicate special trail construction, take pains to use them. Those have been installed to reduce trail-widening and erosion. In areas above the treeline, it is of utmost importance to stay on the Trail. Plants and soil in these areas are extremely sensitive.

Group Hikes and Special Events

Special events, group hikes, or other group activities that could degrade the Appalachian Trail's natural or cultural resources or social values should be avoided. Examples of such activities include publicized spectator events, commercial or competitive activities, or programs involving large groups.

The policy of the Appalachian Trail Conference is that groups planning to spend one or more nights on the Trail should not exceed 10 people, and day-use groups should not exceed 25 people, unless the local maintaining organization has made special arrangements to both accommodate the group and protect Trail values.

Publications

The Appalachian Trail Conference, as part of its commitment to serve as the official clearinghouse of information on the Trail, publishes a number of books other than guides and also sells books from other publishers. ATC members receive a discount on most publications sold through the Conference. Proceeds from sales help underwrite the costs of A.T. maintenance and Trail-corridor management.

A complete list of the publications and merchandise available from ATC can be obtained by writing ATC at P.O. Box 807, Harpers Ferry, WV 25425, or <sales@atconf.org>, or calling (304) 535-6331 or (888) AT STORE); electronic shopping is available at <www.atconf.org> on the Internet .

Those seeking basic information about hiking and equipment might consider joining one of the hiking clubs connected with ATC.

First Aid Along the Trail

By Robert Ohler, M.D., and the
Appalachian Trail Conference

Hikers encounter a wide variety of terrain and climatic conditions along the Appalachian Trail. Prepare for the possibility of injuries. Some of the more common Trail-related medical problems are briefly discussed below.

Preparation is key to a safe trip. If possible, every hiker should take the free courses in advanced first aid and cardiopulmonary-resuscitation (CPR) techniques offered in most communities by the American Red Cross.

Even without this training, you can be prepared for accidents. Emergency situations can develop. Analyses of serious accidents have shown that a substantial number originate at home, in the planning stage of the trip. Think about communications. Have you informed your relatives and friends about your expedition: locations, schedule, and time of return? Has all of your equipment been carefully checked? Considering the season and altitude, have you provided for water, food, and shelter?

While hiking, set your own comfortable pace. If you are injured or lost or a storm strikes, stop. Remember, your brain is your most important survival tool. Inattention can start a chain of events leading to disaster.

If an accident occurs, treat the injury first. If outside help is needed, at least one person should stay with the injured hiker. Two people should go for help and carry with them notes on the exact location of the accident, what has been done to aid the injured hiker, and what help is needed.

The injured will need encouragement, assurances of help, and confidence in your competence. Treat him gently. Keep him supine, warm, and quiet. Protect him from the weather with insulation below and above him. Examine him carefully, noting all possible injuries.

General Emergencies

Back or neck injuries: Immobilize the victim's entire body, where he lies. Protect head and neck from movement if the neck is injured, and treat as a fracture. Transportation must be on a rigid frame, such as a litter or a door. The spinal cord could be severed by inexpert handling. This type of injury must be handled by a large group of experienced personnel. Obtain outside help.

Bleeding: Stop the flow of blood by using a method appropriate to the amount and type of bleeding. Exerting pressure over the wound with the fingers, with or without a dressing, may be sufficient. Minor arterial bleeding can be controlled with local pressure and bandaging. Major arterial bleeding might require compressing an artery against a bone to stop the flow of blood. Elevate the arm or legs above the heart. To stop bleeding from an artery in the leg, place a hand in the groin, and press toward the inside of the leg. Stop arterial bleeding from an arm by placing a hand between the armpit and elbow and pressing toward the inside of the arm.

Apply a tourniquet only if you are unable to control severe bleeding by pressure and elevation. *Warning: This method should be used only when the limb will be lost anyway.* Once applied, a tourniquet should only be removed by medical personnel equipped to stop the bleeding by other means and to restore lost blood. The tourniquet should be located between the wound and the heart. If there is a traumatic amputation (loss of hand, leg, or foot), place the tourniquet two inches above the amputation.

Blisters: Good boot fit, without points of irritation or pressure, should be proven before a hike. Always keep feet dry while hiking. Prevent blisters by responding early to any discomfort. Place adhesive tape or moleskin over areas of developing redness or soreness. If irritation can be relieved, allow blister fluid to be reabsorbed. If a blister forms and continued irritation makes draining it necessary, wash the area with soap and water and prick the edge of the blister with a needle that has been sterilized by the flame of a match. Bandage with a sterile gauze pad and moleskin.

Dislocation of a leg or arm joint is extremely painful. Do not try to put it back in place. Immobilize the entire limb with splints in the position it is found.

Exhaustion is caused by inadequate food consumption, dehydration and salt deficiency, overexertion, or all three. The victim may lose motivation, slow down, gasp for air, complain of weakness, dizziness, nausea, or headache. Treat by feeding, especially carbohydrates. Slowly replace lost water (normal fluid intake should be two to four quarts per day). Give salt dissolved in water (one teaspoon per cup). In the case of overexertion, rest is essential.

Fractures of legs, ankles, or arms must be splinted before moving the victim. After treating wounds, use any available material that will offer firm support, such as tree branches or boards. Pad each side of the arm or leg with soft material, supporting and immobilizing the joints above and below the injury. Bind the splints together with strips of cloth.

Shock should be expected after all injuries. It is a potentially fatal depression of bodily functions that is made more critical with improper handling, cold, fatigue, and anxiety. Relieve the pain as quickly as possible. Do not administer aspirin if severe bleeding is present; Tylenol or other nonaspirin pain relievers are safe to give.

Look for nausea, paleness, trembling, sweating, or thirst. Lay the hiker flat on his back, and raise his feet slightly, or position him, if he can be safely moved, so his head is down the slope. Protect him from the wind, and keep him as warm as possible. A campfire will help.

Sprains: Look or feel for soreness or swelling. Bandage and treat as a fracture. Cool and raise joint.

Wounds (except eye wounds) should be cleaned with soap and water. If possible, apply a clean dressing to protect the wound from further contamination.

Chilling and Freezing Emergencies

Every hiker should be familiar with the symptoms, treatment, and methods of preventing the common and sometimes fatal condition of *hypothermia*. Wind chill and/or body wetness, particularly aggravated by fatigue and hunger, can rapidly drain body heat to dangerously low levels. This often occurs at temperatures well above freezing. Shivering, lethargy, mental slowing, and confusion are early symptoms of hypothermia, which can begin without the victim's realizing it and, if untreated, can lead to death.

Always keep dry, spare clothing and a water-repellent windbreaker in your pack, and wear a hat in chilling weather. Wet clothing loses much of its insulating value, although polypropylene, synthetic pile, and wool are warmer than other fabrics when wet. Always, when in chilling conditions, suspect the onset of hypothermia.

To treat this potentially fatal condition, immediately seek shelter and warm the entire body, preferably by placing it in a sleeping bag and administering warm liquids. The addition of another person's body heat may aid in warming.

Wind Chill Chart

Actual Temperature (°F)

	50	40	30	20	10	0	-10	-20	-30	-40	-50
	Equivalent Temperature (°F)										
0	50	40	30	20	10	0	-10	-20	-30	-40	-50
5	48	37	27	16	6	-5	-15	-26	-36	-47	-57
10	40	28	16	4	-9	-21	-33	-46	-58	-70	-83
15	36	22	9	-5	-18	-36	-45	-58	-72	-85	-99
20	32	18	4	-10	-25	-39	-53	-67	-82	-96	-110
25	30	16	0	-15	-29	-44	-59	-74	-88	-104	-118
30	28	13	-2	-18	-33	-48	-63	-79	-94	-109	-125
35	27	11	-4	-20	-35	-49	-67	-82	-98	-113	-129
40	26	10	-6	-21	-37	-53	-69	-85	-100	-116	-132

Wind Speed (mph)

This chart illustrates the important relationship between wind and temperature.

A sign of *frostbite* is grayish or waxy, yellow-white spots on the skin. The frozen area will be numb. To thaw, warm the frozen part by direct contact with bare flesh. When first frozen, a cheek, nose, or chin can often be thawed by covering with a hand taken from a warm glove. Superficially frostbitten hands sometimes can be thawed by placing them under armpits, on the stomach, or between the thighs. With a partner, feet can be treated similarly. Do not rub frozen flesh.

Frozen layers of deeper tissue beneath the skin are characterized by a solid, "woody" feeling and an inability to move the flesh over bony prominences. Tissue loss is minimized by rapid rewarming of the area in water slightly below 105 degrees Fahrenheit (measure accurately with a thermometer).

Thawing of a frozen foot should not be attempted until the patient has been evacuated to a place where rapid, controlled thawing can take place. Walking on a frozen foot is entirely possible and does not cause increased damage. Walking after thawing is impossible.

Never rewarm over a stove or fire. This "cooks" flesh and results in extensive loss of tissue.

Treatment of a deep freezing injury after rewarming must be done in a hospital.

Heat Emergencies

Exposure to extremely high temperatures, high humidity, and direct sunlight can cause health problems.

Heat cramps are usually caused by strenuous activity in high heat and humidity, when sweating depletes salt levels in blood and tissues. Symptoms are intermittent cramps in legs and the abdominal wall and painful spasms of muscles. Pupils of eyes may dilate with each spasm. The skin becomes cold and clammy. Treat with rest and salt dissolved in water (one teaspoon of salt per glass).

Heat exhaustion, caused by physical exercise during prolonged exposure to heat, is a breakdown of the body's heat-regulating system. The circulatory system is disrupted, reducing the supply of blood to vital organs such as the brain, heart, and lungs. The victim can have heat cramps and sweat heavily. Skin is moist and cold with face flushed, then pale. The pulse can be unsteady, and blood pressure low. He may vomit and be delirious. Place the victim in shade, flat on his back, with feet 8-12 inches higher than his head. Give him sips of salt water—half a glass every 15 minutes—for about an hour. Loosen his clothes. Apply cold cloths.

Heat stroke and *sun stroke* are caused by the failure of the heat-regulating system to cool the body by sweating. They are emergency, life-threatening conditions. Body temperature can rise to 106 degrees or higher. Symptoms include weakness, nausea, headache, heat cramps, exhaustion, body temperature rising rapidly, pounding pulse, and high blood pressure. The victim may be delirious or comatose. Sweating will stop before heat stroke becomes apparent. Armpits may be dry and skin flushed and pink, then turning ashen or purple in later stages. Move victim to a cool place immediately. Cool the body in any way possible (*e.g.*, sponging). Body temperature must be regulated artificially from outside the body until the heat-regulating system can be rebalanced. Be careful not to overchill once temperature goes below 102 degrees.

Heat weakness: Symptoms are fatigue, headache, mental and physical inefficiency, heavy sweating, high pulse rate, and general weakness. Drink plenty of water, find as cool a spot as possible, keep quiet, and replenish salt loss.

Sunburn causes redness of the skin, discoloration, swelling, and pain. It occurs rapidly and can be severe at higher elevations. It can be prevented by applying a commercial sun screen; zinc oxide is the most effective. Treat by protecting from further exposure and covering the area with ointment and a dressing. Give the victim large amounts of fluids.

Artificial Respiration

Artificial respiration might be required when an obstruction constricts the air passages or after respiratory failure caused by air being depleted of oxygen, such as after electrocution, by drowning, or because of toxic gases in the air. Quick action is necessary if the victim's lips, fingernail beds, or tongue have become blue, if he is unconscious, or if the pupils of his eyes become enlarged.

If food or a foreign body is lodged in the air passage and coughing is ineffective, try to remove it with the fingers. If the foreign body is inaccessible, grasp the victim from behind, and with one hand hold the opposite wrist just below the breastbone. Squeeze rapidly and firmly, expelling air forcibly from the lungs to expel the foreign body. Repeat this maneuver two to three times, if necessary.

If breathing stops, administer artificial respiration, as air can be forced around the obstruction into the lungs. The mouth-to-mouth, or mouth-to-nose, method of forcing air into the victim's lungs should be used. The preferred method, protecting yourself with a mask or other cloth barrier, is:

1. Clear the victim's mouth of any obstructions.
2. Place one hand under the victim's neck, and lift.
3. Place heel of the other hand on the forehead, and tilt head backwards. (Maintain this position during procedure.) Use thumb and index finger to pinch nostrils.

4. Open your mouth, and make a seal with it over the victim's mouth. If the victim is a small child, cover both the nose and the mouth.
5. Breathe deeply, and blow out about every five seconds, or 12 breaths a minute.
6. Watch victim's chest for expansion.
7. Listen for exhalation.

Lyme Disease

Lyme disease is contracted from bites of certain infected ticks. Hikers should be aware of the symptoms and monitor themselves and their partners for signs of the disease. When treated early, Lyme disease can usually be cured with antibiotics.

Inspect yourself for ticks and tick bites at the end of each day. The four types of ticks known to spread Lyme disease are smaller than the dog tick, about the size of a pin head, and not easily seen. They are often called "deer ticks" because they feed during one stage of their life cycle on deer, a host for the disease.

The early signs of a tick bite infected with Lyme disease are a red spot with a white center that enlarges and spreads, severe fatigue, chills, headaches, muscle aches, fever, malaise, and a stiff neck. However, one-quarter of all people with an infected tick bite show none of the early symptoms.

Later effects of the disease, which may not appear for months or years, are severe fatigue, dizziness, shortness of breath, cardiac irregularities, memory and concentration problems, facial paralysis, meningitis, shooting pains in the arms and legs, and other symptoms resembling multiple sclerosis, brain tumors, stroke, alcoholism, depression, Alzheimer's disease, and *anorexia nervosa*.

It may be necessary to contact a university medical center or other research center if you suspect you have been bitten by an infected tick. It is not believed people can build a lasting immunity to Lyme disease. For that reason, a hiker who has contracted and been treated for the disease should still take precautions.

Hantavirus

The Trail community learned in the fall of 1994 that—18 months earlier—an A.T. thru-hiker had contracted a form of the deadly hantavirus about the same time (June 1993) the infection was in the news because of outbreaks in the Four Corners area of the Southwest. After a month-long hospitalization, he recovered fully and came back to the A.T. in 1995 to finish his hike.

Federal and state health authorities tested various sites in Virginia that fall—looking for infected deer mice, the principal carriers in the East—but found no mice infected with the virus, which apparently is most often picked up when it is airborne. (The virus travels from an infected rodent through its evaporating urine, droppings, and saliva into the air.)

The health authorities said they themselves would worry more about rabies, never reported on the Trail. Hantavirus is extremely rare and difficult to "catch." Prevention measures for hikers are relatively simple: Air out a closed, mice-infested structure for an hour before occupying it; don't sleep on mouse droppings (use a mat or tent); don't handle mice; treat your water; wash off your hands if you think you have handled droppings.

If you are truly concerned about hantavirus, call ATC for a fact sheet.

Lightning Strikes

Although the odds of being struck by lightning are low, 200 to 400 people a year are killed by lightning in the United States. Respect the force of lightning, and seek shelter during a storm.

Do not start a hike if thunderstorms are likely. If caught in a storm, immediately find shelter. Large buildings are best; tents offer no protection. When indoors, stay away from windows, open doors, fireplaces, and metal objects. Do not hold a potential lightning rod, such as a fishing pole. Avoid tall structures, such as ski lifts, flagpoles, powerline towers, and the tallest trees or hilltops. If you cannot enter a building, take shelter in a stand of smaller trees. Avoid clearings. If caught in the open, crouch down, or roll into a ball. If you are in water, get out. Spread out groups, so that everyone is not struck by a single bolt.

If a person is struck by lightning or splashed by a charge hitting a nearby object, the victim will probably be thrown, perhaps a great distance. Clothes can be burned or torn. Metal objects (such as belt buckles) may be hot, and shoes blown off. The victim often has severe muscle contractions (which can cause breathing difficulties), confusion, and temporary blindness or deafness. In more severe cases, the victim may have feathered or sunburst patterns of burns over the skin or ruptured eardrums. He may lose consciousness or breathe irregularly. Occasionally, victims stop breathing and suffer cardiac arrest.

If someone is struck by lightning, perform artificial respiration (see pages 19 and 20) and CPR until emergency technicians arrive or you can transport the injured to a hospital. Lightning victims may be unable to breathe independently for 15 to 30 minutes but can recover quickly once they can breathe on their own. Do not give up early; a seemingly lifeless individual can be saved if you breathe for him promptly after the strike.

Assume that the victim was thrown a great distance; protect the spine, treat other injuries, then transport him to the hospital.

Snakebites

Reports of bites are extremely rare, but hikers on the Appalachian Trail may encounter copperheads and rattlesnakes on their journey. These are pit vipers, characterized by triangular heads, vertical elliptical pupils, two or less hinged fangs on the front part of the jaw (fangs are replaced every six to 10 weeks), heat-sensory facial pits on the sides of the head, and a single row of scales on the underbelly by the tail. Rattlesnakes have rattles on the tail.

The best way to avoid being bitten by poisonous snakes is to avoid their known habitats and reaching into dark areas (use a walking stick to move suspicious objects). Wear protective clothing, especially on feet and lower legs. Do not hike alone or at night in snake territory; always have a flashlight and walking stick. If you see a snake, walk away; you can outdistance it in three steps. Do not handle snakes. A dead snake can bite and envenomate you with a reflex action for 20 to 60 minutes after its death.

Not all snakebites result in envenomation, even if the snake is poisonous. The signs of envenomation are one or more fang marks in addition to rows of teeth marks, burning pain, and swelling at the bite (swelling usually begins within five to ten minutes of envenomation and can become very severe). Lips, face, and scalp may tingle and become numb 30 to 60 minutes after the bite. (If those symptoms are immediate and the victim is frightened and excited, then they are most likely due to hyperventilation or shock.) Thirty to 90 minutes after the bite, the victim's eyes and mouth may twitch, and he may have a rubbery or metallic taste in his mouth. He may sweat, experience weakness, nausea, and vomiting, or faint one to two hours after the bite. Bruising at the bite usually begins within two to three hours, and large blood blisters may develop within six to 10 hours. The victim may have difficulty breathing, have bloody urine and vomit blood, and collapse six to 12 hours.

If someone you are with has been bitten by a snake, act quickly. *The definitive treatment for snake-venom poisoning is the proper administration of antivenom. Get the victim to a hospital immediately.*

Keep the victim calm. Increased activity can spread the venom and the illness. Retreat out of snake's striking range, but try to identify it. Check for signs of envenomation. Immediately transport the victim to the nearest hospital. If possible, splint the body part that was bitten, to avoid unnecessary motion. If a limb was bitten, keep it at a level below the heart. *Do not apply ice directly to the wound.* If it will take longer than two hours to reach medical help, and the bite is on an arm or leg, place a 2 x 2¼"-thick cloth pad over the bite and firmly wrap the limb (ideally, with an elastic wrap) directly over the bite and six inches on either side, taking care to check for adequate circulation to the fingers and toes. This wrap may slow the spread of venom.

Do not use a snakebite kit or attempt to remove the poison. This is the advice of Maynard H. Cox, founder and director of the Worldwide Poison Bite Information Center. He advises medical personnel on the treatment of snakebites. If you hike in fear of snakebites, carry his number, (904) 264-6512, and when you're bitten, give the number to the proper medical personnel. Your chances of being bitten by a poisonous snake are very, very slim. Do not kill the snake; in most Trail areas, it is a legally protected species.

First-Aid Kit

The following kit is suggested for those who have had no first-aid or other medical training. It weighs about a pound and occupies about a 3" x 6" x 9" space.

Eight 4" x 4" gauze pads
Four 3" x 4" gauze pads
Five 2" bandages
10 1" bandages
Six alcohol prep pads
10 large butterfly closures
One triangular bandage (40")
Two 3" rolls of gauze
Twenty tablets of aspirin-free pain-killer
One 15' roll of 2" adhesive tape
One 3" Ace bandage
Twenty salt tablets
One 3" x 4" moleskin
Three safety pins
One small scissors
One tweezers
Personal medications as necessary

Shelters and Campsites

The A.T. in New Hampshire and Vermont includes a chain of campsites a day's hike or less apart. Most campsites include a shelter or cabin. Shelters are generally three-sided with open fronts. They may have bunks or a wooden floor that serves as a sleeping platform. Water, a toilet, a fireplace, and, in some cases, tent platforms are usually available. Hikers must bring sleeping equipment, cooking utensils, and a stove.

The introductory chapters on Vermont and New Hampshire describe each state's shelter and campsite facilities. [Note: Mileages between campsites start from the site itself (if on the Trail) or from the point where the side trail leaves the A.T. In other words, distances are simply route miles along the A.T. and do not include the length of side trails (see Trail Descriptions for length of side trails).] The "Shelters and Campsites" sections at the beginning of each Trail section describe the shelters and campsites of that section in detail. Those descriptions are ordered from north to south.

The chain of shelters and campsites is broken in the Presidential and Carter-Moriah ranges of New Hampshire. The few shelters available are a day's travel or more apart, because harsh weather in the Presidential Range makes shelters above timberline unfeasible. No shelters or campsites are located between Imp Campsite in the Carter-Moriah Range and Osgood Tentsite in the Presidential Range, a distance of 20 miles. In those areas, camping is often possible, or the hiker may choose to make use of the Appalachian Mountain Club (AMC) huts. In the White Mountains, the AMC hut system extends along the A.T. for approximately 62 miles, from Carter Notch in the Carter-Moriah Range to Lonesome Lake just below (northeast of) Kinsman Ridge. The huts are closed structures with dormitories and blankets. Dinner and breakfast are served. Using the huts permits crossing the White Mountains with minimum equipment. Complete information on the huts appears under "Hiking and Camping Information" in the New Hampshire chapter of this guide, starting on page 52, and in the individual sections where huts are located.

Shelters are provided primarily for the long-distance hiker who may have no other shelter. People planning short overnight hikes are asked to carry tents. This is also good insurance, since the Trail is used heavily during the summer months, and shelters are usually crowded. Organizations are asked to keep their groups small (eight to 10 people, including leaders), carry tents, and not monopolize shelters. Although shelter use is on a first-come, first-served basis, please cooperate and consider the needs of others. If the shelter has a register, please sign it.

The shelters are provided for overnight stays only, and, except in cases of bad weather, injury, or other emergency, please do not stay more than one or two nights. Hunters, fishermen, and other nonhikers are asked not to use the shelters as a base of operation.

Use facilities, maintained by volunteers, with care and respect. Do not carve initials or write on shelter walls. Do not use an axe on any part of the shelter or use benches or tables as chopping blocks. The roofing, especially corrugated aluminum, is easily damaged; do not climb on it. Avoid putting excess weight or strain on wire bunks; the breaking of one wire endangers air mattresses and sleeping bags.

Be considerate of the rights and needs of others around the shelters, especially during meal times. Between nine p.m. and seven a.m., keep noise to a minimum.

Preserve the surroundings and the ecological integrity of the site. Vandalism and carelessness mar the site's pristine nature.

Leave the shelter in good condition. Food left in the shelter may cause damage by animals. Remove unburned trash from the fireplace, including aluminum foil. Pack out excess food and refuse.

Low-Impact Tips

- Travel only on foot.
- Stay on the footpath; short cuts erode the land and make more work for the volunteers who take care of the Trail for you.
- **If you packed it in, pack it out!** Help out by picking up any trash others have left behind, too.
- Travel in small groups. Four to six is ideal; 25 is the maximum for dayhikes.
- Camp at areas established for overnight use.
- Camp in groups of 10 or less. If you have more than five or six people in your group, set up your tents in an appropriate area so all the hikers at a site can use the common facilities. Leave the shelters for solo hikers and smaller groups.
- Purify all drinking and dish-washing water before you use it.

- Take only pictures, leave only the lightest of footprints. Remember, nuts, berries, and flowers may be the only food of the creatures that call this home all the time.
- Use a small backpacking stove instead of building campfires. **Never, ever cut live branches or trees for firewood.**
- Stay on Trail lands; if you wander too far, you may be trespassing on private property.
- Use the privy if the campsite has one nearby. Otherwise, dispose of your waste in a "cathole" 6"-8" deep, 4"-6" wide, at least 50' from the Trail, and 200' from water, campsites, and shelters.
- Don't wash or rinse your dishes in or near open water.
- Respect other hikers—and the wildlife—by traveling and camping quietly.
- Pets are best left at home. If you do bring them, keep them on a leash and away from water sources and clean up after them.

Fires

Increasing Trail use constantly decreases available firewood. In some areas, lack of firewood is a serious problem. Use portable cooking stoves instead of fires whenever possible. If you make a fire, use wood economically. Do not build bonfires.

Fires at campsites and shelters should be built in the fireplaces provided. Permits are not required, but watch for special bulletins about fire use. Details on fire regulations and permits are included where pertinent under "Hiking and Camping Information."

No matter how many people use the fire at each campsite, all must share responsibility for it. Be especially alert for sparks blown from fires during high winds.

If you use wood stored in a shelter or at a campsite, replenish the supply. Many sites have suffered visible deterioration from hikers cutting wood from trees within the site. Use dead or downed wood only, even if this requires searching. Do not cut live trees.

Upon leaving the campsite, even temporarily, make sure your fire is out completely. Douse with water, and overturn the ashes until all underlying coals are extinguished.

Water

The drinking-water supply beside a shelter or campsite may be a lake, a stream, or a spring. Often a hiker mistakenly assumes that water in a natural and relatively uninhabited area is safe to use. The purity of any unprotected water source cannot be guaranteed. All water should be boiled, chemically treated, and/or filtered with a filter claiming to be effective against *giardia*.

Avoid contaminating the water supply and the surrounding area. Dishes, clothes, and hands should never be washed in the water supply. Draw water from the supply, and wash elsewhere.

Animals

Chipmunks, mice, squirrels, and black bears may visit campsites searching for food. Maintain a clean camp. The best precaution is to hang food in a bag between two trees, at least ten feet from the ground and four feet from the nearest tree.

Beaver dams sometimes cause problems in low regions or along streams that flood sections of the Trail. This can be confusing if encountered before the route is detoured. Note where the Trail markings enter the flowage and then detour to one side, following the edge of the water until the Trail markings are seen again.

In some sections, moose frequent the Trail. Hikers should maintain a safe distance from these unpredictable, very large animals, with a handy climbable tree nearby.

Transportation to the Trail

Most sections in New Hampshire and Vermont are accessible by major highways, but the following exceptions are noteworthy.

The northern end of Section One in New Hampshire (the southern Mahoosuc Range), the only section without road access, must be reached by trails. Either follow the A.T. south from Grafton Notch, or approach from the Success Pond Road, beginning in Berlin, New Hampshire, and ascend to the A.T. near the New Hampshire-Maine state line, the northern end of the section, *via* the Success or Carlo Col trails.

The Danby-Landgrove Road, the southern end of Section Five and the northern end of Section Six in Vermont, is paved from Danby on U.S. 7 east to the Trail crossing but is gravel-surfaced onward to Landgrove. The Trail is best approached from Danby but can be reached from either direction. This road is not plowed in winter.

The Arlington-West Wardsboro Road, the southern end of Section Seven and the northern end of Section Eight in Vermont, is gravel-surfaced west of the Trail crossing to East Arlington but paved for much of the distance east of the Trail to West Wardsboro. In spring, the Trail is best approached from West Wardsboro (Vt. 100) but can be easily approached from either direction. The road is not plowed in winter between East Arlington and Stratton.

Except for the Success Pond Road, shown on Map No. 1, roads providing access to section ends are shown on most highway maps. Maps and other information concerning New Hampshire and Vermont are available from the New Hampshire Office of Travel and Tourism Development, 172 Pembrooke Road, P.O. Box 1856, Concord, NH 03302-1856, (603) 271-2665; the Vermont Department of Travel and Marketing, 6 Baldwin Street, Montpelier, VT 05602, (802) 828-3236 or 1-800-VERMONT.

In addition to the major roads at section ends, a number of other roads, often gravel or dirt, intersect the Trail in the middle of sections. Those are shown on the guide maps.

Shuttles

AMC runs a hiker shuttle service in the White Mountains from June to September. You may also write ATC for its shuttle list. For information on AMC schedules and rates, write to AMC Reservations or contact ATC (see "Important Addresses," page 219).

Bus Lines

In New Hampshire and Vermont, daily bus service is available directly to, or within easy access of, the A.T. By using connecting bus lines, transportation can be arranged from most of the United States. Bus lines offering service to the Trail are Concord Trailways, Englander Coach Lines, Greyhound, and Vermont Transit Lines.

Air Service

Commercial air service to cities in New Hampshire and Vermont connects through New York, Albany, or Boston airports. Daily commercial service is available at Rutland, Vermont, 10 miles from the A.T. Airport is 1.4 miles west of Rutland on Vt. 103, and the Lebanon, New Hampshire, airport is five miles south of Hanover, New Hampshire, adjacent to White River Junction, Vermont. Daily commercial service is available to a number of other airports in New Hampshire and Vermont more distant from the Trail.

Taxis

Taxis are available in or near the following cities, with nearby sections listed in parentheses: White River Junction, Vermont (New Hampshire Nine, Vermont One through Three); Lebanon, New Hampshire (New Hampshire Nine); Hanover, New Hampshire (New Hampshire Eight and Nine, Vermont One); Woodstock, Vermont (Vermont One through Three); Rutland, Vermont (Vermont Three through Five); Manchester Center, Vermont (Vermont Six and Seven); Bennington, Vermont (Vermont Eight and Nine); and Williamstown, Massachusetts (Vermont Nine).

Suggested Trips

The A.T. and an extensive side-trail system in New Hampshire and Vermont provide innumerable possibilities for hiking and backpacking trips. The side trails of the White Mountains of New Hampshire and the Green Mountains of Vermont make loop trips possible. The segment of the A.T. between the White and Green mountains has fewer side trails but offers excellent hiking. Trips in this area often require car shuttling to avoid retracing one's steps.

Following are suggested trips arranged according to the approximate number of days required to complete each. The state and A.T. sections are given before each listing. Remember that, in this guide, sections are numbered north to south.

One-day Trips

So many day trips are possible in these states that not all the best could be listed here; the following is just a sample.

New Hampshire One: Mt. Hayes *via* Centennial Trail (A.T.) from Hogan Road.
Mt. Success *via* Success Trail from Success Pond Road.
New Hampshire Two: Carter Dome *via* Nineteen-Mile Brook Trail, Carter Dome Trail, and A.T., beginning at N.H. 16; return on A.T. and Nineteen-Mile Brook Trail *via* Carter Notch (a loop hike).
New Hampshire Three: Mt. Clinton and Mt. Webster *via* Crawford Path and A.T., beginning on U.S. 302; return *via* Webster-Jackson Trail (a loop hike).
New Hampshire Four: Ethan Pond and Thoreau Falls *via* A.T. from U.S. 302.
New Hampshire Five: South Peak of Kinsman Mountain *via* A.T. from U.S. 3; return on A.T. and Kinsman Pond Trail (a loop hike).
New Hampshire Six: Mt. Moosilauke *via* A.T. from N.H. 112 (the most scenic approach).
New Hampshire Seven: Wachipauka Pond and Webster Slide Mountain *via* A.T. and side trail; begin on N.H. 25.
New Hampshire Eight: Mt. Cube *via* A.T. from N.H. 25A.
Smarts Mountain *via* A.T. from Lyme-Dorchester Road.

Vermont Three: The Lookout *via* A.T. from Vt. 12.

Vermont Four: Pico Peak and Killington Peak *via* A.T. from U.S. 4.

Vermont Five: White Rocks Mountain *via* Vt. 140.; return *via* Keewaydin Trail and Vt. 140 (a loop hike).

Vermont Six: Baker Peak *via* Lake Trail and A.T. from U.S. 7; return *via* Baker Peak Trail and Lake Trail (a loop hike).

Styles Peak and Peru Peak *via* A.T. from USFS 21.

Bromley Mountain *via* A.T. from Vt. 11 and 30.

Vermont Seven: Spruce Peak and Prospect Rock *via* A.T. from Vt. 11 and 30.

Stratton Mountain and Stratton Pond *via* the A.T. from Arlington-West Wardsboro Road; return *via* the Stratton Pond Trail (former A.T.). A long loop hike.

Vermont Nine: East Mountain *via* Pine Cobble Trail (beginning from Mass. 2) and A.T.; return on Broad Brook Trail. This is a long loop hike; it is also a good two-day trip.

Two- to Three-day Trips

Listed below are linear and loop trips. Hikers driving to the Trail and choosing a linear trip may need to arrange for a car at each end of their hike or use shuttle services.

New Hampshire One: Southern Mahoosuc Range—Mt. Success to Mt. Hayes to North Road *via* Success Trail from Success Pond Road and A.T.

New Hampshire Two: Carter-Moriah Range—U.S. 2 to Pinkham Notch (N.H. 16).

New Hampshire Three: Southern Presidential Range—U.S. 302 to Pinkham Notch (N.H. 16) *via* A.T. and Tuckerman Ravine Trail.

New Hampshire Four: Franconia Range *via* Greenleaf Trail from U.S. 3 and A.T. Trail passes over Mt. Lafayette, Mt. Lincoln, Little Haystack Mountain, and Mt. Liberty (side trail). This trip begins and ends on U.S. 3, and is almost a loop trip.

New Hampshire Five: Kinsman Ridge—Kinsman Notch (N.H. 112) to Franconia Notch (U.S. 3). Don't underestimate the time for this one.

New Hampshire Eight and Nine: White Mountain Foothills—N.H. 25A to Hanover, passes Mt. Cube, Smarts Mountain, and Holts Ledge (estimated time, three days).

Vermont Three: Green Mountain Foothills—Vt. 12 to U.S. 4, passes The Lookout and goes through Gifford Woods State Park.

Vermont Four: The Coolidge Range—U.S. 4 to Vt. 103, passes Pico and Killington peaks.

Vermont Six: White Rocks Mountain to Bromley Mountain—Vt. 140 to Vt. 11 and 30, passes Little Rock Pond, Baker, Styles, and Peru peaks.

Vermont Seven: The ponds near Stratton—Arlington-West Wardsboro Road to Stratton and Bourn ponds *via* A.T.; return *via* Branch Pond Trail (a loop trip).

Vermont Eight: Glastenbury Mountain *via* A.T. from Vt. 9; return on West Ridge Trail (a nice two-day loop trip).

Extended Trips

The suggestions listed below are all linear, so the hiker with a car must make special plans for return transportation.

Maine Thirteen and New Hampshire One: Mahoosuc Range—Grafton Notch (Maine 26) to North Road (New Hampshire) passes over many open summits and through Mahoosuc Notch (estimated time, three to five days).

New Hampshire Four: Crawfords and Franconias—U.S. 302 to U.S. 3, passes Ethan Pond, Mt. Guyot, Mt. Garfield, Mt. Lafayette, and a number of other peaks (three to five days).

Vermont Seven and Eight: Southern Long Trail—Vt. 11 and 30 to Vt. 9, passing Prospect Rock, Stratton Pond, and Glastenbury Mountain (three to four days).

Natural History

Geology

By Dr. John Creasy
Assistant Professor of Geology
Bates College

Extending from Alabama to Newfoundland, the Appalachian Mountains originated from a complex series of geologic events culminating in a collision of the North American and European/African ("Eurafrican") continents. The crash of those two land masses forcefully closed the ocean separating them (the Proto-Atlantic) and folded, faulted, and uplifted the sediments that had accumulated at their shores. The Appalachian Mountains were pushed skyward. Subsequently, changing forces within the Earth caused the supercontinent formed by this violent union of North America and Eurafrica, known as Pangaea, to split.

The northern Atlantic Ocean, at first a narrow rift, has since grown to its present size and even now continues to widen a few centimeters each year. Meanwhile, erosion and uplift of the Appalachians exposed rocks that took part in this mountain-building, which also continues today.

The Appalachian Trail in Vermont and New Hampshire cuts across the results of those tumultuous billion years of Earth history by traversing the northeasterly oriented geologic and topographic grain of the Appalachian Mountains.

Early Rumblings

The foundation of our continent, the so-called Precambrian "basement" rocks (exposed over large areas of Canada to the northeast of New England), was deformed several times during episodes of mountain-building (orogenies) preceding the formation of the Appalachians.

When the North American continent split, creating an ocean basin, the east coastline of North America was hundreds of miles west of its present position. Shallow water covered what is now eastern New York and western Vermont, then part of the margin of the continent (the submerged continental shelf). Sediment deposited here formed sandstones and limestones.

Farther east, somewhere in central Vermont, the continental shelf abruptly ended at the edge of the continent. Here, where water depth dramatically increased, sediment was deposited in a great wedge, building eastward from the edge of the continent. This wedge formed siltstones, mudstones, and greywackes.

As forces within the Earth changed, the continents reversed their motions, the Proto-Atlantic began closing, and the intervening ocean crust was pushed deep into the Earth (a process termed subduction). An oceanic island arc developing above this zone of subduction began to approach the "quiet" margin of North America. Some 460 million years ago, the island arc and North America collided, strongly folding and faulting the wedge of sediment caught between them. Much of the formerly submerged continental margin, from eastern New York to the Connecticut River, rose above sea level. This completed the Taconic Orogeny, the first stage in the construction of the Appalachians.

From the south, the hiker enters Vermont in the old (Precambrian) basement that pokes through the core of the Green Mountains. With few exceptions, the Trail lies entirely within these billion-year-old gneisses and schists as far north as Sherburne Pass. (The Green Mountains may have resulted from the Taconic Orogeny. The impact of the island arc may have "splintered" the brittle margin of the continent, driving those splinters of basement upward and westward to form them.)

The valley west of the A.T. (Bennington Valley in the south, Champlain Valley further north) is underlain by the limestones and quartzites of the former continental shelf, which were deposited before the continental collision, some 600 to 460 million years ago. Between Seth Warner Shelter and Primitive Camping Area and Vt. 103, a distance of more than 83 miles, the Trail is never far from the juncture (or inconformity) of the continental basement and those overlying "shelf" rocks. The upturned and very resistant white-colored shelf rock known as the Cheshire Quartzite forms much of the high ground (*e.g.*, White Rock Mountain) traversed by the Trail near Manchester and again near South Wallingford. From Killington Peak, Vermont's second-highest mountain, vistas reveal the Champlain Valley, the Taconic Mountains, and the Adirondacks: more continental basement rising above surrounding shelf rocks.

When the Appalachian Trail turns eastward, leaving the Long Trail, it also leaves the continental basement. Between Sherburne Pass and The Lookout (about 15 miles east), the Trail crosses the rocks formed from sediment deposited in deeper water, beyond the continental shelf. High temperatures and pressures arising from the Taconic Orogeny altered the sedimentary character of these rocks. The hiker will see the resulting metamorphic rocks, mostly black and green schists.

The Collision

Even with all the splintering, folding, and faulting that occurred in the Taconic Orogeny, mountain-building in New England still had quite a future—Eurafrica was coasting west toward America. At the end of the Taconic Orogeny, about 460 million years ago, the newly formed continental margin of New England lay near the present-day Connecticut River as far north as Hanover and then cut northeastward into Maine. The volcanic arc along the eastern edge of what was then New England, extinguished by the Taconic Orogeny, eroded and gradually subsided below sea level. Much of the area uplifted during the Taconic Orogeny was thus submerged and remained so for the next 100 million years.

During this time, a variety of rocks, including limestones and sandstones, formed on the submerged continental shelf across western Vermont. Deep-water rocks, forming from a thick wedge of sediment sifting into the deep sea, encroached westward upon the shelf rocks and built eastward across submerged New Hampshire. To the east and northeast of the continent were active volcanic arcs.

Eurafrica continued westward. The Eurafrican continent collided with the sediment-bound margin of North America 360 million years ago. This, the Acadian Orogeny, united Eurafrica and New England as the continent of Pangaea.

The thick package of sediments caught between the two continents folded, faulted, metamorphosed, and locally melted to form granites. Much of New Hampshire and Maine was uplifted above sea level for the first time. The continental margin, which sank below sea level after the Taconic Orogeny, rose and remained above sea level.

From The Lookout, the A.T. goes east across the shelf rocks of the Acadian Orogeny and, at Norwich, Vermont, reaches the old margin of the continent. The Trail does not cut directly east across the deep-water rocks of central New Hampshire but swings northeast to Glencliff, following the fused margin of North America.

The rocks exposed between Hanover and Glencliff are mostly volcanic. Those are rocks from the continental margin moved upward, flexing the overlying and younger shelf and deep-water rocks, analogous to the splintering of the continental basement to form the Green Mountains.

The high ground (*e.g.*, Mt. Cube, Holts Ledge, and Moose Mountain) is held up by one of those upturned shelf rocks—a white resistant quartzite (Clough quartzite). North of Glencliff, the A.T. strikes east, away from the continental margin, crossing the deep-water sediment, known as the Littleton Formation, which was caught between the colliding continents. Those rocks are mostly mica-schists and gneisses; they are well-exposed on Mt. Moosilauke. Granites generated during the collision are found throughout New Hampshire and well-exposed between Kinsman Notch and Lonesome Lake.

The Split

The "supercontinent" of Pangaea, formed in the Acadian Orogeny by the fusion of North America and Eurafrica, began to rift apart about 200 million years ago. The splitting did not follow the "suture" along which the older continents of North America and Eurafrica were joined. The continents were torn apart east of the suture, forming the present-day edge of North America. Coastal Maine, eastern Massachusetts, and Connecticut are probably relics of the Eurafrican continent left behind.

As Pangaea split, volcanoes typical of continental terrains sprang up in a northerly line across northern New Hampshire, then extinguished. Little geologic activity has affected New England since this time, although continued rifting has made North America and Europe more distant neighbors.

Since its opening, the northern Atlantic Ocean has received much of the erosional products from the highlands of the Appalachians. The thick wedge of sediments now lying against the edge of our continent may in time form another chapter in the evolution of the Appalachians.

The White Mountains

Granites and related volcanic rocks underlie the many high peaks and ridges of the White Mountains traversed by the A.T. from Lonesome Lake to Webster Cliffs. Those rocks are the exposed subterranean roots of a volcanic field developed during the early rifting of Pangaea.

North of Webster Cliffs, the Trail traverses the spectacular Presidential Range. Its alpine environment is held up by resistant rocks of the Littleton Formation. Much of the area has distorted layers (or folds) in the mica schists (metamorphosed mudstones) resulting from the forces of the continent-to-continent collision of the Acadian Orogeny.

The Modern Era

The high mountains formed during the Acadian Orogeny have been eroded by water and wind and uplifted several times in the last 360 million years. The present topography is not just a result of that ancient mountain-building; it reflects the differential resistance to erosion of the rock types formed during those orogenic events. Running water is responsible for most of the erosion. The Presidential Range also exhibits evidence of glaciation, rivaled only by Katahdin.

Several continental glaciers, such as those presently developed in Greenland and Antarctica, covered northern New England in the last two million years. Evidence preserved in the Presidential Range reflects the most recent. Valley glaciers, like those in Alaska and Switzerland, once cut cirques and U-shaped valleys (such as Tuckerman Ravine, King Ravine, and the Great Gulf on the eastern side of the Presidential Range), perhaps as recently as 50,000 years ago.

A continental ice sheet, perhaps a mile or more in thickness, subsequently overrode northern New England, including Mt. Washington (6,288 feet). This ice sheet scoured and sculpted the mountains to their present forms. The many U-shaped "notches" or "gulfs" traversed by the A.T. in northern New England resulted.

The continental ice sheet retreated through the Presidential Range about 12,000 years ago, leaving a thick blanket of debris in the lowlands. On mountain peaks and flanks, bedrock pokes through, offering clues to the mountains' origins.

Debris is easily eroded by running water and by footsteps where the vegetation is cleared to form trails or roads. By man's measure, the mountain's ongoing history is timeless. It is the fragile environment of the mountains that is not.

References

The Evolution of North America, by P.B. King, third ed., Princeton, New Jersey, Princeton University Press, 1977 (includes many figures and maps).

Tectonics of the Appalachians, by John Rodgers, Wiley Interscience, New York, 1970.

Maps

Centennial Geologic Map of Vermont, 1961, scale 1:250,000. Geologic maps and reports are also available for each of the 15-minute quadrangles of Vermont.

Geologic Map of New Hampshire, 1955, scale 1:250,000. Geologic maps and accompanying reports, written for the layman, are also available (index upon request) from Vermont Department of Commerce and Community Development, National Life Building, Montpelier, VT 05620-0501, and from New Hampshire Department of Environmental Services, 6 Hazen Drive, P.O. Box 95, Concord, NH 03302-0095.

Plant Life
By Roger Stern, Appalachian Mountain Club,
and Suzanne Crowley

The hiker passes a wide array of plant life while walking along the A.T. in New Hampshire and Vermont. The vegetation varies from field to forest and from valley to summit.

Trees

The trees throughout the lower elevations of the White Mountains in New Hampshire, as well as where the A.T. crosses the Green Mountains in Vermont, are predominantly northern hardwoods. This forest, which extends up to 2,500 feet above sea level, is composed mainly of sugar maple, beech, birch trees, white pine, red oak, red maple, hemlock, white ash, and basswood.

In spring, the shrubby mountain ash and shadbush bloom. The mountain ash displays cream-white flowers after its large leaves unfold in early June. This small tree, seldom reaching 30 feet, is short-lived and prefers moist, sunny spots. In the fall, it decorates the woods with hanging clusters of bright orange-red berries. The mountain ash is not related to true ashes. The name comes from the similarity between its leaves and those of the ash trees. The mountain ash is actually a member of the rose family.

Thriving in the sun or shade, another understory tree, the service-berry, or shadbush (maximum height of 50 feet), shows its white flowers before, or as, its leaves unfold. It buds in April and May when the shad ascend the New England rivers to spawn, hence its name. Its berry-like, purplish fruit matures in late June.

Forest Flowers

Most of the herbaceous flowers in the hardwood forest are peren-nials that bloom only a short time. The trout lily, or adder's tongue, which blooms in March, is most common in wet woods or meadows. From each stalk hangs a pendant yellow flower, resembling a minia-ture lily, with two mottled leaves at its base. Soon after blooming, the plant withers as its bulb begins to prepare for next spring's growth.

Trillium also blooms in moist areas of hardwood forests. Its name is derived from the Latin word for three. The trillium boasts a flower with three petals and three large, parallel-veined leaves, a sign of the lily family. Three varieties of trillium, white, purple, and painted, grow along the A.T. in New Hampshire and Vermont.

In clearings or areas that border an open field, day-lilies and meadow rue grow. Day-lilies are not true lilies, but the shape of their yellow or orange flowers resembles that of the lily family. The scientific name, *Hemerocallis*, originates from Greek words meaning "beautiful" and "day." The flowers, which bloom from May to July, are quite beautiful, but each bloom appears for only one day. The meadow rue exhibits graceful, lacy small leaves. It forms a bushy plant one to two feet tall. It, too, is an early bloomer, sporting a crown of numerous small, white flowers. The plant's resemblance to the herb rue is the basis for its name.

Bluets have small, pale-blue flowers forming large patches in sunny openings. Hepatica bears small white, pink, lavender, or blue blooms on a low plant named for its liver-shaped, lobed leaves. Violets historically have been used for medicinal purposes, from preventing hangovers to "strengthening the heart."

Midsummer flowers bloom in July and August. Partridgeberry, orchids, and Indian pipes are a few. Partridgeberry has small pink or white, four-lobed flowers in pairs at each end of its creeping stem. The leaves, too, are small, paired, and rounded. The fruit, a single red berry, often develops by late July. The fragrance of the orchid's flowers is sometimes noticed before its blossoms come into view.

Lady's-slipper usually grows in coniferous forests along edges of streams. The orchis is more common. It prefers coniferous swamps, bogs, spruce forests, and peaty soil. Growing to only four to 10 inches in height, the Indian pipe is pipe-shaped, as its name implies. The stem is a single, translucent, waxy tube ending with a nodding white or pink flower, which later turns black. Like mushrooms, this shade dweller is a saprophyte—receiving its energy from decaying organic matter rather than from the sun. Green chlorophyll, which produces carbohydrates (sugars) from sunlight, is absent, leaving the Indian pipe an unusual white color.

In late summer and fall, asters and goldenrods replace the summer flowers. The woods of New Hampshire and Vermont have several varieties of these members of the daisy family. Goldenrods are spikes two to five feet high. Many of the asters, which may have purplish, blue, pink, or white flowers, also bloom late.

Ferns

Ferns are a common groundcover in northern hardwood forests. In most wooded sections of the Northeast, 15 to 20 fern species can be found easily.

Wood fern and lady fern are similar in appearance and common in the hardwoods. Both form lacy plumes, and spores develop on the backs of the leaflets. A stem cut at the base and looked at in cross-section will show two small crescent shapes on the lady fern and five dots on the wood fern. They are the vascular bundles that transport water and nutrients through the fern.

Along hillsides or in meadows, hay-scented ferns often form great masses of feathery two- to three-foot foliage. This light-green fern looks more fragile than the lady fern. Standing separately, the fronds turn to follow the sun. The hay-scented fern smells sweet when crushed or dried.

The common polypody, one of the most abundant of the ferns, grows on shaded rocks. It is small, a few inches to a foot tall, but its dark, leathery leaflets are easily spotted.

Subalpine Plants

At elevations above the northern hardwood forest stands the spruce-fir or subalpine forest, beginning at about 2,500 feet above sea level. At this elevation, between the hardwood and alpine cover, black spruce and balsam fir replace the hardwood species. The diversity of species declines as elevation increases. The subalpine forest occasionally includes mountain ash or striped maple but is mainly composed of spruce and fir, which are easily discerned. Spruce needles are sharp to the touch, and spruce cones hang as pendants. Fir needles are soft, and its cones stand on the branches.

Subalpine plants include mayflower, goldenthread, clintonia, bunchberry, starflower, woodsorrel, twinflower, and large-leaved aster. In boggy areas, sphagnum moss often grows with pale laurel, blueberry, and wild raisin.

At 4,000 feet, the spruce and fir become shrubby. This community of dwarfed trees is called krummholz. The dwarfing probably resulted from windborne ice destroying the growing tips. Repeated removal of vertically growing tips results in lateral growth. The krummholz reflects the depth of winter snow, as any tip above snowline for a winter probably will not survive. Because the krummholz is so dense, there is no groundcover, except in breaks in the canopy.

Alpine Plants

Above the twisted krummholz, at about 4,700 feet, lies the true alpine vegetation. Here, where the landscape is chiefly characterized by the absence of trees, grows a variety of fragile, often rare plants. Strong winds, which cause drifting snow, determine which plants will grow.

In snow-free areas, the dense, low-growing cushion plants such as *diapensia* grow. Its dense mat of tiny, overlapping leaves protects it from windblown ice. Its shape also deflects wind from the cushion.

Behind rocks and in depressions, protected from wind and abundant moisture, lie the snowbank communities. Mountain heath, dwarf willow, moss plant (not a true moss, but a flowering plant), and painted cup are some of the plants found here.

To maintain themselves through the harsh winters, most alpine plants have large storage sites for nutrients, many underground. Evergreen plants often have storage sites in their leaves. The round-leaved sundew, on the other hand, is insectivorous. A sticky substance on its leaves captures small insects. The leaves slowly close, and the plant digests the insect for its nutrients.

North of Mt. Washington and the Presidential Range, the A.T. traverses the Mahoosuc Range, which begins in New Hampshire and continues northeastward into Maine. On the peaks of this range, between the krummholz and the more alpine communities, are heath-shrub communities with pockets of tundra bog. The heath is dominated by pale laurel and Labrador tea. In bedrock depressions, under the sphagnum-moss cover, lie lenses of frozen peat. Those often remain intact well into the growing season. In mid-July, the depth of those lenses is about 15 inches. They persist because of the insulating properties of dry sphagnum in warm, dry weather. The frozen peat cools the plant-root environment above it, creating a growing medium characteristic of higher elevations. In this way, tundra species grow although the elevations are much lower than the alpine zone in the Presidentials. Baked appleberry, black crowberry, and cotton grass are three such species.

All hikers should take pains to preserve the forest and flowers for others to enjoy. Many plants are rare or endangered. In alpine areas, stay on the established pathway. Plants here have adapted themselves to withstand the weather, but not crushing footsteps. Take home only pictures. Be a steward of the natural beauty along the Trail.

References

A Field Guide to Ferns, Peterson Field Guide Series, by Boughton Cobb. Houghton Mifflin, Boston, 1956.

A Field Guide to Wildflowers, Peterson Field Guide Series, by Roger Peterson and Margaret McKenny. Houghton Mifflin, Boston, 1968.

Trees of Eastern and Central United States and Canada, by William Harlow. Dover Publications, New York, 1957.

Wildlife
By Dr. Rebecca Field
U.S. Fish and Wildlife Service

A variety of birds and animals lives along the Appalachian Trail in New Hampshire and Vermont. The leaf-strewn hardwood forest, shrubby abandoned pastures, spruce-covered knolls, bogs, marshes, and ponds are among the many different habitats, each providing a place for a wealth of animal species.

Some creatures ramble from one spot to another, but each demonstrates habitat preferences, adapting to its surroundings through evolution.

This section highlights some of the animals most likely to be seen while hiking the A.T. in New Hampshire and Vermont, arranged according to six easily identifiable habitats: the open water of lakes and ponds; bogs and marshes; the drier grasslands; open woodlands, thickets, and edges; deciduous forests; and coniferous or evergreen forests.

Lakes, Streams, Ponds, and Shores

During their spring and fall migrations, waterfowl use ponds and lakes as resting and feeding areas. Ducks (mallards, shovelers, black ducks, teal) prefer shallow water, where they feed on bottom vegetation. Other waterfowl (mergansers, goldeneyes, and rudy ducks) dive for their food. They eat both plants and underwater invertebrates. Since most waterfowl migrate through northern New England, the hiker will see them only during spring and fall.

Another bird, the loon, may be seen on a pond or lake and then suddenly plunge out of view. These birds, like diving waterfowl, find both protection and food beneath the surface. They are best known for a yodeling, laugh-like call, one of the four in their repertoire. Loons live in open water, except when they breed and nest, and will dive deeply in search of fish.

The kingfisher is a small bird often seen flying over open water. It usually hovers, searching for fish, and then dives, catching its prey with its long, sharp beak.

Many birds can be seen standing in shallow water along pond and lake shores, where they feed on small fish and invertebrates in the water and mud. Most conspicuous is the tall, long-necked great blue heron, which spears fish with its sharp beak. The smaller green heron also may be seen along the edge of ponds and streams. On the shore, the spotted sandpiper, a summer resident, walks along the edge of the water looking for food. As it looks, it constantly bobs its tail, giving it the nickname "teeter-tail."

Many mammals come to the edges of streams or ponds to drink or feed. Three small carnivores, the weasel, mink, and river otter, frequent wooded areas along streams and ponds. The river otter, which prefers open water, is the most aquatic of the three. Opossums and raccoons usually are not far from water. In shallow northern waters, as in the Mahoosuc Range of New Hampshire, you may see a moose. Since mammals are often nocturnal, you may be more successful at finding indirect signs of activity along a shore: pawprints in a muddy bank, scat along the shore, or chewed bark.

Beavers are the largest rodents in the area. They build dams along streams and ponds in the midst of woodlands. They feed on hardwood trees at the water's edge and make shelter in lodges of mud and sticks. Ordinarily, beavers are not seen, but signs of their work—gnawed trees, dams, lodges, and ponds—are common. Their ponds create a new aquatic habitat for many other creatures.

Amphibians and reptiles are most abundant in aquatic or moist habitats. Many species require water for laying their eggs. Turtles are found in still, shallow streams or creeks. Painted turtles are the most likely to be basking in the sun, though snapping turtles also may be seen. The stinkpot turtle sometimes climbs limbs that extend over the water. Newts and salamanders live in quiet, shallow water along the water's edge. Look carefully under small logs or rocks along the shore of creeks or streams, and you may see a salamander. Several snakes also are found around quiet water or marshes, but the poisonous snakes of the wetlands in the southern United States are not found in northern New England.

Toads and frogs are more often heard than seen. On a spring evening, areas of still, shallow water can be alive with the choruses of several species. The high whistle of the spring peeper and the deep resonating tones of the bullfrog are most familiar. Also in the spring, look for egg masses or schools of tadpoles along the water's edge.

Bogs and Marshes

Freshwater bogs and marshes provide many of the habitat benefits of lakes, streams, and ponds: abundant moisture and some of the same food and shelter, but more vegetation, such as dense sphagnum, cattails, sedges, or reeds. Marshes may form a continuum of habitats in succession from open water to more wooded areas.

Wading birds, such as herons, bitterns, or rails, may be found in marshes. If you startle an American bittern, it points its bill straight up; this posture and the striped coloration make this bird hard to see. Rails are elusive birds but have distinctive voices of piping notes or metallic rattles.

The marsh hawk, as its name implies, frequents the marshy habitat. It often flies low over the ground, tilting from side to side, searching for prey, usually rodents. Sexes are easy to distinguish: The females are brown, and the males are grey. Barred owls and short-eared owls also may be seen over marshes. They are most active at dusk, flying silently, hunting for rodents and other small mammals.

The marsh wrens are also part of this community. Look for the short, vertical tail, but you are more likely just to hear their rattling trill. A few of the warblers are summer residents of marshes, particularly the palm warbler and the northern waterthrush. The redwing and rusty blackbirds can also be seen in marshes.

Mammals of the marsh are similar to those species found near ponds and streams. In addition, you may find signs of bobcats (rare and solitary), black bears, and snowshoe hares.

Most amphibians and reptiles seen along edges of open water also like marshy conditions. The eastern garter snake, northern water snake, and the smaller northern brown snake may be found in bogs or marshes. The four-toed salamander, a resident of sphagnum bogs, has a black-spotted white belly and a tail that breaks off when seized.

Grasslands

Grasslands in the eastern United States are open areas that usually are cleared and maintained. Unlike the West, the East lacks vast natural prairies, yet the many farmlands, pastures, and clearings along the Trail offer valuable habitats for a number of species.

Some birds of the open bogs, such as the marsh hawk, also are found in the open grasslands. In addition, the rough-legged and red-tailed hawks are typical of the open country. These large hawks generally soar high overhead and then dive upon their prey. The small sparrow hawk (or kestrel) perches on utility wires, watching for small animals, but primarily eats insects.

The killdeer, which calls its name, builds its nest on the ground in grasslands. If you should get too close, the adult will feign an injured wing, as it does to lure a predator from the nest area. The ruffed grouse also may be seen crouching or strutting through woodsy clearings in the summer. The ring-necked pheasant may be flushed from farmlands; its loud, metallic honking is a frequent sound.

Songbirds of the grasslands include the fly-catching eastern kingbird, the eastern phoebe (with its raspy call of its name), and the white-rumped yellow-bellied sapsucker. Eastern bluebirds perch on utility wires. Watch for the swooping flight of the barn swallow, cliff swallow, and purple martin. Eastern meadowlarks and bobolinks can be spotted on fence posts or on the ground. The melodious call of the meadowlark is a familiar sound in a pasture. The savannah, vesper, chipping, and field sparrows are all summer residents of the grasslands. In the winter, you may see another sparrow, the snow bunting.

Open grasslands provide little cover for most mammals. Some small mice, voles, and moles live in this habitat. They are usually too quick to be seen by the passing hiker. Most other mammals of the grasslands stay near shelter, in thickets or brushpiles, although rabbits hop across open fields between spots of better cover.

The dryness of grasslands makes those areas unattractive for most amphibians and reptiles. The animals in that group that can endure drier conditions are more likely found in woodlands or in rocky, mountainous areas. However, you may come across an occasional wood turtle or leopard frog in the summer.

Woodlands, Edges, and Thickets

Woodlands are open, often second-growth, forests that may be in transition between fields and dense woods. Low shrubs and brushy thickets may be found here. Where a forest is directly adjacent to an open area, it is called an edge habitat. Those edges provide abundant cover for a great diversity of animals.

Many birds are found in woodlands and the edges of forests. If water is nearby, you may see a colorful wood duck or hear its whistle call. Those ducks nest in tree holes. The Cooper's hawk, sharp-shinned hawk, broad-winged hawk, and red-shouldered hawk are a few of this group of birds in Vermont or New Hampshire woodlands. Another common group, the owls, are represented by the screech owl or long-eared owl. During the day, you may be lucky to spot an owl sitting close to a tree trunk. They spit up pellets of the indigestible hair and bones of their prey to the woodland floor.

Many songbirds like the woodland and edge habitats. Yellow-bellied sapsuckers are a common woodpecker. Several flycatchers, such as the least flycatcher, the olive-sided flycatcher, and the eastern wood pewee, feed on the many insects in thickets. Chickadees can be found all year long. The grey catbird is a good mimic and may fool you with its imitations of other birds' calls. Several warblers, such as the yellow warbler, chestnut-sided warbler, mourning warbler, and common yellow throat frequent the thicket. The indigo bunting is a small blue bird found in edge habitats. The common rufous-sided towhee sings "drink your tea" or calls with a loud "chat." Several sparrows such as tree sparrow, white-throated sparrow, and song sparrow, also are common along forest edges.

A brushy area provides plenty of cover for small mammals. Mice, voles, squirrels, chipmunks, and rabbits escape predators in the dense thicket. The spine-covered porcupine curls up in woodland trees in the day and prowls for food at night, often gnawing on woody plants. Foxes, either the red or grey, can be spotted in sparsely wooded areas. White-tailed deer feed on the vegetation of woodlands or nearby meadows. Watch for them especially at dusk; as they bound away, they flip their white tails in the air.

Wherever there is moist soil, you may find some amphibians and reptiles. Wood turtles may stray some distance from open water. The garter snake, ringneck snake, and milk snake live in woodlands. The red-backed salamander is one of the most terrestrial salamanders, usually hiding under rocks or logs. Few frogs leave wetland areas for drier habitats, although the spring peeper, pickerel frog, and wood frog wander into moist woodlots.

Deciduous Forests

Deciduous forests are made up of broad-leafed trees that usually lose their leaves in the fall. Mature forests in northern New England may include beech, birch, maple, oak, and elm.

Several types of birds are common in deciduous forests. Where the forest is moist, you may see a red-shouldered hawk, or flush the elusive woodcock, ordinarily hard to spot with its effective camouflage. The peregrine falcon and golden eagle, now endangered species, can still be seen in higher country. Open, deciduous forest is a favorite habitat for the screech owl and the broad-winged hawk.

Woodpeckers are common in these woods and often are heard hammering for insects on dead or dying trees. The downy woodpecker, the similar but larger hairy woodpecker, the pileated woodpecker, the northern flicker, and the yellow-bellied sapsucker all frequent these forests.

Many kinds of songbirds frequent deciduous woods. The eastern wood pewee and the great crested flycatcher feed on flying insects. The blue jay, American robin, American crow, and black-capped chickadee are year-round residents.

The small nuthatches can be spotted climbing along the tree bark. The brown creeper is well-camouflaged but also may be seen climbing the tree bark. Where the forest has a thick understory, you may hear the long, flutelike song of the wood thrush. The veery also has a flutelike call, consisting of descending notes.

As a group, warblers prefer deciduous or coniferous woods. A common one, the ovenbird, calls "teacher, teacher." Another group common in deciduous forests is the insect-eating vireos.

The male scarlet tanager is easily spotted by its bright red body and contrasting black tail and wings. The rose-breasted grosbeak has a distinctive red bib.

Deciduous forests are home to several types of mammals. Where the soil is moist and soft, shrews and moles burrow extensive tunnel networks. Weasels, martens, fishers, and raccoons also prefer moist habitats and seldom are far from water. Bats spend the days in caves in wooded areas, coming out in the early evening to feed on insects. When the forested area is open and near meadows, you may see white-tailed deer, especially in the evening or morning. Unlike most mammals, squirrels, chipmunks, and woodchucks are active during the day in the forest. The terrestrial amphibians and reptiles mentioned in the last section are also found in deciduous forests.

Coniferous Forests

Coniferous trees, commonly known as evergreens, do not shed their leaves seasonally. Their leaves are shaped like needles, and the surrounding soil tends to be acidic.

Hawks are common in coniferous forests. The goshawk prefers mature forests while the sharp-shinned hawk and merlin are found in open forest. Grouse are found in coniferous woods all year long. In the spring, you can hear their deep, muffled drumming, part of their courtship ritual. The long-eared owl and the great-horned owl are active at night in this habitat. In thickets of evergreen forests, the tiny saw-whet owl can be found all year.

Ravens are seen soaring at high elevations in coniferous habitats. They are distinguished from crows by their larger size, wedge-shaped (rather than rounded) tail, and distinctive croaking call. The boreal chickadee of higher elevations has a brown cap, rather than the black cap of its relative, the black-capped chickadee, of lower country. You may hear the winter wren singing; look for its short, stiff tail. Dark-eyed juncos and white-throated sparrows migrate vertically, ascending into the mountains during the summer to nest and raise young and descending to lower country to pass the winter.

Among mammals, black bears are active at night in coniferous forests. Near swamps, the bobcat is a rare sight, but it is worth watching for tracks. Porcupines can be spotted in the daytime as a ball of spines curled up on a tree branch.

Few amphibians and reptiles are specific to coniferous habitats. Those previously listed as terrestrial species also can be found in evergreen forests. The timber rattlesnake, a rare sight in New England, can be found in mountainous regions. In winter, several rattlers congregate in dens, often with other snakes. Most often, rattlers are found in second-growth forests where rodents are plentiful.

Despite the large number of animals mentioned, this description has been only a brief overview of the fauna along the A.T. in New Hampshire and Vermont. Only the most common habitats have been covered, and the hiker will undoubtedly come across other species.

The hiker should take time to watch, listen, and explore each habitat to increase the chances of seeing wildlife. Hikers wishing to have complete information about identification, distribution, and characteristics of animals along the Trail should obtain one of the field guides mentioned below. In addition to these references, it is wise to contact authorities of national or state forests and parks in the area for information on specific flora and fauna.

References

The Peterson Field Guide Series from Houghton Mifflin Company gives information on a wide variety of fauna. Guides are available on amphibians and reptiles, mammals, birds, butterflies, animal tracks, insects, and birds' nests.

Birds of North America, by C.S. Robbins, *et al.* Golden Press, New York, 1966.

The Audubon Society Field Guide to North America's Birds (Eastern Region), by J. Bull and J. Farrand. Alfred A. Knopf, New York, 1977.

The Appalachian Trail in New Hampshire

Through the eastern part of New Hampshire "north" on the Trail), the Appalachian Trail follows the lofty ridgecrests of the White Mountains. In the western part, it traces a route through the hardwood country of the eastern slope of the Connecticut River Valley. Through the White Mountains, the A.T. is rugged, often steep, and sometimes wet but passes through a variety of habitats. The route ascends high, rocky, and barren ridges divided by deep notches or valleys, often also cut by sharp cols between high peaks. It follows footpaths and woods roads through dense hardwood and coniferous forests and crosses rushing mountain streams. Along the Connecticut River Valley, in the western part of the state, the Trail passes through a succession of pastures, cleared hills, patches of timber, ravines, and peaks as it traverses the broken ridgecrest of the White Mountain foothills. The rough terrain makes hiking in New Hampshire strenuous, yet rewarding.

In the New Hampshire part of this guide, each section generally describes one range.

The Maine-New Hampshire state line crosses the Trail through the middle of the Mahoosuc Range of eastern New Hampshire and western Maine, which has no easy road access. For this reason and because the range is usually hiked as a unit, this guide begins at Grafton Notch in Maine and covers the last (southern) section of the Trail described in the *Appalachian Trail Guide to Maine*.

The southbound Trail ascends from Grafton Notch and traverses the remote and rugged Mahoosuc Range, with many open summits. Along the way, the hiker must wind, crawl, and jump through the boulder-clogged and cave-ridden Mahoosuc Notch. The Trail descends from the range and crosses the Androscoggin River Valley and then climbs to the crest of the Carter-Moriah Range, which it follows to the open Carter Dome before dropping at Carter Lakes into Carter Notch. From Carter Notch, the Trail rises sharply to Wildcat Mountain, then descends steeply over exposed ledges into Pinkham Notch, where the Pinkham Notch Visitor Center and the North Country headquarters of the Appalachian Mountain Club are located.

From Pinkham Notch, the Trail ascends and then drops through the Great Gulf Wilderness, climbing to the rocky summit of Mt. Madison, which marks the northern end of the alpine Presidential Range, a rocky, tundra-covered ridge. The Trail passes close to the summits of Mt. Adams, Mt. Jefferson, and Mt. Clay, and then ascends to Mt. Washington (6,288 feet), the highest peak in the northeastern United States. From the summit of Mt. Washington, the Trail descends south, skirting Mt. Monroe, where it passes over Mt. Franklin, skirting Mt. Eisenhower, passing over Mt. Pierce (Mt. Clinton), and reentering woods. It continues on the ridge, passing over Mt. Jackson and Mt. Webster before dropping into Crawford Notch State Park.

From Crawford Notch, the Trail climbs to cross the lower flank of the Willey Range, passes through Zealand Notch, and then ascends to cross Zealand Ridge, Garfield Ridge, and the alpine Franconia Range, where it passes over Mt. Lafayette (5,249 feet), the highest peak in the area. The Trail drops from Franconia Ridge into Franconia Notch and Franconia Notch State Park.

From Franconia Notch, the Trail once again ascends. It follows the crest of the wooded Kinsman Ridge to Kinsman Notch, where evidence of intensive glacial activity is preserved in the Lost River Reservation. From Kinsman Notch, the Trail makes a spectacular ascent to the summit of the massive, bald Mt. Moosilauke (4,802 feet), the southwestern edge of the White Mountains. From the summit, the Trail descends to Glencliff.

Between Glencliff and the Connecticut River, the physical and cultural features characteristic of upland northern New England become strikingly evident. Many of the low ridges and rolling hills have reverted to woodland. The many large fields and clearings, cellar holes, stone fences, lilac and apple trees, cemeteries, and abandoned roads are evidence of a time, more than a century ago, when this was a prosperous area of farms and small hamlets.

Beginning at Glencliff, the Trail climbs Wyatt Hill, where it passes Wachipauka Pond and crosses the summit of Mt. Mist, before descending to cross N.H. 25C. The Trail passes over the summit of Ore Hill and descends to N.H. 25A.

From the highway, the A.T. climbs Mt. Cube (2,911 feet), crosses Eastman Ledges, and then climbs to the firetower on Smarts Mountain (3,240 feet). The Trail descends steeply from the firetower, over Lambert Ridge to the Dartmouth Skiway, and then climbs Holts Ledge. Continuing on trails and woods roads through hardwood forest, pastures, and fields, the Trail passes over the north and south peaks of Moose Mountain and over Velvet Rocks to Hanover, home of

Dartmouth College. At Hanover, the Trail descends to the Connecticut River (400 feet), the border between New Hampshire and Vermont.

The Appalachian Mountain Club is responsible for maintaining the Trail from Grafton Notch (Maine 26) to Kinsman Notch (N.H. 112), although parts are maintained also by the U.S. Forest Service (USFS). The Gulfside Trail, in the northern Presidential Range (above treeline), is marked with yellow paint in addition to the standard white blazes. For further information on those sections of Trail, contact the AMC, Pinkham Notch Visitor Center, Box 298, Gorham, NH 03581, (603) 466-2721.

The Dartmouth Outing Club (DOC) maintains the Trail from the Connecticut River to Kinsman Notch (N.H. 112). This portion is blazed with standard A.T. white and DOC orange-and-black blazes. For further information on this section, contact the Dartmouth Outing Club, P.O. Box 9, Hanover, NH 03755, (603) 646-2428.

Hiking and Camping Information

White Mountain National Forest

For two-thirds of its length in New Hampshire, the A.T. crosses the White Mountain National Forest (WMNF). The WMNF covers 730,000 acres in Maine and New Hampshire, accommodating timber and wildlife management, watershed protection, and recreation. Most of the land in the White Mountains in northern New Hampshire is a part of the WMNF. Instructions for using the forest in each section are listed under "Regulations."

In recent years, use of backcountry trails and facilities in the White Mountains has increased dramatically. Soil erosion, loss of vegetation, water pollution, and disposal of human waste have become major problems. In certain areas, scarred trees, eroded trails, and hardened campsites indicate that use is causing steady deterioration. Some areas of the forest may never recover. An example is Franconia Ridge, where compaction and erosion from hikers' footsteps has left a broad, gutted footway. In other places, campers have cut trees, trampled vegetation, and polluted water. These problems have necessitated regulations to lessen the impact camping and hiking have on plant life, soils, and water.

Forest Protection Areas (FPA)

To prevent harming the forest's fragile ecosystems and to allow damaged areas to rehabilitate, the USFS has designated parts of the A.T. as Forest Protection Areas (FPA). FPA information can be found under "Regulations."

Camping and fires are prohibited inside FPAs. Outside FPAs off-Trail camping and wood fires are limited to areas below timberline (where trees are at least eight feet tall), at least 200 feet off the Trail, and one-quarter mile from any road, hut, shelter, lake, or stream. Federal citations are issued for violations.

FPA information is posted at Trailheads. In the summer, USFS ridgerunners patrol the FPAs, offering assistance. For further information, contact the Supervisor's Office, White Mountain National Forest, or AMC's Pinkham Notch Visitor Center (see "Important Addresses," page 219).

Wildernesses

The Trail passes through the Great Gulf Wilderness. No facilities exist in this area, but off-Trail camping is permitted. The Trail also skirts the northern boundary of the Presidential Range–Dry River Wilderness and closely parallels the northern and western borders of the Pemigewasset Wilderness. Those lands were set aside by Congress to preserve distinctive natural resources.

Caretakers

AMC summer caretakers maintain and supervise several back-country shelters and campsites in the White Mountains. At those areas, described in the shelter portion of each section, a fee is charged to partially defray costs. Please cooperate with caretakers and use trails and shelters in an ecologically sound manner.

Carry In/Carry Out

Carry out all trash and garbage. AMC and DOC-maintained facilities do not permit trash to be left behind by visitors. Please adhere to carry-in/carry-out policies in all backcountry areas.

State Parks

The A.T. passes through three state parks within the White Mountain National Forest: Franconia Notch State Park (Section Four), Crawford Notch State Park (Section Three), and the summit of Mt. Washington (Section Three). Those parks were established by the state of New Hampshire to ensure that those scenic areas would always be public domain. In state parks, camping is permitted only at designated campgrounds, huts, or shelters. Camping is not permitted on Mt. Washington's summit.

Campsites

A campsite generally refers to a site with a shelter, water, toilet facilities, fireplace, and tent platforms. Platforms allow tenting in rugged or steep terrain. They also concentrate, or at least localize, soil compaction. Caretakers are in residence at the following campsites and a $6 overnight fee (1998) is charged: Kinsman Pond, Liberty Spring, Garfield Ridge, 13 Falls, Guyot, Ethan Pond, Nauman, Imp, and Speck Pond (Maine). The remaining campsites are available to backcountry travelers at no charge.

At AMC-maintained campsites where a fee is charged, A.T. thru-hikers may be able to work off their stay. "Work-for-stay," as it is known, allows thru-hikers to work for about one hour in lieu of paying the fee. The work-for-stay option is limited to two thru-hikers per night and is offered on a first-come/first-served basis; no reservations are accepted. Work-for-stay is at the discretion of the caretaker, and, as a courtesy to other thru-hikers, AMC requests that individuals limit their use of the work-for-stay option to no more than three campsites and three huts.

Tentsites

Tentsites have only tent platforms or tent pads, with a fireplace, toilet, and water. Some have a caretaker, and a fee is charged to help defray costs.

Shelters

A number of Adirondack shelters (three walls, open front) that accommodate five to 14 people are located along the Trail. Shelters are near water and have fireplaces and toilet facilities; many sites have tent platforms as well. At some sites, a caretaker is in residence, and a fee is charged.

Cabins

A cabin is a closed shelter with water, fireplace, and toilet. Some have more elaborate facilities, such as bunks and stoves, and some sites have a caretaker, and a fee is charged. Complete details are available from the Appalachian Mountain Club (see "Important Addresses," page 219).

AMC Huts

These large, enclosed structures sleep anywhere from 36 to 90 people and are open as early as May, closing in late September or mid-October, depending on the hut. Two levels of service are provided; the "full-service" season lasts from the first Friday in June to late September or mid-October, depending on the hut. During the full-service season, a hut "croo," consisting primarily of college-aged outdoor enthusiasts, staffs each hut except Carter Notch, which offers a simpler "caretaker service." During the full-service season, an overnight stay includes bunkspace, bathroom privileges (no showers), breakfast, and dinner, prepared by the croo. The huts cater mainly to families and weekend hikers, and usually, the croo schedules nightly entertainment programs or games. The self-service or "caretaker season" starts in early May and lasts until the first Friday in June at Lonesome Lake, Greenleaf, Galehead, and Mizpah huts. Carter Notch and Crawford huts operate on caretaker service year-round, including the busy summer season. Zealand Hut offers caretaker service from late October through the winter months and then switches to full service from June through late October. Caretaker service offers no meals, no bedding, and a single caretaker present in the morning and evening. With the caretaker service, guests are required to bring their own sleeping bag and food but are welcome to use the kitchen facilities, including the oven, pots, serving dishes, and utensils. In 1998, the caretaker season rate was $14 per person per night.

AMC has a long tradition of providing room and board to A.T. thru-hikers in exchange for work at AMC facilities in the White mountains. "Work-for-stay," as it is known, is usually available at the huts or Camp Dodge volunteer center. Work-for-stay usually proves to be beneficial for both facility staff and thru-hikers; crews and caretakers appreciate the extra help, and thru-hikers enjoy a soft bed and some-body else's cooking. Each of the huts can accommodate two thru-hikers (four at Lakes of the Clouds and Camp Dodge) if there is work available. Work-for-stay is offered on a first-come, first-served basis; no reservations accepted. Thru-hikers are offered work at the discre-tion of the hut croo or caretaker. Thru-hikers working off their stay can expect to work two hours at full-service sites and one hour at caretaker sites. As a courtesy to other A.T. thru-hikers, AMC requests that individuals limit their use of the work-for-stay option to no more than three huts and three campsites.

At the Pinkham Notch Visitor Center, public-health regulations now require that only kitchen staff be allowed in the kitchen. Since kitchen work is what AMC used to offer thru-hikers in exchange for lodging, AMC no longer offers this service. Thru-hikers can stay at regular guest quarters at the reduced member rates, whether or not they are members of the AMC.

At Camp Dodge, four miles north of Pinkham on N.H. 16, the available work is usually light facilities maintenance or a brief talk to volunteers about your A.T. experience. AMC can accommodate up to four thru-hikers per night. Please call (603) 466-9469 before stopping in.

Any thru-hiker interested in staying at an AMC facility will be offered the reduced rate given to AMC members ($7 savings per night). Rates are higher on Saturdays, holidays, and during the month of August at all facilities. It is wise to make reservations as far ahead as possible, because all facilities are heavily used. Reservations open in November for the following year. For more information and to make reservations, call (603) 466-2727, Monday-Saturday, 9:00 a.m.-5:00 p.m., or write Reservations, AMC, P.O. Box 298, Gorham, NH 03581.

An AMC hiker shuttle (fee) operates daily from June to October. The shuttle services such points as Pinkham Notch Visitor Center, Crawford Notch Hostel and Visitor Center, Ammonoosuc Ravine

Trail, Lafayette Place West, Foster's Store (U.S. 3 and 302), 19 Mile Brook, Webster Cliff, and Zealand, Gale River, Garfield, and Liberty trailheads.

Public Accommodations

In addition to the huts, a wide range of commercial accommodations is available along the public roads the Trail crosses. Those are described in each section.

Grafton Notch (Maine 26) to Maine-New Hampshire State Line
The Mahoosuc Range in Maine
14.6 Miles

The Mahoosuc Range

The Mahoosuc Range is a long, northeast-to-southwest mountain chain extending from Grafton Notch, Maine, to the Androscoggin Valley of New Hampshire. Its many alpine bogs and open ledges provide splendid views of this wild area of northeastern New Hampshire and northwestern Maine.

Two guide sections of the Trail traverse this range, crossing eight major mountain peaks. The range is accessible by road only at its ends, and it is usually hiked in its entirety (two sections, 31.1 miles). The total climb in either direction is approximately 8,000 feet.

The range is wild and rugged. Be prepared for frequent climbs and descents and a rough, wet footway. Do not underestimate the time necessary to traverse the range (three to five days). The range has no major stream crossings, and water might be scarce.

The Trail crosses wet, boggy areas along the range, both high on the ridge and in sags between peaks. Although those bogs appear stable, even limited trampling breaks down the vegetation and soil structure, leading to unpleasant, muddy areas. To keep hikers from widening the footway, extensive log walkways or bog bridges have been installed. Use the walkways to prevent further harm and allow regeneration of the parts of the bogs already damaged.

The A.T. follows the Mahoosuc Trail, a rugged crestline footpath, along the ridge. At the northern end of the range, from Grafton Notch to Old Speck, the Trail follows the Old Speck Trail. At the southern end, from the Androscoggin Valley to Mt. Hayes, it follows the Centennial Trail. East of the Maine-New Hampshire state line, the Trail passes through Grafton Notch State Park. West of the state line, the A.T. is on U.S. Forest Service land managed jointly by USFS and AMC, with the exception of the lower mile of the Centennial Trail, which is in New Hampshire's Leadmine State Forest. Most of the side trails are on private land.

Brief Description of Section

The Trail in this section crosses rugged, mountainous terrain. It passes Speck Pond, a scenic tarn. At its northern end in Grafton Notch, it skirts the cliffs of the Eyebrow. In this section, the A.T. traverses the following major peaks from north to south:

Old Speck, 4,180 feet (0.3 mile on side trail)
Mahoosuc Arm, 3,765 feet
South Peak, Fulling Mill Mountain, 3,395 feet
North Peak, Goose Eye Mountain, 3,680 feet
West Peak, Goose Eye Mountain, 3,854 feet
Mt. Carlo, 3,565 feet

The Trail also passes through Mahoosuc Notch, a deep cleft between Mahoosuc Arm and Fulling Mill Mountain. Giant boulders from the notch's sheer walls have clogged the floor. Ice is found in caves here as late as July. Hikers must climb around and under boulders and through caves and, in some places, must remove their packs to do so. Although the notch is only about one mile long, a few hours should be set aside for its traverse.

Four side trails from north of the range, and one from the east intersect the A.T. in this section and lead to Success Pond Road. This long, gravel road is reached from Berlin, New Hampshire. (see "Road Approaches" on next page and directions on pages 66-67). All the trails are maintained by AMC. From north to south, they include:

Speck Pond Trail (intersects the A.T. 4.6 miles from the northern end of the section)
Mahoosuc Notch Trail (intersects the A.T. 8.2 miles from the northern end of the section)
Goose Eye Trail (intersects the A.T. 12.3 miles from the northern end of the section)
Carlo Col Trail (intersects the A.T. 14.1 miles from the northern end of the section)

In addition, the Wright Trail approaches the A.T. from Sunday River Road east of the range. Its two branches intersect the Trail 11.8 and 12.0 miles from the northern end of the section.

For a description of all trails on the range, refer to the *White Mountain Guide* or *Maine Mountain Guide*, available from AMC. The Trail northward in Maine is covered on *Appalachian Trail Guide to Maine* maps, available from ATC or the Maine Appalachian Trail Club (see "Important Addresses," page 219).

Road Approaches

Only the northern end of this section on Maine 26 is directly accessible by car. Parking is available where Maine 26 intersects the A.T. in Grafton Notch, 12 miles from U.S. 2. It is 18 miles from the town of Bethel, Maine, to the Trail *via* U.S. 2 and Maine 26. The small village of Upton, near Umbagog Lake, is seven miles north on Maine 26.

The Trail may be approached from gravel Success Pond Road, which parallels the Mahoosuc Range to the north. This road, a private Crown Vantage Company Road open to public use, begins in Berlin, New Hampshire. From this road, hikers can ascend any of the four AMC side trails mentioned on the previous page.

The Trail may also be approached from the Sunday River Road, which leaves U.S. 2 north of Bethel and threads its way through the Sunday River ski complex east of the range. The Wright Trail, mentioned above, leaves the south fork of this road about two miles northwest of Ketchum.

Maps

Map One (this guide)
MATC Map No. 7, Maine 17 to Maine-New Hampshire Line
AMC Carter-Mahoosuc Map

The A.T. route might not be current on the following:
USGS 15-minute topographic quadrangles:
        Old Speck, Maine
        Bethel, Maine
        Milan, New Hampshire
        Gorham, New Hampshire
USGS 7½-minute topographic quadrangle:
        Shelburne, New Hampshire

Shelters and Campsites

This section has two shelters and a campsite with a shelter. Because of heavy use at the Speck Pond site, AMC provides a caretaker there during the summer to maintain and manage the shelter and tentsites. A fee is charged at campsites and shelters.

Speck Pond Shelter and Campsite: Shelter built and maintained by AMC; 4.6 miles from northern end of section; shelter accommodates 10; also five tent platforms; caretaker in residence; water from small spring or from pond, a scenic mountain tarn; fee.

Next shelter or campsite: north 6.9 miles (Baldpate Lean-to); south 5.1 miles.

Full Goose Shelter: Rebuilt in 1970 and maintained by AMC; 9.7 miles from northern end of section; accommodates 12; also four tent platforms; on short side trail; water from small spring down side trail. Do not camp near spring.

Next shelter or campsite: north 5.1 miles; south 4.4 miles.

Carlo Col Shelter: Rebuilt in 1976 and maintained by AMC; 0.5 mile from southern end of section; down Carlo Col Trail 0.3 mile from A.T.; accommodates 14; also four tent platforms; water from small stream; Carlo Col Trail continues 2.6 miles past shelter to Success Pond Road.

Next shelter or campsite: north 4.4 miles; south 5.2 miles (Gentian Pond Campsite).

Regulations

Throughout this section, camping should be limited to the shelter sites and away from water sources. Off-Trail camping is limited. Do not camp in the fragile alpine bogs. State fire laws require that wood and charcoal fires be built only at designated shelter sites. At other places along the Trail, only gas stoves are permitted.

Supplies and Services

The nearest supply point to this section is Gorham, N.H. (ZIP Code 03581, telephone, supermarket, laundromat, restaurants, equipment, bus stop), 20.1 miles from the southern end of the section, reached by continuing 16.5 miles on the A.T. to U.S. 2 and, from there, 3.6 miles west into Gorham.

From the northern end of the section in Grafton Notch, it is 18 miles south on Maine 26 and U.S. 2 to the town of Bethel (ZIP Code 04217, telephone, groceries, bus stop).

Public Accommodations

Gorham has a number of motels, hostels, a guest house (inexpensive); 20.1 miles from the southern end of the section, reached by continuing 16.5 miles on the A.T. to U.S. 2 and, from there, 3.6 miles west into Gorham.

Trail Description, North to South

Miles	Data
0.0	Just north of Grafton Notch State Park trails parking area on Maine 26, leave road on western side. (Leave cars in parking area.) A.T. (Old Speck Trail) skirts northern side of parking area. Pass prominent directional signs near parking area.
0.1	Bear left on A.T. at trail junction. (Trail to right is Eyebrow Trail, which ascends northern side of the prominent cliffs on side of notch. This trail again intersects A.T. near top of cliffs.)
0.3	Cross brook. Beyond, Trail parallels brook up southern side of Eyebrow over several wide switchbacks. Ascend steadily.
1.1	In small box canyon, turn right, and cross brook. This is last reliable water source until Speck Pond in 3.5 miles.
1.2	Reach upper junction of Eyebrow Trail. A.T. turns left and ascends toward North Ridge. (It is 0.1 mile to right on Eyebrow Trail to the top of Eyebrow Cliffs, with a sheer 800-foot drop to floor of notch.)
1.5	Reach crest of North Ridge. Trail swings southwest on ridge, climbing steadily toward Old Speck.
3.0	Cross wooded knob, and descend into small col on ridge.
3.1	Reach junction with Link Trail to left (trail descends for 0.3 mile to a brook and start of East Spur Trail). A.T. continues ahead along northern ridge.
3.4	Begin steep ascent up side of east-west summit ridge.
3.5	After passing meadow area, reach junction with Mahoosuc Trail. A.T. turns right (west) along this trail and descends gradually. (To left is a gentle climb of 0.3 mile to the summit

of Old Speck Mountain, 4,180 feet, with high observation tower; view of western Maine mountains. From summit, East Spur Trail leads down mountain along open East Spur, then swings back to meet Link Trail.)

3.7 Descend steeply along open, scrubby boulder slope.

4.0 Intermittent spring is located 100 feet to left in small sag. Ascend gradually beyond.

4.3 At top of knob, descend steeply toward Speck Pond.

4.6 At junction of trails, reach **Speck Pond Shelter and Campsite** (caretaker, fee) on right. (To right is Speck Pond Trail, leading 3.3 miles west to Success Pond Road.) A.T. (Mahoosuc Trail) makes sharp left and skirts eastern side of Speck Pond.

4.9 Cross outlet of Speck Pond, and bear right. Ascend steadily.

5.5 Reach open summit of Mahoosuc Arm (3,765 feet). (May Cutoff to Speck Pond Trail leads 0.3 mile west.) Descend over ledges, gradually at first, then steeply. *Use caution in wet weather.*

6.6 Cross brook. Mahoosuc Notch 2 (smaller version of main notch) is to right, upstream. Beyond, slab southern slope of sheer-walled Mahoosuc Mountain.

7.1 At the eastern end of Mahoosuc Notch, turn right, and follow Bull Branch of Sunday River upstream. Route through notch is difficult and dangerous. *Take care to avoid slipping on damp moss.* Follow blazes over and under boulders.

8.2 At western end of Mahoosuc Notch, reach trail junction. A.T. (Mahoosuc Trail) turns sharply left and ascends steeply uphill. (Ahead, Mahoosuc Notch Trail leads west off range 2.5 miles to Success Pond Road.)

9.2 Reach bare crest of South Peak of Fulling Mill Mountain (3,395 feet). Bear right, and descend.

9.7 Just past bottom of sag, pass **Full Goose Shelter.** (Side trail leads southeast 250 yards to water.) A.T. beyond ascends steeply for 0.2 mile, then less steeply.

10.3 Emerge from woods at treeline on North Peak of Goose Eye Mountain.

10.7 Reach open North Peak of Goose Eye Mountain (3,675 feet), and turn left along line of cairns into sag ahead.

11.8 Just before steep ascent, reach north fork of Wright Trail (This trail descends 1.5 miles to meet its southern branch and another 1.5 miles to the Sunday River Road.)

11.9	Reach summit of East Peak of Goose Eye Mountain (3,794 feet). Turn right, and descend into col.
12.0	In col, reach southern branch of Wright Trail. (This trail descends 2.5 miles to meet its northern branch and another 1.5 miles to Sunday River Road.)
12.3	Reach trail junction. A.T. turns left and bypasses West Peak of Goose Eye Mountain, descending steeply into sag. (Ahead, Goose Eye Trail ascends 0.1 mile to summit of West Peak of Goose Eye Mountain, 3,854 feet, then descends west off the range 3.2 miles to the Success Pond Road.)
13.1	Reach bottom of sag. Begin ascent of Mt. Carlo.
13.7	Reach open summit of Mt. Carlo (3,565 feet). Bear right, and descend toward col ahead.
14.1	At junction of trails at floor of Carlo Col, A.T. (Mahoosuc Trail) continues ahead. (To right is Carlo Col Trail, leading northwest off range 2.6 miles to Success Pond Road. **Carlo Col Shelter** is down this side trail 0.3 mile.) Ahead, A.T. ascends steeply over ledges, then levels out.
14.6	Reach Maine-New Hampshire state line (2,972 feet) at clear-cut strip with boundary line marked by yellow blazes; end of section. To continue ahead, cross clear-cut strip, and descend. (See New Hampshire Section One.)

Trail Description, South to North

Miles   **Data**

0.0	Maine-New Hampshire state line is marked by yellow blazes along clear-cut strip (2,972 feet). A.T. follows Mahoosuc Trail, ascending gradually from state line, then descending steeply into Carlo Col, a small box canyon.
0.5	At junction of trails at floor of Carlo Col, A.T. continues ahead. (To left is Carlo Col Trail that leads northwest off range 2.6 miles to Success Pond Road. **Carlo Col Shelter** is down this side trail 0.3 mile.) A.T. beyond ascends steeply out of col.
0.9	Reach open summit of Mt. Carlo (3,565 feet). Bear left, and enter woods, descending into sag ahead.
1.5	Cross bottom of sag, and begin ascent toward Goose Eye Mountain.

2.0   Emerge from woods, and continue to ascend, crossing heath and scrub.

2.3   At trail junction, turn right, and descend gradually. (To left is Goose Eye Trail, which ascends 0.1 mile to the summit of West Peak of Goose Eye Mountain, 3,854 feet, then descends west off the range, 3.2 miles to the Success Pond Road.)

2.6   Reach junction with the southern fork of Wright Trail. (Wright Trail descends east 2.5 miles to the junction with its northern branch and another 1.5 miles to a branch of the Sunday River Road.) Trail ascends.

2.7   Reach East Peak of Goose Eye Mountain (3,794 feet). Bear left toward North Peak of Goose Eye Mountain, descending into sag between two peaks on open alpine ridge.

2.8   Reach junction with northern fork of Wright Trail. (Wright Trail descends east 1.5 miles to the junction with its southern branch.) Trail continues along ridge through two sags.

3.9   Reach North Peak of Goose Eye Mountain (3,675 feet). Turn right, and descend.

4.3   Reach treeline of North Peak of Goose Eye Mountain.

4.9   Near bottom of sag, pass **Full Goose Shelter**. Side trail leads southeast 250 yards to water. Beyond, A.T. ascends steeply toward Fulling Mill Mountain.

5.4   Reach bare crest of South Peak of Fulling Mill Mountain (3,395 feet). Descend gradually at first, through scrub growth, then very steeply 0.5 mile toward Mahoosuc Notch.

6.4   At bottom of descent, at western end of Mahoosuc Notch, reach trail junction. A.T. makes sharp right and proceeds easterly into notch. (Mahoosuc Notch Trail on left leads west off range 2.5 miles to Success Pond Road.) Route through notch is difficult and dangerous. *Take care to avoid slipping on damp moss.* Follow blazes over and under boulders.

7.5   At eastern end of Mahoosuc Notch, turn left, away from Bull Branch of Sunday River. With huge boulder on right, bear left across southern slope of sheer-walled Mahoosuc Mountain. Cross brook. Mahoosuc Notch 2 (smaller version of main notch) is to left, upstream. Ascend very steeply beyond for 0.9 mile. *Use caution in wet weather.*

9.1   Reach open summit of Mahoosuc Arm (3,765 feet). Descend steadily through woods. (May Cutoff Trail leads 0.3 mile west to Speck Pond Trail on left.)

9.7	Cross outlet of Speck Pond, and skirt eastern side of pond.
10.0	At trail junction, reach **Speck Pond Campsite.** (Speck Pond Trail leads left west 3.6 miles off range to Success Pond Road.) A.T. bears right and ascends away from pond.
10.6	In small sag, intermittent spring is 100 feet to right. Ascend along old, open, scrubby slide. Beyond, gradually ascend along ridge leading easterly toward summit of Old Speck.
11.1	Make sharp left, leaving Mahoosuc Trail. (Ahead, trail continues 0.3 mile to summit of Old Speck Mountain, 4,180 feet with high observation tower. From summit, East Spur Trail leads down mountain along open East Spur, then swings back to meet Link Trail.) A.T. skirts a meadow, then descends steeply north along ridge.
11.5	In small col on ridge, reach upper junction with Link Trail to right (which descends 0.3 mile to brook and lower end of East Spur Trail). Ahead, ascend over wooded knob, then descend gradually along North Ridge.
13.1	Bear right, and leave North Ridge. Trail swings southeast and descends to lower ridge.
13.4	In level area, reach upper junction of Eyebrow Trail. (To left, it is 0.1 mile to top of Eyebrow Cliffs, with sheer 800-foot drop to floor of Grafton Notch below. Eyebrow Trail continues beyond top of cliffs around northern end and descends to rejoin A.T. near floor of notch.) Ahead, A.T. continues to descend into small box canyon.
13.5	Cross small brook (last water for 3.4 miles), then descend, paralleling brook to south over series of switchbacks.
14.3	Cross mountain brook at bottom of main descent.
14.5	Reach lower junction with Eyebrow Trail that enters on left. Short distance beyond, pass prominent sign for Grafton Notch State Park. A.T. then skirts north of trails parking area.
14.6	Reach Maine 26 and end of section; parking available. To continue on Trail, cross road. (See *Appalachian Trail Guide to Maine* maps.) North from this point, it is:

> 0.8 mile to Table Rock Trail
> 3.1 miles to West Peak of Baldpate Lean-to
> 4.0 miles to East Peak of Baldpate Lean-to
> 5.8 miles to Frye Notch Lean-to
> 10.3 miles to Andover B-Hill (Upton) Road

Maine-New Hampshire State Line to Androscoggin Valley (U.S. 2)
New Hampshire Section One
16.5 Miles

Brief Description of Section

See the description of the Mahoosuc Range in the previous section. The Trail in this section passes four scenic mountain tarns: Gentian Pond, Moss Pond, Dream Lake, and Page Pond. The major peaks from north to south are:

Mt. Success, 3,565 feet
Cascade Mountain, 2,631 feet
Mt. Hayes, 2,555 feet (0.2 mile on side trail)

Four side trails, all maintained by AMC, intersect the A.T. From north to south, they are:

Success Trail—intersects the A.T. 1.3 miles from the northern end of the section.
Austin Brook Trail—intersects the A.T. 4.7 miles from the northern end of the section.
Peabody Brook Trail—intersects the A.T. and Dryad Falls Trail 6.9 miles from the northern end of the section.
Mahoosuc Trail—intersects the A.T. 3.9 miles from the southern end of the section.

For a description of all trails on the range, refer to the AMC *White Mountain Guide.* For current Trail information, contact the Appalachian Mountain Club (see "Important Addresses," page 219).

Road Approaches

The Trail is not directly accessible by road at the northern end. It can be reached 1.3 miles south of the Maine-New Hampshire border *via* the Success Trail, which begins on gravel Success Pond Road, 8.7 miles from Berlin, New Hampshire. The road is a Crown Vantage Company Road, open to public use but accessible only from Berlin and sometimes difficult to find. (Leave N.H. 16 just south of Berlin, 4.5 miles north of the eastern junction of U.S. 2 and N.H. 16 in Gorham, and cross the Androscoggin on the Cleveland Bridge. At the eastern end of the bridge, the road—Unity Street—swings left and passes through traffic lights in 0.7 mile from N.H. 16. At 0.8 mile, the road bears right across railroad tracks and becomes Hutchins Street. It turns sharply left at 1.6 miles, at Franks Village Store and continues past the Crown Vantage mill yard. At 1.9 miles, where there has usually been a large sign that reads "OHRV P 1 M," Success Pond Road begins on the right, east. Watch for trucks entering from the right. The first part of the road may be difficult to distinguish from branch roads, but, once out of the open area, it is well-defined.)

At the southern end of the section, the Trail crosses U.S. 2, 3.6 miles east of Gorham. Parking is available 0.8 mile north of U.S. 2 on Hogan Road, where the Trail turns right into the woods on the Centennial Trail, or at the junction of Hogan and North roads.

Maps

Map One (this guide)
AMC Carter-Mahoosuc Map

The A.T. route might not be current on the following:
USGS 7½-minute topographic quadrangles:
      Shelburne, New Hampshire
      Berlin, New Hampshire

Shelters and Campsites

This section has one campsite with shelter and one tentsite:
Gentian Pond Campsite: Shelter rebuilt in 1974 and maintained by AMC; 4.7 miles from northern end of section; accommodates 14; 4 tent platforms; water available from brook 500 feet north of shelter.

Next shelter or campsite: north 5.2 miles (Carlo Col Shelter); south 4.9 miles.

Trident Col Tentsite: Primitive site rebuilt in 1978 and maintained by AMC; 9.6 miles from northern end of section on short side trail; accommodates 8; tent platforms only; water available from spring (sometimes unreliable), 500 feet west of tentsite.

Next shelter or campsite: north 4.9 miles (Gentian Pond Campsite); south 8.8 miles (Rattle River Shelter).

In addition to those sites, Carlo Col Shelter is a half-mile north of the Maine-New Hampshire border, 0.3 mile down the Carlo Col Trail.

Regulations

Throughout this section, the Trail is mostly on a corridor jointly managed by the USFS and AMC. Camping is limited to designated sites, and off-trail camping opportunities are limited. Do not camp in fragile alpine bogs. State fire laws require wood and charcoal fires be built only at designated sites, and at some sites, only camping stoves are permitted. Use dead and downed wood only.

Supplies and Services

The nearest supply point is Gorham, New Hampshire (ZIP Code 03581, telephone, supermarket, laundromat, restaurants, bus stop, equipment), 3.6 miles west of the southern end of the section. Supplies are also available in Berlin (11.7 miles; 3.0 miles on Success Trail to Success Pond Road, then 8.7 miles to the end of Success Pond Road.

From the Trail crossing of U.S. 2 camping is available, and it is 2.0 miles west to a restaurant.

In an emergency, call the New Hampshire State Police, (603) 846-5517 or (603) 846-3333, or AMC Pinkham Notch Visitor Center, (603) 466-2721.

Public Accommodations

Gorham, 3.6 miles west on U.S. 2 from the southern end of the section has a number of motels, hostels, a guest house (inexpensive), and camping, as does Berlin, at the end of the Success Pond Road. Tourist cabins and a camping area are available on U.S. 2, 2.0 miles west of the Trail crossing.

Trail Description, North to South

Miles	Data

0.0   Section begins at Maine-New Hampshire state line (2,972 feet). The boundary is designated by yellow blazes along a cleared strip. Descend southwest to rough col, and ascend along flank of unnamed 3,335-foot peak north of Mt. Success.

1.3   Reach junction. (Success Trail descends right, 3.0 miles, to Success Pond Road.) Ascend northern ridge of Mt. Success.

1.9   Reach summit of Mt. Success (3,565 feet). Descend southwest to ledges of lower peak of Mt. Success, and enter woods.

3.3   Cross brook in col. Climb southwest over two humps, then to ridgetop. Drop generally south down ridge and through spruce grove.

4.7   Reach **Gentian Pond Campsite** on left (2,166 feet). (Austin Brook Trail descends left 3.3 miles to North Road in Shelburne.) Water is available from a small inlet brook at the northeastern side of pond; follow a path 300 yards northeast from shelter. Beyond shelter, follow southwest side of Gentian Pond, pass around northwest corner of pond, and climb steeply.

5.4   Pass along northwestern shore of Moss Pond. Ascend northwest and west, then descend through swampy woodland. Cross inlet brook of Dream Lake, and briefly follow lumber road.

6.9   Reach junction. (Peabody Brook Trail leads left, passes Dryad Falls Trail in 100 yards, and descends 3.1 miles to North Road. Dryad Falls Trail descends past a series of cascades to North Road.) Just beyond junction, recross inlet brook of Dream Lake, and continue around lake's northern end. Climb around end of small ridge, descend to cross upper (west) branch of Peabody Brook, and then climb west.

8.0   Reach Wocket Ledge, a spur of Bald Cap. (Side trail leads northwest 50 feet to ledges.) Descend steeply southwest, then gradually west.

8.6   Pass to south of Page Pond and cross outlet on beaver dam. Descend west over southern flank of peak west of Page Pond. Continue traversing side of two additional peaks. These three peaks form the trident. Climb briefly northwest.

9.6   Reach Trident Col. **Trident Col Tentsite** is 175 yards to right on side trail. Water is available from spring 50 yards west of campsite. A.T. climbs steeply southwest beside ledges to eastern peak of Cascade Mountain, continuing west and southwest, rising gradually.

10.7   Reach summit of Cascade Mountain (2,631 feet). Veer sharply northwest back into woods, and then descend the southwest ridge of Cascade Mountain. Pass through col between Cascade Mountain and Mt. Hayes. (Water is just east of Trail.) Climb northern ridge of Mt. Hayes.

12.6   A.T. diverges left from Mahoosuc Trail to follow Centennial Trail (constructed in 1976, AMC's centennial year). (Mahoosuc Trail continues straight ahead 0.2 mile to summit of Mt. Hayes, 2,555 feet, then descends 3.1 miles to N.H. 16, 1.3 miles north of Gorham.) Descend southeast on Centennial Trail over series of open ledges, and then climb slightly.

12.9   Reach eastern summit of Mt. Hayes on open ledges with views of Carter-Moriah Range and northern Presidentials. Descend southeast to small valley, then climb briefly. Resume descent, and cross a logging road.

15.0   Cross brook (reliable water). Continue on woods road. Soon, turn right off woods road. Descend gradually, then more steeply on stone steps. Join woods road, and follow right.

15.7   Turn left onto gravel Hogan Road at lower end of Centennial Trail.

16.0   Turn right onto paved North Road.

16.2   Cross Androscoggin River on Leadmine Bridge with small dam and power plant on right. Cross railroad tracks.

16.5   Reach section end at U.S. 2, 3.6 miles east of Gorham (760 feet). To continue on Trail, turn left, cross Rattle River on highway bridge, and then turn right onto Rattle River Trail (see New Hampshire Section Two).

Trail Description, South to North

Miles   **Data**

0.0   From U.S. 2, 3.6 miles east of Gorham (760 feet), take North Road to the north. Soon, cross railroad tracks.

0.3	Cross Androscoggin River on Leadmine Bridge, with small dam and power plant on left.
0.5	Turn left from North Road onto gravel Hogan Road.
0.8	Turn right onto woods road, beginning of Centennial Trail, opposite clearing and parking area. (Trail was constructed in 1976, AMC's centennial year.) A.T. turns left off woods road in 50 yards, heads northwest, and climbs steeply on stone steps, then more gradually. Turn left onto a woods road.
1.5	Cross small brook (reliable water). Cross logging road. Climb, then turn sharply left; ascend moderately to open ledges.
3.6	Reach eastern summit of Mt. Hayes with views of Carter-Moriah Range and northern Presidentials. Continue across open ledges.
3.9	Reach junction with Mahoosuc Trail to left. Mt. Hayes (2,555 feet), is 0.2 mile left on this trail, with N.H. 16 (1.3 miles north of Gorham) 3.1 miles beyond. Bear right, and descend north to col between Mt. Hayes and Cascade Mountain. (Water may be found in col just east, to right of Trail.) Beyond col, climb Cascade Mountain by southwest ridge.
5.8	Reach summit of Cascade Mountain (2,631 feet). Veer sharply left back into woods, heading northeast and east. Cross eastern peak of Cascade Mountain, then descend steeply to northeast and east.
6.9	Reach Trident Col. **Trident Col Tentsite** is 175 yards left on side trail, with water from spring 50 yards west. About 0.3 mile beyond col, briefly follow old logging road. Turn left (southeast), and descend, traversing ridge past three peaks that form Trident. Beyond Trident, continue east, cross three gullies (possible water), and begin ascent.
7.9	Pass to south of Page Pond, and cross outlet on beaver dam. Climb gradually east, then steeply northeast.
8.5	Reach Wocket Ledge, a spur of Bald Cap. (Side trail leads northwest 50 feet to ledges.) Descend steeply southwest, then gradually west. Descend east, cross upper (left) branch of Peabody Brook, climb around end of small ridge, and then gradually descend to Dream Lake. Bear left, continuing around northern end of lake.
9.6	Cross inlet brook of Dream Lake. Just beyond, reach junction. (Peabody Brook Trail descends right, passing Dryad Falls Trail in 100 yards, 3.1 miles to North Road. Dryad Falls Trail

descends right past series of scenic cascades to North Road.) From Dream Lake, A.T. follows old lumber road 100 yards, recrosses inlet brook, and continues northeast through sometimes swampy woodland, ascending initially, then descending.

11.1   Reach Moss Pond, and follow northwestern shore. About 0.3 mile past pond, turn abruptly right, and descend to Gentian Pond. Pass along southwestern shore of pond.

11.8   Reach **Gentian Pond Campsite** (2,166 feet) on the right. Water is available at small brook at northeastern side of pond, reached by side path 300 yards northeast from the shelter. (Austin Brook Trail descends right 3.3 miles to North Road in Shelburne.) Beyond shelter, A.T. ascends through spruce grove to ridge, crosses small col, then climbs over two steep humps.

13.2   Cross small brook in col after second hump. Ascend steeply northeast, leave woods, and head onto open ledges.

14.6   Reach summit of Mt. Success (3,565 feet), and descend north to col.

15.2   Reach junction. (Success Trail descends left 3.0 miles to Success Pond Road.) Climb northwest along the flank of unnamed 3,335-foot peak north of Mt. Success. Pass through col, and continue northwest.

16.5   Reach Maine-New Hampshire state line (2,972 feet), where section ends. Border is marked by yellow blazes along cleared strip. From this point, A.T. continues north on Mahoosuc Trail (see "The Mahoosuc Range in Maine," page 60).

Androscoggin Valley (U.S. 2) to Pinkham Notch (N.H. 16)
New Hampshire Section Two
21.1 Miles

Brief Description of Section

The Carter-Moriah Range offers rugged hiking on an uninterrupted footpath. The Trail drops precipitously into Carter Notch and passes the Carter Lakes but traces a high ridgecrest route for the rest of its length. From the Androscoggin Valley (approximately 800 feet above sea level) in the north, the Trail follows the Rattle River Trail up the ridge and the Kenduskeag Trail, Carter-Moriah Trail, and Wildcat Ridge Trail along the ridge, then descends across the Wild Kittens (small peaks) and the Lost Pond Trail to Pinkham Notch (approximately 2,000 feet). The major peaks the Trail traverses in this section are, from north to south:

Mt. Moriah, 4,049 feet
North Carter Mountain, approximately 4,530 feet
Middle Carter Mountain, approximately 4,600 feet
South Carter Mountain, 4,458 feet
Mt. Hight, 4,675 feet
Carter Dome, 4,832 feet
Wildcat Mountain, 4,380 feet

Allow three days to traverse this section. Water may be scarce on the ridge.

This section has a number of side trails, described briefly in the Trail data, that provide interesting side or loop hikes. Five trails provide access to the A.T. from N.H. 16 on the western side of the range, and five trails on the eastern side lead to different parts of the White Mountain National Forest. Hikers may ride the Wildcat Gondola, when it is in operation, from Pinkham Notch to Peak E of Wildcat Mountain. For more information, see the AMC *White Mountain Guide*. For current trail conditions, contact the information desk at Pinkham Notch Visitor Center (see "Important Addresses," page 219).

Road Approaches

Both the northern and southern ends of this section are accessible from major highways. At the northern end, the Trail crosses U.S. 2, a major east-west highway, 3.6 miles east of Gorham (parking). At the southern end, the Trail crosses N.H. 16 at Pinkham Notch (parking), 8.0 miles north of Jackson and 12.0 miles south of Gorham.

Theft and vandalism have been reported at both parking areas. Do not leave valuables in cars.

Maps

Map Two (this guide)
AMC Carter-Mahoosuc Map
White Mountain National Forest Map (1:250,000)
AMC Mt. Washington Range Map

The A.T. route might not be current on the following:
USGS 15-minute topographic quadrangles:
North Conway, New Hampshire
Crawford Notch, New Hampshire
Mt. Washington, New Hampshire
USGS 7½-minute topographic quadrangles:
Carter Dome, New Hampshire
Wild River, New Hampshire

Shelters and Campsites

This section has two shelters:
Rattle River Shelter: Built and maintained by USFS; 1.9 miles from northern end of section; accommodates 8; water from river.

Next shelter or campsite: north 8.8 miles (Trident Col Tentsite); south 6.1 miles.

Imp Campsite: Shelter built and maintained by AMC; 8.0 miles from northern end of section; 0.1 mile down side trail; shelter accommodates ten; five tent platforms; caretaker in residence; water from brook by shelter; fee.

Next shelter or campsite: north 6.1 miles (Rattle River Shelter); south 17.9 miles (Osgood Tentsite).

Carter Notch Hut is located 7.2 miles south of Imp Campsite and 5.9 miles north of Pinkham Notch at the section's southern end (see "Public Accommodations" below).

Regulations

Except for its northern 0.8 mile, where camping is not permitted, this section is within the White Mountain National Forest.

Camping and wood or charcoal fires are prohibited in the following areas, except at designated sites: above treeline (defined as areas where trees are less than eight feet tall), within one-quarter mile of Imp Campsite and Carter Notch Hut, within one-quarter mile of intersection of the Carter-Moriah Trail (A.T.) and the Carter Dome Trail (Zeta Pass) in Cutler River Drainage, and within one-quarter mile of N.H. 16 in Pinkham Notch.

Campfire permits are required for open fires outside White Mountain National Forest lands. They can be obtained from AMC at Pinkham Notch (see "Important Addresses," page 219).

Supplies and Services

This section's nearest supply point is Gorham, 3.6 miles west of the northern end of the section (ZIP Code 03581, telephone, supermarket, laundromat, restaurants, hardware store, bus service, doctor, bank, vet, and equipment).

Limited supplies and services (cafeteria, showers, rest rooms, snacks, phone, rooms, bus stop) are available at Pinkham Notch Visitor Center at the southern end of the section.

In an emergency, contact the Imp Campsite caretaker, Carter Notch Hut, Pinkham Notch Visitor Center, (603) 466-2721, or New Hampshire State Police, (603) 846-5517 or (603) 846-3333.

Public Accommodations

Gorham, 3.6 miles west on U.S. 2 from the northern end of the section, has motels, hostels, guest houses, and camping areas. On U.S. 2, 2.0 miles west of the Trail crossing, cabins and a camping area are available.

AMC built and maintains two facilities where lodging is available. Reservations may be made by calling or writing the reservations secretary, Pinkham Notch Visitor Center (see "Important Addresses," page 219).

Carter Notch Hut: oldest hut still in use, erected in 1914, 5.9 miles from southern end of section on short side trail; reservations strongly recommended; self-service year-round; caretaker in residence; fee; accommodates 40; ample water; self-service year-round.

Pinkham Notch Visitor Center: extensive mountain facility and AMC's North Country operations base, located on N.H. 16 at the southern end of section; reservations required; meals served; information desk; limited equipment; hot drinks and snacks; pack-up room; telephone; showers; accommodates 107.

Trail Description, North to South

Miles	Data
0.0	From junction of U.S. 2 and North Road, 3.6 miles east of Gorham, proceed east on U.S. 2, crossing highway bridge over Rattle River.
0.2	Turn right through parking lot onto Rattle River Trail, and ascend gradually on woods road. A snowmobile trail enters from right, then diverges left.
1.9	Pass **Rattle River Shelter** on left, built and maintained by USFS. Water available from river.
2.3	Take right fork, and cross East Rattle River. Ascend steeply.
3.4	Cross Rattle River, and climb steeply.
4.5	Reach junction where A.T. turns right onto Kenduskeag Trail. (Kenduskeag Trail also leads left to Shelburne Trail, which leads north to U.S. 2 and south to Wild River.) A.T. continues over wooded summit of Middle Moriah Mountain, passes through a sag, and ascends steeply.
5.9	Reach junction where Kenduskeag Trail ends. A.T. turns left onto Carter-Moriah Trail and descends south, swinging west along the wooded ridge. (At junction, Carter-Moriah Trail leads right, north, soon reaching rocky summit of Mt. Moriah, 4,049 feet. From summit, Carter-Moriah Trail continues north, descending 4.5 miles to U.S. 2 in Gorham.)
7.3	Reach junction in col. (Stony Brook Trail descends right 3.5 miles to N.H. 16, and Moriah Brook Trail descends left to

Wild River.) A.T. ascends ahead on Carter-Moriah Trail, passes across an open knob, then descends southwest.

8.0   Reach junction where side trail descends right 0.1 mile to **Imp Campsite and shelter**. Trail continues across stream, turns sharply left, then climbs south, first gradually, then steeply.

9.7   Pass over wooded summit of North Carter Mountain (4,530 feet).

9.9   North Carter Trail descends right, west, 1.2 miles to Imp Trail, which descends 2.3 additional miles to N.H. 16. Cross boggy area, and continue over many minor knolls with occasional views. Pass open ledges on Mt. Lethe.

10.5 Cross wooded summit of Middle Carter Mountain (4,600 feet), and descend to col, then ascend.

11.8 Pass over wooded summit of South Carter Mountain (4,458 feet), and descend.

12.6 Reach Zeta Pass (3,990 feet). (Carter Dome Trail descends right 1.9 miles to Nineteen-Mile Brook Trail, which leads 1.9 miles to N.H. 16.) Water is generally found near path in Zeta Pass. (In other direction, Carter Dome Trail coincides with the Carter-Moriah Trail for 150 feet, then diverges right and ascends, bypassing Mt. Hight.) A.T. bears left and ascends steeply toward Mt. Hight.

13.2 Make a sharp right turn on the open summit of Mt. Hight (4,675 feet). Descend slightly, and continue southwest through scrub growth.

13.6 Carter Dome Trail enters from right and rejoins A.T. (One hundred feet beyond, Black Angel Trail descends left, east, to Wild River.) A.T. continues ahead, climbing open slope.

14.0 Reach open summit of Carter Dome (4,832 feet). (Rainbow Trail descends left, east, to Perkins Notch and Wild River.) A.T. descends southwest, first moderately to a side trail to a spring, then very steeply.

15.2 Reach junction in Carter Notch where Carter-Moriah Trail ends and A.T. turns right onto Nineteen-Mile Brook Trail, skirts shore of pond, and ascends steeply. (Left of junction, Nineteen-Mile Brook Trail passes between Carter Lakes and reaches **Carter Notch Hut** in 0.1 mile. From hut, Wildcat River Trail descends south toward Mt. Jackson.)

15.4 Reach height of land (3,388 feet) and junction where Trail turns left onto Wildcat Ridge Trail and ascends steeply on switchbacks. (Nineteen-Mile Brook Trail continues ahead, descending in 3.5 miles to N.H. 16.)

16.1 Reach Peak A of Wildcat Mountain (4,380 feet). Continue south through woods along ridge, cross wooded peaks B and C (both 4,272 feet), and descend over many humps to Wildcat Col. Begin ascent of Peak D.

18.1 Swing around northern end of Peak D (4,063 feet), passing wooden observation platform with views of Tuckerman (left) and Huntington (right) ravines on Mt. Washington, as well as northern Presidential Range. (The Wildcat Mountain gondola terminal building is 0.1 mile beyond, with open area for hikers. When in operation, the gondola descends north-west to N.H. 16. Also, any number of ski trails may be descended to N.H. 16.) A.T. continues southwest on ridge.

18.4 Cross summit of Peak E (4,041 feet). Pass over lower Peak E, descend gradually to upper ledges (fine views), then begin an exceptionally steep decent, *requiring extra care.* Pass over middle and lower ledges, and continue descent at a more moderate grade.

20.2 Reach junction where Trail turns right onto Lost Pond Trail. (Ahead, Wildcat Ridge Trail descends 0.1 mile to N.H. 16 at Glen Ellis Falls.) Follow Trail around eastern edge of Lost Pond, and descend gradually to Ellis River. Where Square Ledge Trail bears right, A.T. turns left across small marsh on wooden bridge.

21.1 Reach N.H. 16 at Pinkham Notch Visitor Center on left and end of section. To continue on A.T., cross highway, and follow Tuckerman Ravine Trail for 250 feet, where A.T. branches right (see New Hampshire Section Three).

Trail Description, South to North

Miles   **Data**

0.0 From Pinkham Notch Visitor Center, cross N.H. 16, and follow Lost Pond Trail. Cross wooden bridge over small bog. Square Ledge Trail leads left. A.T. goes along eastern bank of Ellis River. Ascend slightly from river, pass around eastern edge of Lost Pond, and continue along outlet stream.

0.9   Reach junction where A.T. turns left onto Wildcat Ridge Trail. (To right, Wildcat Ridge Trail leads 0.1 mile to N.H. 16 at Glen Ellis Falls.) Trail shortly begins an exceptionally steep ascent *requiring extra care*. Pass lower, middle, and upper ledges, all with fine views. Ascent then moderates. Pass over lower summit of Wildcat Peak E.

2.7   Cross summit of Peak E (4,041 feet). Swing north, descend slightly. Pass near Wildcat Mountain gondola terminal building. (Any number of ski trails may be descended west to N.H. 16. When in operation, the gondola descends northwest to N.H. 16.) Ascend northeast from terminal building.

3.0   Reach Peak D (4,063 feet), passing wooden observation platform with views of Tuckerman (left) and Huntington (right) ravines on Mt. Washington, as well as northern Presidential Range. Descend to Wildcat Col, then ascend, crossing many small humps, then Peaks C and B (both 4,270 feet).

5.0   Reach Peak A, summit of Wildcat Mountain (4,380 feet). Descend on switchbacks into Carter Notch.

5.7   Reach junction in Carter Notch (3,388 feet). (Nineteen-Mile Brook Trail descends left 3.5 miles to N.H. 16.) A.T. turns right here, descending to lake on Nineteen-Mile Brook Trail.

5.9   Reach junction where A.T. turns left and follows Carter-Moriah Trail. (Nineteen-Mile Brook Trail continues ahead, passes between two small Carter Lakes, and reaches **Carter Notch Hut** in 0.1 mile. From hut, Wildcat River Trail descends south toward Jackson.) A.T. ascends very steeply east, passing side trails to a view and, farther, a spring, then ascends more moderately.

7.1   Reach open summit of Carter Dome (4,832 feet). (Rainbow Trail descends right to Perkins Notch and Wild River.) A.T. descends north on Carter-Moriah Trail.

7.5   Reach junction. Black Angel Trail descends right, east, to Wild River. One hundred feet farther, where Carter Dome Trail leads left, bypassing summit of Mt. Hight, A.T. ascends right through scrub growth.

7.9   Reach summit of Mt. Hight (4,675 feet). Turn sharply left at summit (can be obscure in bad weather), and descend steeply.

8.5   Carter Dome Trail reenters from left. Beyond, in low point of Zeta Pass (3,990 feet), reach junction. (Carter Dome Trail descends left 1.9 miles to Nineteen-Mile Brook Trail, which descends 1.9 miles to N.H. 16.) Water usually is found near path in Zeta Pass. From pass, A.T. ascends north steadily.

9.3 Reach wooded summit of South Carter Mountain (4,458 feet), and continue north through woods along ridge, descending to col, then ascending.

10.6 Pass over wooded summit of Middle Carter Mountain (4,600 feet) to open ledges on Mt. Lethe. From this viewpoint, descend, and cross boggy area.

11.2 Reach junction. (North Carter Trail descends left, west, 1.2 miles to Imp Trail, which descends an additional 2.3 miles to N.H. 16.) A.T. ascends northeast.

11.4 Reach wooded summit of North Carter Mountain (4,530 feet). Descend steeply, with rough footing, then more gradually, passing through a wet area.

13.1 Cross stream, and reach junction. (Side trail descends left 0.1 mile to Imp Campsite.) A.T. climbs over an open knob and descends northeast.

13.8 Reach junction in col. (Stony Brook Trail descends left 3.5 miles to N.H. 16, and Moriah Brook Trail descends right to Wild River.) A.T. continues on Carter-Moriah Trail, ascending northeast along ridge through woods with good views.

15.2 Reach junction where A.T. turns right onto Kenduskeag Trail. (Carter-Moriah Trail continues ahead, just beyond the summit of Mt. Moriah, 4,049 feet. From summit, Carter Moriah Trail continues north, descending 4.5 miles to U.S. 2 in Gorham.) A.T. descends steeply northeast, passes through a sag, and continues over Middle Moriah Mountain.

16.6 Reach junction where of A.T. and Rattle River Trail and descends steeply. (Kenduskeag Trail continues to Shelburne Trail, that leads north to U.S. 2 and south to Wild River.)

17.7 Cross Rattle River, and descend less steeply.

18.8 Cross East Branch of Rattle River.

19.2 Pass **Rattle River Shelter.** From shelter, Trail follows old logging road north. A snowmobile trail enters from right, then diverges left.

20.9 Cross through parking lot. Reach U.S. 2, and turn left (west), crossing Rattle River on highway bridge.

21.1 Reach North Road and end of section, 3.6 miles east of Gorham on U.S. 2. To continue on Trail, turn right onto North Road (see New Hampshire Section One).

Pinkham Notch (N.H. 16) to Crawford Notch (U.S. 302)
New Hampshire Section Three
26.0 Miles

Brief Description of Section

The Presidential Range is the highest mountain group traversed by the A.T. north of Clingmans Dome on the North Carolina-Tennessee border. For most of the nearly 12-mile distance between Mt. Madison and Mt. Pierce (Mt. Clinton), the Trail is above treeline. From Pinkham Notch (approximately 2,000 feet above sea level) in the north, the Trail gradually ascends on the Old Jackson Road to the Mt. Washington Auto Road. It crosses the Auto Road into the Great Gulf Wilderness, descends gradually on the Madison Gulf Trail, follows the Osgood Cutoff, and then ascends steeply on the Osgood Trail to a ridge above treeline. From Madison Springs Hut, it continues to follow the ridgecrest on the Gulfside Trail to the summit of Mt. Washington, where P.T. Barnum declared the view "the second-greatest show on earth!"

The Trail gradually descends on Crawford Path, past Lakes of the Clouds, to Mt. Pierce. It reenters the woods and follows the Webster Cliff Trail across a sometimes-open ridge and Webster Cliffs to Crawford Notch (1,277 feet), the southern end of this section. Most of the section is within the White Mountain National Forest. The southern end lies within Crawford Notch State Park.

The elevation change in this section is enormous, but it is mostly at the ends of the ridge. Many less significant climbs are along the ridgecrest. The A.T. passes over the highest Presidential summits but bypasses many others that can be reached by short loop trails, scarcely increasing the total distance traveled. The major peaks traversed in the section, from north to south, are:

Mt. Madison, 5,363 feet
Mt. Washington, 6,288 feet
Mt. Franklin, 5,004 feet
Mt. Pierce (Mt. Clinton), 4,310 feet
Mt. Jackson, 4,052 feet
Mt. Webster, 3,910 feet

The alpine ridge of the Presidential Range is exposed to storms that rise rapidly and are often violent, with hurricane-force winds and freezing conditions, even in summer. The above-treeline sections of the Gulfside Trail and Crawford Path are marked with frequent cairns, topped by yellow-painted stones; nonetheless, it is still possible to lose the Trail in fog or bad weather. Carry ample extra clothing, and, if weather becomes threatening, promptly descend to shelter by the shortest route. If severe weather is predicted (forecasts available at Pinkham Notch Visitor Center and Madison Springs Hut, Lakes of the Clouds Hut, and Mizpah Hut), take the shortcut between Lakes of the Clouds and Pinkham Notch *via* Tuckerman Ravine and Hermit Lakes (shelter), which eliminates crossing the northern Presidential Range. Even this route can be forbidding in bad weather (about one death per year occurs) and should be approached cautiously.

Treeline in the Presidential Range is at about 4,200 feet. Above this elevation, only stunted krummholz (spruce) and alpine plants survive the severe weather. The vegetation is extremely vulnerable to damage by foot traffic, evident in many places where the obliteration of the alpine tundra has given way to erosion, visibly scarring the mountainside. To prevent trampling vegetation and erosion and allow successful regeneration of damaged areas, rock steps and borders have been installed in several parts of the section. Closely follow the established treadway to keep impact to a minimum.

The system of side trails in this section is comprehensive and offers hikers many choices for exploring the Presidential Range. Many of those trails are briefly noted in the Trail description. For complete information, refer to the AMC *White Mountain Guide* or AMC *Guide to Mt. Washington and the Presidential Range*; both describe the region in detail. For information on these books, current trail conditions, and answers to questions concerning material not in this guide, contact the information desk at AMC Pinkham Notch Visitor Center (see "Important Addresses," page 219).

Mt. Washington Summit

Mt. Washington (6,288 feet), the highest U.S. peak north of the Carolinas and east of the Mississippi, is part of the New Hampshire state park system. The Mt. Washington Cog Railway, the world's first mountain-climbing railway, ascends from Marshfield Station three miles up the western ridge of the mountain to the summit. The Mt.

Washington Auto Road (toll road), beginning on N.H. 16, winds eight miles up the eastern side of the mountain to the summit.

The Sherman Adams Building, on the summit just north of the highest point on the mountain, is owned by the state and has a snack bar, souvenir shop, toilets, telephone, and post office. It also houses the Mt. Washington Observatory and Museum. Southwest of the summit is the transmitter building, with two broadcasting towers and a radio and television station. The old Tip-Top House, built in 1853, is west of the summit building and is usually open daily as a museum during the park's season.

Mt. Washington has long been a center of attention. The first path to the summit was cut in 1819 by a father-and-son team, Abel and Ethan Allen Crawford, who later established the first tourist hostelries in the notch now bearing their name. In 1839, Thomas, a younger son of Abel, converted Crawford Path into a bridle path, the first of its kind to the summit. The first bridle path from the east was constructed between 1851 and 1861 and started at the Glen House, where the Auto Road begins.

The summit stands well above treeline and, with the 20-mile ridge of the Presidential Range, forms an arctic island in New England, with permafrost, arctic flora resembling that of northern Labrador, and some of the worst weather in the world. The severe weather is caused by high winds and frequent sharp temperature changes influenced by air masses flowing from the south, west, and the St. Lawrence River Valley in the north.

The first weather observatory was established on the summit in 1870 and staffed by the U.S. Signal Corps until 1892. The present observatory was initiated in 1932 by Joe Dodge, former AMC hut-system manager, and Bob Monahan, Dartmouth College weather buff. In 1934, the observatory measured a wind velocity of 231 miles per hour, the strongest wind ever recorded on land in the world. The observatory is staffed throughout the year, carrying out scientific experiments and recordings, including a morning report on the summit weather conditions. The observatory is not open to the public, but a museum on the lower floor of the Sherman Adams Building contains summit artifacts and exhibits of unusual flora and fauna. A museum admission fee supports the observatory.

Because of the violent weather, the Crawfords provided crude stone huts for shelter. The first summit house was built in 1852; the Tip-Top House, in 1853. Those small structures became inadequate, and the first large summit house was opened in 1874. A fire swept the summit in 1908, destroying the summit house and damaging the Tip-Top House.

Construction of the Carriage Road began in 1851, and it opened in 1861. Today, thousands of cars ascend the eight miles to the summit at grades of up to 12 percent.

The cog railway began operating in 1869. Its trestle over Jacob's Ladder, at a 37.4-percent grade, is the steepest in the world. Sylvester Marsh built the 3.5-mile railroad and powered it by a coal-fired steam engine, which is still used by the present owner, Ellen Teague. The railway was honored at its 100th birthday by designation as a national historical mechanical and civil-engineering landmark.

In 1937-38, a radio tower was installed on the summit. FM radio broadcasts from the summit began as early as 1941, and, in 1954, the current television transmitter was added. Small buildings for those operations were built and maintained under the most trying weather conditions. A snow vehicle is used for the weekly change of personnel in the winter.

Until recently, the summit was privately owned. From early grants and purchases, it passed to Colonel Henry Teague of the cog railway, who left it to Dartmouth College. Most of it is now owned by the state of New Hampshire.

For additional information about Mt. Washington, see *"Mt. Washington and the Heart of the Presidential Range"* by the Boston Museum of Science.

Crawford Notch State Park

In 1777, Timothy Nash spied a defile, in what was then considered an impassable wall of mountains, while he was hunting moose on Cherry Mountain.

Soon after Nash's discovery, a road was built through Crawford Notch. It was rough, crossing the Saco River 32 times. In some places, horses had to be lifted or lowered by ropes. As poor as it was, the route was far preferable to traveling around the White Mountains. The first shipment sent from the coast through the notch was a barrel of rum, that was sampled freely during the venture and arrived a great deal lighter than when it began its voyage.

In 1825, Samuel Willey and his family moved into the notch and opened a hostel. The next year, the calamitous "Willey Slide" shook the notch, taking the lives of the entire family. Tons of debris suddenly and violently slid and fell from the valley walls, partly determining the shape of the notch today. Despite the devastation of the slide, activity in the notch did not slow down; it was an important commercial route and a prime spot for summer tourists.

Today, the notch is preserved in Crawford Notch State Park. The Willey House Site and Willey Slide are still visible one mile north of the Trail crossing. A snack bar and souvenir shop are nearby; open mid-May to mid-October. AMC operates the recently renovated Crawford Hostel and an information center 3.7 miles north of the Trail crossing on U.S. 302.

Road Approaches

Both ends of this section are accessible by major highways. At the northern end, the Trail crosses N.H. 16 at Pinkham Notch (parking), eight miles north of Jackson and 12 miles south of Gorham. At the southern end, the Trail crosses U.S. 302 in Crawford Notch opposite the road to the former Willey House Station (parking), eight miles north of Bartlett and 10 miles south of Twin Mountain. Theft and vandalism have been reported at both ends. Do not leave any valuables in vehicles.

Maps

Map Two (this guide)
AMC Mt. Washington Range Map
White Mountain National Forest Map (1:250,000)

The A.T. route might not be current on the following:
USGS 15-minute topographic quadrangles:
    Mt. Washington, New Hampshire
    Crawford Notch, New Hampshire

Shelters and Campsites

Because of the alpine nature of this section, few overnight facilities are available. Anticipate long hiking days.

One shelter and two cabins, or huts, all some distance off the Trail, three campsites, and one public campground (on U.S. 302) are located in this section. AMC's Lakes of the Clouds Hut, in addition to its regular services (see "Public Accommodations"), offers lodging for backpackers; reservations suggested.

Osgood Tentsite (USFS): Four tent platforms, spring; near junction of Osgood Trail and Osgood Cutoff; 4.8 miles from northern end of section.

Next shelter or campsite: North 17.9 miles (Imp Campsite); south 3.0 miles.

Valley Way Tentsite (USFS): Four tent platforms, spring; 0.6 mile down Valley Way side trail.

Next shelter or campsite: north 3.0 miles; south 0.9 miles.

Crag Camp: Closed cabin; maintained by Randolph Mountain Club (RMC); 8.7 miles from northern end of section, 1.1 miles down spur trail; blankets, cooking utensils, gas stove; accommodates 12; caretaker; fee; ample water.

Gray Knob: Closed cabin; maintained by RMC and town of Randolph; 8.7 miles from northern end of section; 1.2 miles down Lowe's Path; blankets, cooking utensils, gas stove; accommodates 14; caretaker; fee; ample water.

Next shelter or campsite: north 0.9 miles; south 0.6 mile.

The Perch Shelter: Built and maintained by RMC; 9.3 miles from northern end of section; 0.9 mile down side trail; accommodates 8; caretaker; fee; ample water.

Next shelter or campsite: north 0.6 mile; south 9.6 miles.

Nauman Tentsite: Built and maintained by AMC; adjacent to Mizpah Spring Hut; 6.4 miles from southern end of section; 6 tent platforms; accommodates 20; fee; ample water; caretaker in attendance.

Next shelter or campsite: north 9.6 miles; south 6.4 miles.

Dry River Campground: Operated and maintained by New Hampshire Division of Parks in Crawford Notch State Park; on U.S. 302, 1.5 miles south of Trail crossing; 24 tentsites; ample water.

Next shelter or campsite: north 6.4 miles; south 2.9 miles.

This section also has four AMC mountain huts, described under "Public Accommodations."

Regulations

The southern part of this section lies in Crawford Notch State Park, where camping and fires are not permitted, except at Dry River Campground. The rest of the Trail passes through White Mountain National Forest, where special regulations apply.

Camping and wood or charcoal fires are prohibited within one-quarter mile of Madison Springs Hut, the Perch Shelter, Gray Knob Cabin, Crag Camp Cabin, Lakes of the Clouds Hut, and Mizpah Spring Hut, except at designated areas.

Camping and wood or charcoal fires are prohibited above treeline. The A.T. from Mt. Madison to Mt. Pierce, a distance of 11.5 miles, is mostly above treeline. (Treeline is an area where trees are less than eight feet tall.)

Camping and fires are prohibited in the Cutler River Drainage (this includes the 1.9-mile section of Trail between Pinkham Notch Visitor Center and the Mt. Washington Auto Road) or within one-quarter mile of N.H. 16 in Pinkham Notch. In the Great Gulf Wilderness, between the Auto Road and Osgood Tentsite, only off-Trail camping, at least 200 feet from the Trail, is allowed, and fires are prohibited.

Campfire permits are required for open fires outside White Mountain National Forest lands. Permits can be obtained at Pinkham Notch Visitor Center, in Crawford Notch State Park at the Willey House, and from other cooperators (inquire locally).

The A.T. passes along the border of, but does not enter, the Presidential Range–Dry River Wilderness in the southern part of the section.

Supplies and Services

Gorham is 12.0 miles north of Pinkham Notch on NH 16 (ZIP Code 03581, with telephone, supermarket, laundromat, restaurants, bus stop, equipment, hardware store, bank, doctor, vet). Nine miles south is Jackson (ZIP Code 03846, telephone, basic supplies, restaurants, bus stop). Eight miles south of Jackson is North Conway, a large business center with most major services (supermarkets, restaurants, specialty hiking equipment, hospital, cobbler, bus stop).

From the Trail crossing at U.S. 302, it is 1.0 mile north to the Willey House (telephone, snacks), 3.7 miles north to Crawford Notch (information, lodging, hostel), and 10.0 miles north to Twin Mountain (ZIP Code 03595, phone, groceries, restaurants, bus stop). Bartlett is 13.0 miles south (ZIP Code 03812, telephone, groceries, meals, bus stop). North Conway, *via* U.S. 302 and N.H. 16, is 12.0 miles south of Bartlett.

In an emergency, contact the New Hampshire State Police, (603) 846-5517 or (800) 846-3333, or AMC Pinkham Notch Visitor Center, (603) 466-2721.

Public Accommodations

AMC in this section maintains the following four huts, where lodging and family-style meals are available. The huts may be the only conveniently located shelter on the ridge. Reservations are usually necessary and may be made at any hut or by calling or writing the Reservations Secretary, Pinkham Notch Visitor Center, (see "Important Addresses," page 219).

Pinkham Notch Visitor Center: Extensive mountain facility located on N.H. 16 at northern end of the section; reservations required; meals served; information desk; hot drinks and snacks; pack-up room; telephone; showers; accommodates 107.

Madison Springs Hut: At treeline, built on site of first AMC refuge; 7.8 miles from northern end of section; full-service, no caretaker, reservations recommended; accommodates 50; water.

Lakes of the Clouds Hut: Above treeline; 14.8 miles from northern end of section; backpacker rates in 8-person refuge room (cellar); reservations strongly recommended; accommodates 90; water available; full charge.

Mizpah Spring Hut: Built and maintained by AMC; 6.4 miles from southern end of section; reservations strongly recommended; full-service; fee; accommodates 60; water available.

Crawford Hostel: Built and maintained by AMC; 6.4 miles from the southern end of the section on a 2.9 mile side trail; reservations strongly recommended; accommodates 24; fee; self-service year-round; water available.

Lodgings also are available in Gorham, Jackson, and Bartlett and at inns south of the Trail crossings of both U.S. 302 and N.H. 16.

Trail Description, North to South

Miles	Data

0.0 From N.H. 16, pass AMC Pinkham Notch Visitor Center, and follow Tuckerman Ravine Trail west for 250 feet. Turn right onto Old Jackson Road (trail), and ascend. (Tuckerman Ravine Trail continues ahead, ascending gradually 2.4 miles to **Hermit Lake Shelter** and steeply through the ravine 4.8 miles to Tuckerman Junction. One-half mile farther is summit of Mt. Washington, where trail rejoins A.T.; it is 0.8 mile across Bigelow Lawn on Tuckerman Crossover to Lakes of the Clouds, where it also meets A.T. The route to Lakes of the Clouds, eliminating the northern the Presidential Range, is recommended in bad weather but should be approached with caution, too.) Trail passes numerous side trails and ski trails and eventually, after crossing large brook, makes sharp left away from the old roadbed and climbs steeply. Raymond Path soon leads left (climbing southwest across mountainside to Tuckerman Ravine Trail). After A.T. crosses a brook, Nelson Crag Trail leads left (ascends past Nelson Crag and continues to Mt. Washington Auto Road near summit).

1.9 Cross Mt. Washington Auto Road near its two-mile post, and follow Madison Gulf Trail into Great Gulf Wilderness. Shortly, a side trail leads right 200 yards to Lowe's Bald Spot (2,860 feet), a rocky knob with fine views. Trail ascends briefly, then descends, crossing several brooks.

4.0 A.T. (Madison Gulf Trail) intersects Great Gulf Trail, and those trails coincide for 0.1 mile. Cross West Branch of Peabody River via suspension bridge, and go up ridge.

4.1 Madison Gulf Trail turns left. (From this junction, Madison Gulf Trail climbs two miles to Star Lake Trail, which, in 0.2 mile, rejoins A.T. at Madison Springs Hut. This route avoids ascending Mt. Madison by Osgood Ridge but involves rock scrambles in places.) Trail, now following the Great Gulf Trail east, descends to and crosses Parapet Brook. Climb steep bank on other side of brook.

4.2 Reach Osgood Cutoff junction. Great Gulf Trail leaves sharply right at top of bluff (continues downstream 2.6 miles to Great Gulf trailhead on N.H. 16). Trail follows Osgood Cutoff as it leaves sharply left, then, in a short distance, turns sharply right and continues along the contour.

4.8 Reach intersection of Osgood Cutoff with Osgood Trail, where **Osgood Tentsite** is located on right. Spring on right is last sure water. Turn left onto Osgood Trail, and ascend steeply. (Osgood Trail continues right 0.8 mile to Great Gulf Trail, which continues 1.8 miles to N.H. 16.)

6.1 Reach treeline on crest of Osgood Ridge. For next 12.7 miles, most of Trail is above treeline (climb should be attempted only in favorable weather).

6.8 Reach Osgood Junction. (Here, Daniel Webster Trail descends right 3.5 miles to Dolly Copp Campground. Parapet Trail leads left and contours southern side of Mt. Madison. It is sheltered from winds, avoids ascent of Mt. Madison, and still leads to AMC **Madison Springs Hut** in 1.0 mile.) A.T. continues up ridge on Osgood Trail, passing junction with the Howker Ridge Trail (descends right, north, 4.4 miles to Dolly Copp Road near Randolph).

7.3 Reach summit of Mt. Madison (5,363 feet). (Watson Path descends right, north, 3.4 miles to Valley Way and Appalachia parking lot on U.S. 2.) A.T. descends southwest ridge of Mt. Madison.

7.8 Reach **Madison Springs Hut**. Parapet Trail descends 0.2 mile south to Star Lake. Among trails descending north, Valley Way reaches **Valley Way Tentsite** and spring, 0.6 mile from hut and Appalachia parking lot on U.S. 2, in 3.5 miles. From hut, A.T. follows Gulfside Trail, marked with yellow-topped cairns, crosses nearby Snyder Brook and ascends southwest.

8.1 Air Line descends right (3.3 miles to Appalachia parking lot on U.S. 2). Two hundred feet farther on A.T., Air Line climbs left (0.8 mile to summit of Mt. Adams, 5,798 feet). A.T. ascends gradually southwest.

8.7 Reach Thunderstorm Junction, marked by massive rock cairn more than 10 feet high. (Lowe's Path ascends left 0.3 mile to summit of Mt. Adams. It descends right 1.2 miles to **Gray Knob Cabin** and 4.5 miles to U.S. 2 at Lowe's Service Station. Spur Trail descends north 1.1 miles to **Crag Camp Cabin**. Great Gully Trail descends north into King Ravine.) A.T. continues on Gulfside Trail, passes grassy area in saddle between Mt. Adams on left and Mt. Sam Adams on right, and soon passes the northern junction of Israel Ridge Path (leads left 0.4 mile to summit of Mt. Adams) and various springs.

9.3   Reach junction. (Israel Ridge Path descends right 0.9 mile to **The Perch Shelter** and 4.4 miles to Bowman on U.S. 2.) A.T. follows narrow ridge between Castle Ravine on right and Jefferson Ravine on left, with fine view of latter.

10.0   Reach Edmands Col. (Randolph Path leads right 0.2 mile to Spaulding Spring and descends 1.1 miles to **The Perch Shelter.** To left, Edmands Col Cutoff passes reliable Gulfside Spring in 30 yards.) A.T. slabs up eastern side of Mt. Jefferson, soon passing northern end of Jefferson Loop. (It leads 0.3 mile to summit of Mt. Jefferson, 5,715 feet. From summit, Caps Ridge Trail descends west 2.4 miles to Jefferson Notch Road.) A.T. continues along eastern flank of summit.

10.4   Reach junction. (Six Husbands Trail descends very steeply left, east, into Jefferson Ravine and Great Gulf Wilderness, passing spring in 100 yards. Six Husbands Trail also climbs right to summit of Mt. Jefferson.) A.T. continues ahead, and reaches the grassy plateau called Monticello Lawn, where the Jefferson Loop enters from right, 0.3 mile from summit. Trail then begins gradual descent.

10.9   Pass Cornice Trail, descending right. (This trail and Caps Ridge Trail descend 2.4 miles to Jefferson Notch Road.)

11.4   Reach Sphinx Col. (Sphinx Trail descends steeply left into Great Gulf Wilderness, reaching the treeline shelter in a few hundred yards.) Trail rises out of col. It soon reaches the Mt. Clay Loop (leads left and passes over summits of Mt. Clay, 5,532 feet; better views). Graded A.T. (Gulfside Trail) continues across western side of ridge, passing loop trail to unreliable Greenough Spring.

12.3   Pass junction. (Jewell Trail descends right, 2.9 miles to Marshfield Station.) A.T. descends slightly, and shortly Mt. Clay Loop enters from left. Trail continues around head wall, ascending gradually.

12.7   Westside Trail diverges right, contouring around summit of Mt. Washington and rejoining A.T. (a shortcut). A.T. ascends between edge of gulf and Mt. Washington Cog Railway.

13.1   Reach junction. Great Gulf Trail descends steeply left into Great Gulf. A.T. turns right, crosses railway, and continues across side of Mt. Washington to junction with Trinity Heights

Connector. (Gulfside continues straight and ends at Crawford Path 0.1 mile farther.) A.T. follows Connector uphill to left.

13.4   Reach summit of Mt. Washington (6,288 feet), highest point on A.T. north of Tennessee; actual summit is south of the summit house. (From summit, Mt. Washington Auto Road descends east 8.0 miles to Glen House site on N.H. 16. Tuckerman Ravine Trail descends east 1.7 miles to **Hermit Lake Shelters** and **tentsite** and 2.4 additional miles to **Pinkham Notch Visitor Center** on N.H. 16.) A.T. descends on Crawford Path, passing stone horse corral and Gulfside Trail, then steeply down southwestern side of Mt. Washington.

13.9   Westside Trail enters from right. Just beyond, Davis Path leads left and follows Montalban Ridge 14.4 miles south to U.S. 302. A.T. descends more gradually, passing between two Lakes of the Clouds. (Here, Camel Trail to Boott Spur and Tuckerman Crossover enter from left. Tuckerman Crossover leads 0.8 mile east to Tuckerman Junction where Tuckerman Ravine Trail descends east, steeply and treacherously, 1.2 miles to **Hermit Lake Shelters** and **tentsite** and 2.4 miles farther to **Pinkham Notch Visitor Center** on N.H. 16 and A.T.)

14.8   Reach AMC **Lakes of the Clouds Hut**. (From hut, Ammonoosuc Ravine Trail descends right 2.5 miles to Marshfield Station, base station of Mt. Washington Cog Railway). A.T. continues on Crawford Path, climbing gradually, soon passing Monroe Loop (diverges right and climbs two sharp peaks of Mt. Monroe, 5,385 feet). A.T. contours around eastern side of peak, passing Dry River Trail (which descends left down head wall of Oakes Gulf and into Presidential–Dry River Wilderness). Monroe Loop enters from right. A.T. continues on Crawford Path, passes just west of the summit of Mt. Franklin (5,004 feet), and then descends quite steeply.

16.8   Reach junction. (Mt. Eisenhower Trail descends left into Oakes Gulf and Presidential–Dry River Wilderness.) One hundred feet farther, Edmands Path descends right (2.9 miles to Mt. Clinton Road). Beyond, Mt. Eisenhower Loop diverges right. (In pleasant weather, this loop is recommended for views from summit of Mt. Eisenhower, 4,761 feet.) A.T. skirts eastern side of summit through scrub growth. A.T. contours eastern side of Eisenhower to where the Eisenhower Loop enters from right, then descends gradually to col.

18.7   Reach junction where A.T. turns left onto Webster Cliff Trail. (Crawford Path continues straight, descending 2.9 miles to U.S. 302 at AMC's Crawford Hostel (see page 91). As an alternative to A.T., follow Crawford Path to U.S. 302, continue from Crawford Hostel site, climbing west 1.4 miles on Avalon Trail to A-Z Trail, which may be followed 3.7 miles to Zealand Trail. Here, alternate route turns left and rejoins A.T. in 0.3 mile at Zealand Pond, just below Zealand Falls Hut.)

18.8   Reach summit of Mt. Pierce (Mt. Clinton, 4,310 feet). Descend through scrub, and enter woods. Cross meadow-like summit of southern peak of Mt. Pierce, and descend steeply through woods.

19.6   Reach AMC **Mizpah Spring Hut** and **Nauman Tentsite** on left. (To left, Mt. Clinton Trail descends into Oakes Gulf and Presidential Range–Dry River Wilderness. To right, Mizpah Cutoff descends 0.8 mile to Crawford Path and 1.8 miles farther to U.S. 302 at Crawford Hostel site.) A.T. continues along wooded summit of the divide, passing through several open meadows, then ascends.

21.3   Reach summit of Mt. Jackson (4,052 feet). (Jackson fork of Webster-Jackson Trail descends right 2.7 miles to U.S. 302 at Saco Lake, 0.2 mile east of AMC's Crawford Hostel.) From summit, A.T. crosses three small humps and descends steeply. It then follows ridge, ascends gradually, and eventually reaches the Webster fork of Webster-Jackson Trail (which descends right, joins Jackson fork, and continues down to U.S. 302 for a total of 2.3 miles). A.T. ascends slightly.

22.7   Reach summit of Mt. Webster (3,910 feet). Follow edge of Webster Cliffs, passing last viewpoint, and begin steep, winding descent through hardwood forest. At the valley floor, cross the Saco River on bridge.

26.0   Reach U.S. 302 and end of section, 1.0 mile south of Willey House site in Crawford Notch State Park. **Dry River Campground** is 1.5 miles left (south). To continue on the Trail, cross highway, and ascend on road to former Willey House Station (see New Hampshire Section Four).

Trail Description, South to North

Miles   **Data**

0.0   Opposite road to former Willey House Station on U.S. 302
      (1,277 feet), 1.0 mile south of Willey House site in Crawford
      Notch State Park and 1.5 miles north of **Dry River Camp-
      ground,** A.T. follows Webster Cliff Trail east. In 150 yards,
      cross Saco River on bridge. Ascend through hardwood for-
      est, and begin steep, winding climb. Reach first viewpoint
      from Webster Cliffs. For next 1.5 miles, follow edge of cliffs.

3.3   Reach summit of Mt. Webster (3,910 feet), and descend
      slightly. Pass Webster fork of Webster-Jackson Trail (de-
      scends left 2.3 miles to U.S. 302 at Saco Lake, 0.2 mile east of
      AMC's Crawford Hostel). A.T. follows ridge to sharp ascent,
      crosses three small humps, and then ascends northeast.

4.7   Reach summit of Mt. Jackson (4,052 feet). (Jackson fork of
      Webster-Jackson Trail descends left, joins Webster fork, and
      continues down to U.S. 302 for a total of 2.7 miles.) A.T.
      descends over ledges, through woods and through several
      meadows.

6.4   Reach AMC **Mizpah Spring Hut** and **Nauman Tentsite.** (To
      right, Mt. Clinton Trail descends into Oakes Gulf and the
      Presidential Range–Dry River Wilderness. To left, Mizpah
      Cutoff descends 0.8 mile to Crawford Path and 1.8 additional
      miles to U.S. 302 at Crawford Hostel site.) A.T. continues on
      Webster Cliff Trail, climbing steeply through woods beyond
      hut to alpine summit of south peak of Mt. Pierce. Trail then
      reenters woods and ascends through scrub.

7.2   Reach summit of Mt. Pierce (Mt. Clinton, 4,310 feet). From
      summit, route is mostly above treeline for next 12.7 miles
      (*should be attempted only in favorable weather*). Continue straight
      ahead.

7.3   Reach junction where Webster Cliff Trail ends and A.T.
      continues northeast along ridge on Crawford Path. (It is 2.9
      miles west *via* Crawford Path to U.S. 302 at AMC's Crawford
      Hostel.) Trail climbs gradually, passing a spring and the Mt.
      Eisenhower Loop, which diverges left. (In pleasant weather,
      this loop is recommended for fine views from summit of Mt.

Eisenhower, 4,761 feet). A.T., on Crawford Path, skirts summit through scrub growth (better route in foul weather).

9.2 Reach junction where northern end of Mt. Eisenhower Loop enters from left. (Beyond, Edmands Path descends left 2.9 miles to Mt. Clinton Road. One hundred feet farther, Mt. Eisenhower Trail descends right into Oakes Gulf and Presidential Range–Dry River Wilderness.) A.T. continues along ridge, passes a spring, and climbs steeply, then more gradually, and passes just west of the summit of Mt. Franklin (5,004 feet). Trail continues on Crawford Path with views into Oakes Gulf. Monroe Loop diverges left (climbs two sharp peaks of Mt. Monroe, 5,385 feet). A.T. contours around eastern side of peak, passing Dry River Trail (which descends right down head wall of Oakes Gulf and into Presidential Range–Dry River Wilderness). Monroe Loop reenters from left.

11.2 Reach AMC **Lakes of the Clouds Hut.** (From hut, Ammonoosuc Ravine Trail descends left, 2.5 miles to Marshfield Station, base station of Mt. Washington Cog Railway.) A.T. continues northeast on Crawford Path between two Lakes of the Clouds, passing junction where Camel Trail to Boott Spur and Tuckerman Crossover diverge right. (Tuckerman Crossover leads 0.8 mile east across Bigelow Lawn, flat area south of cone of Mt. Washington, to Tuckerman Junction. From Tuckerman Junction, Tuckerman Ravine Trail descends east, steeply and *treacherously*, 1.2 miles to **Hermit Lake Shelter** and **Tentsites** and 2.4 miles farther to AMC **Pinkham Notch Visitor Center** to rejoin the A.T. This route, eliminating northern Presidential Range, is recommended in bad weather but should be approached with caution, too.) From Lakes of the Clouds, A.T. continues north, crossing western side of Bigelow Lawn.

12.1 Reach junction where Davis Path leads right and follows Montalban Ridge 14.4 miles south to U.S. 302. Just beyond, Westside Trail contours left 0.9 mile around western side of cone of Mt. Washington to rejoin A.T. north of summit. A.T. climbs steep cone of Mt. Washington, passing old stone horse corral and Gulfside Trail (leading left).

12.6 Reach summit of Mt. Washington (6,288 feet), the highest point on the A.T. north of Tennessee (actual summit is just south of summit house). (From summit, Mt. Washington Auto Road descends east 8.0 miles to Glen House site on N.H. 16. Tuckerman Ravine Trail descends east 1.7 miles to **Hermit Lake Shelter** and **tentsite** and 2.4 additional miles to **Pinkham Notch Visitor Center** on N.H. 16, where it rejoins the A.T.) From summit, descend *via* Trinity Heights Connector (0.1 mile) to Gulfside Trail, which the A.T. then follows north.

12.9   Just after crossing cog railway, reach junction where the A.T. makes a sharp left to continue on Gulfside Trail. (Ahead, Great Gulf Trail descends into Great Gulf Wilderness.)

13.3   Westside Trail on left contours around Mt. Washington to Crawford Path. A.T. descends into Clay-Washington Col. Mt. Clay Loop diverges right, passing over summits of Mt. Clay (5,532 feet). A.T. continues along ridge on western side of summits.

13.7   Pass junction. (Jewell Trail descends left 2.9 miles to Marshfield Station.) Trail continues slabbing descent, passing loop trail leading left to unreliable Greenough Spring. Just before trail enters Sphinx Col, Mt. Clay Loop enters from right.

14.6   East end of Sphinx Col. (Sphinx Trail descends steeply right into Great Gulf Wilderness.)

15.1   Cornice Trail descends left, crossing Caps Ridge Trail (which descends 2.4 miles to Jefferson Notch Road and contours north to Castellated Ridge). A.T. continues rising along ridge to the grassy plateau known as Monticello Lawn, where the Jefferson Loop leads left over summit of Mt. Jefferson (5,715 feet). A.T. contours around eastern side of Mt. Jefferson.

15.6   Reach Six Husbands Trail, which descends steeply east, right, into Jefferson Ravine and Great Gulf Wilderness. It passes a spring in 100 yards and ascends west to summit of Mt. Jefferson. Descend past northern end of Jefferson Loop.

16.0   Reach Edmands Col. (Randolph Path leads left 0.2 mile to Spaulding Spring and descends 1.1 miles to **The Perch Shelter**. To right, Edmands Col Cutoff passes reliable Gulfside Spring in 30 yards.) From col, A.T. ascends on narrow ridge between Castle Ravine on left and Jefferson Ravine on right, with fine views of latter.

16.7   Reach junction. (Israel Ridge Path descends left 0.9 mile to **The Perch Shelter** and 4.4 miles to Bowman on U.S. 2.) In a half-mile, pass several springs and the north junction of the Israel Ridge Path (diverges on right, leading 0.4 mile to summit of Mt. Adams, 5,798 feet). A.T. passes a grassy area in saddle between Mt. Sam Adams on left and Mt. Adams on right.

17.3   Reach Thunderstorm Junction, marked by massive rock cairn more than 10 feet high. (Lowe's Path ascends right 0.3 mile to summit of Mt. Adams. It descends left 1.2 miles to **Gray Knob Cabin** and 4.5 miles to U.S. 2 at Lowe's Service Station. Spur Trail descends north 1.1 miles to **Crag Camp Cabin**, and Great Gully Trail descends north into King Ravine.) A.T. continues on Gulfside Trail, descending gradually northeast.

17.9   Reach junction. (Air Line climbs right 0.8 mile to summit of Mt. Adams, 5,798 feet. Beyond, Air Line descends left 3.3 miles to Appalachia parking lot on U.S. 2.)

18.2   Cross Snyder Brook, and reach AMC **Madison Springs Hut**, and the end of the Gulfside Trail. (Valley Way reaches **Valley Way Tentsite** and spring 0.6 mile from hut and Appalachia parking lot on U.S. 2 in 3.5 miles. Ascending south, Parapet Trail passes Star Lake and contours around southern side of Mt. Madison, joining the Osgood Trail in 1.0 mile, thus missing the summit of Madison. Starting at Star Lake, rugged Gulfside Trail descends steeply and very roughly into Great Gulf Wilderness and rejoins A.T. in approximately two miles, avoiding Osgood Ridge altogether). On the Osgood Trail from **Madison Springs Hut**, A.T. climbs steep southwest ridge of Mt. Madison.

18.7   Reach summit of Mt. Madison (5,363 feet). (Watson Path descends left, north, 1.0 mile to Valley Way, which leads 2.1 miles to Appalachia parking lot.) A.T. descends along crest of eastern ridge on Osgood Trail and soon passes Howker Ridge Trail (which descends left 4.4 miles north to Dolly Copp Road near Randolph). A.T. continues on ridgecrest on Osgood Trail, southeast.

19.2   Reach Osgood Junction. (Parapet Trail enters on right from **Madison Springs Hut**, 1.0 mile. Daniel Webster Trail descends 3.5 miles left, east, to Dolly Copp Campground.) Descend Osgood Ridge on Osgood Trail.

19.9   Enter woods, and continue steep descent.

21.2   At junction of Osgood Trail and Osgood Cutoff is **Osgood Tentsite** and spring. Turn right onto Osgood Cutoff, and enter Great Gulf Wilderness. Spring is on left at boulder. (Ahead, Osgood Trail continues 0.8 mile to Great Gulf Trail, which continues 1.8 miles to N.H. 16.) Trail contours, then turns left and descends.

21.8   Meet Great Gulf Trail at end of Osgood Cutoff. (Straight ahead, Great Gulf Trail descends 2.6 miles to Great Gulf Trailhead on N.H. 16.) A.T. follows Great Gulf Trail sharply right, downhill, crosses Parapet Brook, and climbs slightly to ridge.

21.9   Madison Gulf Trail joins from right. A.T. continues left on Madison and Great Gulf trails and descends ridge, crosses West Branch of Peabody River *via* suspension bridge, and climbs briefly.

22.0   A.T. turns left on Madison Gulf Trail, and Great Gulf Trail turns right, upstream. A.T. ascends gradually, crossing several brooks, reaches a ridge, climbs over a small ledge, and passes a short side trail leading left 200 yards to Lowe's Bald Spot (2,860 feet), a rocky knob with fine views. A.T. continues south, leaving Great Gulf Wilderness.

24.1   Cross Mt. Washington Auto Road. A.T. now follows Old Jackson Road (trail). Pass through old gravel pit, and enter woods. Nelson Crag Trail leads right (ascending past Nelson Crag and continuing to Auto Road). Beyond, after A.T. crosses brook, Raymond Path leads right (climbing southwest across mountainside to Tuckerman Ravine Trail). A.T. drops steeply and then makes sharp right onto roadbed of abandoned Jackson Road. It follows this road, descending gradually and passing several ski trails.

26.0   Turn left onto Tuckerman Ravine Trail, and reach AMC **Pinkham Notch Visitor Center** on N.H. 16. To continue on Trail, cross highway, and follow Lost Pond Trail (see New Hampshire Section Two).

Crawford Notch (U.S. 302) to
Franconia Notch (U.S. 3)
New Hampshire Section Four
27.7 Miles

Brief Description of Section

Crossing the Willey Range and Zealand, Garfield, and Franconia ridges, this is the longest section of uninterrupted footpath on the A.T. in New Hampshire or Vermont. The A.T. traces a route partly through dense hardwood and coniferous forests and partly across high ridges and summits.

Most of the Trail lies along the edges of the Pemigewasset Wilderness. Beginning on Ethan Pond Trail, the A.T. climbs steeply from the floor of Crawford Notch (1,277 feet), crosses a low point in Willey Range (2,907 feet), passes Ethan Pond and Thoreau Falls, and follows an old logging-railroad bed through Zealand Notch. Ascending Zealand Ridge, north of the Pemigewasset Wilderness on the Twinway Trail, it continues, always high on the ridge, on the northern, then western sides of the Pemigewasset area on Garfield Ridge Trail and Franconia Ridge Trail. For two miles, on sometimes narrow and precipitous Franconia Ridge, the Trail passes above treeline, providing a vista from the summit of Mt. Lafayette (5,249 feet), the highest peak in this section. The Trail descends from Franconia Ridge on Liberty Spring Trail into Franconia Notch State Park to U.S. 3 (1,450 feet). Water is scarce on the ridgecrests.

Franconia Ridge is exposed to the full force of storms, which rise rapidly and violently, producing winds of hurricane force and freezing conditions, even in summer. Carry extra clothing, and, if the weather becomes threatening, promptly descend to shelter by the shortest route.

This section is within White Mountain National Forest except the southern end, within Franconia Notch State Park, and the northern end, in Crawford Notch State Park.

Many steep ascents and descents are encountered at the section ends and on a number of peaks. The Trail in this section passes over seven major peaks, which are, from north to south:

Mt. Guyot, 4,560 feet
South Twin Mountain, 4,902 feet
Mt. Garfield, 4,488 feet
Mt. Lafayette, 5,249 feet
Mt. Lincoln, 5,089 feet
Little Haystack Mountain, approximately 4,760 feet
Mt. Liberty, 4,459 feet (on short side trail)

Treeline on Franconia Ridge occurs at approximately 4,200 feet. Above this elevation, only stunted krummholz (spruce) and a wealth of alpine species prevail against severe weather. This vegetation is extremely vulnerable to damage by foot traffic. In many places, obliteration of alpine tundra has given way to erosion, visibly scarring the mountainside. To prevent trampling vegetation and to allow successful regeneration of damaged areas, rock steps and low stone walls have been installed in many places. Closely follow established treadway in order to keep impact to a minimum.

The extensive system of side trails in this section gives hikers a variety of possibilities for loop hikes, side trips, and alternate routes to the A.T. Most side trails are briefly noted in the Trail description, but, for complete information, consult the AMC *White Mountain Guide*. This guide and current Trail information are available from AMC, Pinkham Notch Visitor Center (see "Important Addresses," page 219).

The Pemigewasset Wilderness

In this section, the A.T. passes through the valley and along the ridges making up the western and northern edges of the Pemigewasset Wilderness, an 18,560-acre tract of now-undeveloped mountain land where forests were once extensively logged. In 1969, the U.S. Forest Service established much of this tract as the Lincoln Woods Scenic Area. It became a congressionally approved wilderness area in 1986.

Logging began before 1900 and continued until just after World War II. On a clear day, hikers can see south from Zealand, Garfield, and Franconia ridges into a densely forested landscape that was once a clear-cut area. The most striking evidence of past logging activity is the striated appearance of the forest where logging roads once cut across the mountainside. In Zealand Notch, hikers walk along the bed of the former Zealand Valley Railroad, used to transport timber out of the notch before 1900.

Most of the timber logged in the White Mountains, including Zealand Notch and the "Pemi," was removed by one of 17 railroads, and many other trails in the wilderness area follow former railroad rights-of-way. The Lincoln and East Branch Railroad (now the Kancamagus Highway), leading from Lincoln northeast into the wilderness area, was the largest, with more than 60 miles of track. The Zealand branch was known as the steepest and most crooked in New England. Relics of logging and the railroads are still found in the forest.

During the logging years, forest fires swept the "Pemi" and left marks still visible today. In 1903, the Zealand Notch area burned. In 1907, a fire ravaged much of the "Pemi," burning Zealand and Garfield ridges, on which the A.T. now passes. Mt. Guyot and Mt. Garfield, now open summits, were both wooded until fire burned their forest cover. The forest is still in the succession stage of regrowth.

Franconia Notch State Park

This park was established to protect the area's spectacular natural features and geologic curiosities. The Basin, located one mile north of the Trail crossing at the bottom of the Basin-Cascades Trail, is a glacial pothole 20 feet in diameter, carved in granite at the base of a waterfall some 25,000 years ago. The Old Man of the Mountains, a 40-foot stone profile of a man's face formed by five ledges of Cannon Cliff, stands 1,200 feet above Profile Lake and is best viewed from Profile Clearing, 4.9 miles north of the Trail crossing on U.S. 3. Just north of the clearing is an aerial tramway to the summit of Cannon Mountain.

The Flume, 0.9 mile south of the Trail crossing, is a natural chasm 800 feet long, with granite walls 60 to 70 feet high and 12 to 20 feet apart. Boardwalk views are available within the gorge itself (fee charged).

Road Approaches

Both the northern and southern ends of this section are accessible from major highways. At the northern end, the Trail crosses U.S. 302 in Crawford Notch opposite Willey House Station Road, 8.0 miles north of Bartlett and 9.0 miles south of Bretton Woods. Southbound hikers should leave their cars at the end of Willey House Station Road (ample parking), 0.3 mile west of U.S. 302.

At the southern end of the section, A.T. crosses U.S. 3 at Whitehouse Bridge, 5.8 miles north of North Woodstock and 10.2 miles south of

Franconia. A parking lot is just north of the New Hampshire State Park Flume Complex, with access to the A.T. *via* the one-mile-long Whitehouse Trail.

Theft and vandalism have occurred at these locations. Do not leave valuables in vehicles.

Maps

Map Three (this guide)
AMC Franconia Map
White Mountain National Forest Map (1:250,000)
Franconia Notch State Park Map

The A.T. route might not be current on the following:
USGS 15-minute topographic quadrangle:
      Crawford Notch, New Hampshire
USGS 7½-minute topographic quadrangles:
      South Twin Mountain, New Hampshire
      Franconia, New Hampshire
      Lincoln, New Hampshire

Shelters and Campsites

Three campsites, with shelters, two tentsites, and two public campgrounds are located in this section:

Dry River Campground: In Crawford Notch State Park on U.S. 302; 1.5 miles southeast of Trail crossing; 24 tentsites; ample water.

Next shelter or campsite: north 6.4 miles (Nauman Tentsite); south 2.9 miles.

Ethan Pond Campsite: Shelter built and maintained by AMC at Ethan Pond; 2.9 miles from northern end of section on short side trail; accommodates 10; 5 tent platforms accommodate 28; water from brook by site; caretaker; fee.

Next shelter or campsite: north 2.9 miles; south 9.0 miles on a 0.7-mile side (Bondcliff) trail.

Guyot Campsite: Shelter rebuilt in 1977 and maintained by AMC; 11.9 miles from northern end of section, on a 0.7-mile side trail; accommodates 12; 6 tent platforms accommodate 24; caretaker in residence; fee; water from spring at site.

Next shelter or campsite: north 9.0 miles; south 5.0 miles.

13 Falls Tentsite: Maintained by AMC; 10.8 miles from southern end of section, on 1.2-mile side trail; caretaker; fee; water on site.

Next shelter or campsite: north 5.0 miles; south 0.5 mile.

Garfield Ridge Campsite: Shelter rebuilt in 1970 and maintained by AMC; 10.3 miles from southern end of section, on a 0.1 mile side trail; accommodates 12; 6 tent platforms accommodate 24; caretaker in residence; fee; water from spring on A.T.

Next shelter or campsite: north 0.5 mile; south 7.7 miles.

Liberty Spring Tentsite (no shelter): Built and maintained by AMC; 2.6 miles from southern end of section; 11 tent platforms accommodate 42; caretaker in residence; fee; water from spring at site.

Next shelter or campsite: north 7.7 miles; south 2.6 miles.

Lafayette Place Campground: Operated and maintained by New Hampshire Division of Parks in Franconia Notch State Park; 6.4 miles from the southern end of the section (on bridle path off A.T., approximately 2.5 miles north of Trail crossing of U.S. 3); also accessed by Greenleaf and Falling Waters side trails at 21.3 and 23.0 miles from the northern end of the section; 98 tentsites; fee; limited provisions; showers; telephone; ample water.

Next shelter or campsite: north 2.6 miles; south 8.4 miles (Kinsman Campsite).

The three AMC mountain huts in this section are described under "Public Accommodations."

Regulations

The northern 2.5 miles of this section lie in Crawford Notch State Park; the last southern mile, in Franconia Notch State Park. Camping and fires are prohibited in those parks except at the two campgrounds.

The remainder of the Trail in this section lies within White Mountain National Forest. Camping and wood or charcoal fires are prohibited above treeline, defined as an area where trees are less than eight feet tall.

Camping and wood or charcoal fires are prohibited within one-quarter mile of Ethan Pond Campsite, Zealand Falls Hut, Mt. Guyot Campsite, Galehead Hut, 13 Falls Tentsite, Garfield Ridge Campsite, Greenleaf Hut, or Liberty Springs Campsite, except at designated areas. Camping and wood or charcoal fires are prohibited within 200 feet of the A.T. from Galehead Hut to Liberty Springs Tentsite and anywhere on Liberty Springs Trail to state park lands.

Supplies and Services

From the Trail crossing at U.S. 302, at the northern end of the section, it is 1.0 mile north to Willey House (telephone, snacks), 3.7 miles north to AMC's Crawford Hostel (showers, phone, limited provisions), and 10.0 miles north to Twin Mountain (ZIP Code 03595; telephone, basic groceries, restaurants, bus stop). Bartlett is 13.0 miles south (ZIP Code 03812; telephone, basic groceries, meals, bus stop). Twelve miles south of Bartlett is North Conway (ZIP Code 03860; full services, specialty hiking stores, cobbler, hospital).

From the Trail crossing at U.S. 3 at the southern end of the section, it is approximately 2.5 miles north to Lafayette Place Campground (limited provisions, showers, telephone), 4.9 miles to Franconia Notch State Park headquarters (aerial tramway, telephone, snacks, souvenirs, bus stop), 10.2 miles to Franconia (ZIP Code 03580; restaurants, supermarket, laundromat, telephone, equipment, bus stop), and 20.0 miles to Littleton (ZIP Code 03561; full services, hospital, cobbler, bus stop). Also from the Trail crossing on U.S. 3, it is 0.8 mile south to the Flume Store (snacks, telephone, souvenirs, bus stop), 5.8 miles to North Woodstock (ZIP Code 03262; telephone, supermarket, restaurants, specialty backpacking store, laundromat, bus stop), and 6.8 miles to Lincoln (ZIP Code 03251; groceries, laundromat, telephone, Linwood Medical Center).

In an emergency, contact any AMC hut or shelter caretaker or the New Hampshire State Police, (603) 846-5517 or (603) 846-3333.

Public Accommodations

Lodging and family-style meals are available at the following three huts in this section, built and maintained by AMC. Reservations are necessary and may be made at any AMC hut or by contacting the Reservations Secretary, Pinkham Notch Visitor Center (see "Important Addresses," page 219).

Zealand Falls Hut: 7.7 miles from northern end of section; accommodates 36; ample water.

Galehead Hut: 14.7 miles from northern end of section; accommodates 46; ample water.

Greenleaf Hut: at treeline, 6.4 miles from southern end of section, 1.1 miles down side trail; accommodates 46; ample water.

From A.T. crossing at U.S. 3, it is 10.2 miles north to Franconia (motels, cabins), 1.6 miles south to roadway with motels and cabins, and 5.8 miles south to North Woodstock (motels, guest house). Lodging also available south of the Trail crossing on U.S. 302 and in Bartlett.

Trail Description, North to South

Miles   **Data**

0.0	From U.S. 302 in Crawford Notch, proceed uphill on Willey House Station Road. (**Dry River Campground** is 1.5 miles east on U.S. 302 in Crawford Notch State Park.) Ascend path at right of parking area for 50 yards, cross railroad tracks, and follow Ethan Pond Trail, ascending through woods.

0.5	Pass Arethusa-Ripley Falls Trail (leading left 0.4 mile to Ripley Falls, 2.5 miles to Arethusa Falls, and 3.8 miles back to U.S. 302). For next half-mile, Trail ascends steeply and then more gradually.

1.6	Pass Kedron Flume Trail (which descends very steeply right, northeast, to Willey House on U.S. 302).

1.9	Reach junction. A.T. turns left onto Ethan Pond Trail and ascends. (Ahead, Willey Range Trail leads across Kedron Brook and ascends 1.0 mile to Mt. Willey, 2.3 miles to Mt. Field, and farther to A-Z Trail and Avalon Trail.) Soon, reach height of land, and descend; enter former logging road.

2.9	Side trail leads right 250 yards, past Ethan Pond, to **Ethan Pond Campsite.** A.T. continues on level terrain, eventually crosses a brook, bears right, and merges with an old rail bed.

4.9	Shoal Pond Trail leads left on railroad grade. (This trail leads south 0.8 mile to Shoal Pond and continues to Stillwater Junction in Pemigewasset Wilderness.) Trail soon crosses the North Fork on a bridge and turns left.

5.4	Reach junction. (Thoreau Falls Trail leads left, passes falls, and continues 5.1 miles to Wilderness Trail, which leads 6.5 miles to Kancamagus Highway. Camping is prohibited at falls.) A.T. follows old railroad grade on gradual curve north into Zealand Notch and then along Whitewall Mountain.

6.2 Pass Zeacliff Trail (which leads left across brook and climbs very steeply, rejoining A.T. in 2.7 mile at top of Zeacliff). A.T. continues along side of Whitewall Mountain.

7.5 Reach junction where Ethan Pond Trail ends. A.T. turns left onto Twinway, passes left of Zealand Pond, and ascends steeply. (To right, Zealand Trail descends gradually 0.3 mile to A-Z Trail and 2.5 miles to Zealand Road, passable by car, 6.3 miles from U.S. 302 at Zealand Campground. A-Z Trail leads right, east, from Zealand Trail 3.7 miles to Avalon Trail, which leads 1.4 miles to U.S. 302.)

7.7 Pass AMC **Zealand Falls Hut** on left, and ascend less steeply.

7.8 Lend-a-Hand Trail diverges right. (It ascends to Mt. Hale in 2.5 miles. From there, Hale Brook Trail descends 2.4 miles to Zealand Road, leading to U.S. 302.) Beyond Lend-a-Hand junction, A.T. crosses Whitewall Brook and ascends southwest, moderately, through woods toward the top of Zeacliff.

8.9 At the crest of the rise, a 100-yard side loop to A.T. swings left to spectacular lookout east at edge of Zeacliff. Trail turns west and follows ridge on level. Zeacliff Trail soon enters from left.

9.4 Side trail descends left (0.1 mile to Zeacliff Pond). Pass view with Zeacliff Pond below, and continue along Zealand Ridge.

10.6 Cross knob. (Obscure side trail leads right to Zealand Mountain.) Descend into minor col, and ascend to southwest.

11.9 Reach open summit of Mt. Guyot (4,560 ft.). Beyond, reach Bondcliff Trail. (It leads left 0.5 mile to side trail descending left 0.2 mile to **Guyot Campsite** and spring. From shelter side trail, Bondcliff Trail continues south 1.3 miles to Mt. Bond, 2.8 miles to Bondcliff, 6.0 miles to Wilderness Trail at Camp 16, and 5.0 additional miles by this trail to Kancamagus Highway.) At junction with Bondcliff Trail, A.T. follows ridge northwest.

13.9 Reach summit of South Twin Mountain (4,902 feet). Just below summit, turn left. (North Twin Spur leads right, north, 1.3 miles to summit of North Twin. From there, North Twin Trail descends 7.5 miles to U.S. 3, 2.3 miles west of Twin Mountain.) From South Twin Mountain, A.T. descends steeply west over rocky slope.

14.7   Reach junction where Twinway ends and A.T. continues ahead, descending through forest on Garfield Ridge Trail. Forty yards to left of this junction is AMC **Galehead Hut.**

15.3   Gale River Trail descends right (5.8 miles to U.S. 3 at "Five Corners," opposite Trudeau Road). A.T. follows wooded ridge, soon passes outlook on knob (3,590 feet), and continues along ridge.

16.9   Reach junction. (Franconia Brook Trail descends left, south, 1.2 miles to **13 Falls Tentsite** and 5.0 miles to Wilderness Trail, which leads 2.8 additional miles through Pemigewasset Wilderness to Kancamagus Highway.) A.T. descends to col and then ascends steeply.

17.4   Side trail leads right 0.1 mile to **Garfield Ridge Campsite** with **shelter.** Water from spring located at junction. A.T. ascends steeply.

17.6   Garfield Trail descends right, 5.6 miles to U.S. 3 at Gale River. A.T. continues to ascend steeply.

17.8   Pass 150 feet north of summit of Mt. Garfield (4,488 feet). Descend steeply west on cone of Mt. Garfield, pass to left of Garfield Pond, and continue along Garfield Ridge, passing over several humps. Eventually, begin climb of Mt. Lafayette.

20.6   Reach treeline on Franconia Ridge. Skookumchuck Trail descends right (3.6 miles west to junction of U.S. 3 and I-93). Next 2.0 miles are narrow and above treeline (*should be hiked only in favorable weather*). A.T. continues up rocky ridge and passes over North Peak of Mt. Lafayette.

21.3   Reach summit of Mt. Lafayette (5,249 feet). Remains of summit-house foundation are just below summit. (Greenleaf Trail descends right, west, 300 yards to spring, 1.1 miles to AMC **Greenleaf Hut**, and 3.3 miles to U.S. 3 at Profile Clearing. From Greenleaf Hut, bridle path descends to **Lafayette Place Campground** on U.S. 3.) From summit, A.T. descends south, passing over minor summit in a half-mile.

22.3   Pass over summit of Mt. Lincoln (5,089 feet). Beyond, drop on each side of ridge is precipitous, and Trail passes many rocky points.

23.0   Pass over summit of Little Haystack Mountain (approximately 4,760 feet). (Falling Waters Trail descends right 2.8

miles to **Lafayette Place Campground** on U.S. 3.) Enter woods, and descend steeply over rough ledges.

24.8 Reach junction where A.T. turns right onto Liberty Spring Trail and descends steeply. (Ahead, Franconia Ridge Trail continues south 0.3 mile to summit of Mt. Liberty, 4,459 feet, 1.4 miles to summit of Mt. Flume, and 1.5 miles to Flume Slide Trail. Here, Osseo Trail begins and descends south along ridge, 5.3 miles to Kancamagus Highway east of Lincoln.)

25.1 Pass **Liberty Spring Tentsite** with spring, just off Trail to left. Descend steeply on switchbacks through evergreens and then hardwoods, joining an old logging road and crossing several brooks.

27.1 Reach trail junction (Flume Slide Trail leads left 3.8 miles to summit of Mt. Flume). A.T. continues descent.

27.7 Cross two small brooks. Section ends in Franconia Notch State Park where paved bike trail intersects Liberty Spring Trail. To continue on A.T., turn left onto bike trail, cross steel bridge over creek, and turn right under U.S. 3 onto Cascade Brook Trail. To reach Flume Complex, follow bike path south to Whitehouse Trail, which leads one mile to parking and nearby park visitors center. (See New Hampshire Section Five. To reach Lafayette Place Campground, follow bike path to right 2.5 miles).

Trail Descriptions, South to North

Miles   **Data**

0.0 From intersection of paved bike path and Liberty Spring Trail in Franconia Notch State Park near U.S. 3, enter woods on Liberty Spring Trail. Cross two small brooks. Soon, follow old logging road.

0.6 Reach trail junction. (Flume Slide Trail leads right 3.8 miles to summit of Mt. Flume.) A.T. ascends steadily straight ahead on an old logging road, crosses a large brook, and, 0.3 mile later, turns sharply left off the logging road. Continue a steepening, switchbacking ascent.

2.6 Pass **Liberty Spring Tentsite**, with spring just off Trail to right. Ascend steeply.

2.9   Reach Franconia Ridge Trail. (South, right, on this trail, it is 0.3 mile to summit of Mt. Liberty, 1.4 miles to Mt. Flume, and 1.5 miles to upper end of Flume Slide Trail. There, Osseo Trail begins and descends south on ridge, 5.3 miles to Kancamagus Highway east of Lincoln.) A.T. turns north (left) onto Franconia Ridge Trail and ascends gradually, then steeply, over rough ledges.

4.7   Reach Little Haystack Mountain (4,760 feet). (Falling Waters Trail descends left 2.8 miles to **Lafayette Place Campground** on U.S. 3.) A.T. continues ahead. The footpath on the next 2.0 miles, Franconia Ridge, is narrow and above treeline and should be traversed only in favorable weather. *Particular care should be taken if electrical storms threaten.*

5.4   Pass over Mt. Lincoln summit (5,089 feet) and another minor peak in 0.4 mile. Ascend steeply rocky cone of Mt. Lafayette.

6.4   Reach summit of Mt. Lafayette (5,249 feet). Remains of summit-house foundation are just below summit. (Greenleaf Trail descends left, west, 300 yards to spring, 1.1 miles to MAC **Greenleaf Hut**, and 3.3 miles to U.S. 3 at Profile Clearing. From Greenleaf Hut, bridle path descends 2.5 miles to **Lafayette Place Campground** on U.S. 3.) From summit, A.T. descends north on Garfield Ridge Trail, passes over North Peak of Mt. Lafayette in 0.4 mile, and descends steeply.

7.1   Skookumchuck Trail descends left (3.6 miles west to junction of U.S. 3 and I-93). A.T. descends northeast, passes through treeline, and begins the long traverse of Garfield Ridge, over many small humps, eventually passing to right (south) of Garfield Pond and ascending steeply east.

9.9   Pass 150 feet north of summit of Mt. Garfield (4,488 feet). Descend northeastern side of cone of Mt. Garfield.

10.1   Reach junction. (Garfield Trail descends left 5.6 miles to U.S. 3 at Gale River.) A.T. descends steeply east.

10.3   Reach junction and spring. (Side trail leads left 0.1 mile to **Garfield Ridge Campsite**.) Trail descends into col.

10.8   Reach junction. (Franconia Brook Trail descends south, right, 1.2 miles to **13 Falls Tentsite** and 5.0 miles to Wilderness Trail, which leads 2.8 miles through Pemigewasset Wilderness to Kancamagus Highway.) A.T. continues straight, ascending along ridge, eventually passing outlook on knob (3,590 feet).

12.4   Gale River Trail descends left 5.8 miles to U.S. 3 at "Five Corners," opposite Trudeau Road to Bethlehem Junction. A.T. ascends southeast through forest.

13.0   Garfield Ridge Trail ends, and A.T. continues ahead, climbing steeply east on Twinway. Forty yards to right of this junction is AMC **Galehead Hut.**

13.8   Just short of South Twin Mountain summit (4,902 feet), reach North Twin Spur. (It leads left, north, 1.3 miles to North Twin summit. From there, North Twin Trail descends 7.5 miles to U.S. 3, 2.3 miles west of Twin Mountain.) A.T. continues on Twinway, descending southeast from South Twin Mountain on ridge.

15.8   Reach junction. (Bondcliff Trail leads right 0.5 mile to side trail that descends to left 0.2 mile to **Guyot Shelter** and spring. From shelter side trail, Bondcliff Trail continues south 1.3 miles to Mt. Bond, 2.8 miles to Bondcliff, and 6.0 miles to Wilderness Trail at Camp 16, which leads 5.0 miles to Kancamagus Highway.) At junction with Bondcliff Trail, A.T. turns left, crosses open summit of Mt. Guyot (4,560 feet), descends its northeastern ridge, passes through minor col, and ascends steeply.

17.1   Reach junction at knob (an obscure side trail leads left to Zealand Mountain), and continue along Zealand Ridge, eventually passing viewpoint with nearby Zeacliff Pond below.

18.3   Side trail descends right 0.1 mile to Zeacliff Pond, and A.T. continues east on ridge. In 0.3 mile, reach junction with Zeacliff Trail, which descends steeply right 1.5 miles and rejoins A.T. on Ethan Pond Trail.

18.8   One-hundred-yard side loop leads right to spectacular lookout east at edge of Zeacliff. Trail turns northwest, descends steeply through woods, crosses a brook, and continues through woods.

19.9   Cross Whitewall Brook. (Two hundred feet beyond, Lend-a-Hand Trail leaves left, ascending to Mt. Hale in 2.5 miles. From there, Hale Brook Trail descends 2.4 miles to Zealand Road, which leads to U.S. 302.)

20.0   Pass AMC **Zealand Falls Hut,** and descend east; pass to right of Zealand Pond.

20.2   Reach junction where Twinway ends and A.T. turns right onto Ethan Pond Trail. (Zealand Trail continues left 0.3 mile to A-Z Trail and 2.5 miles to Zealand Road, which is passable by automobile, 6.3 miles from U.S. 302 at **Zealand Campground**. An alternate to A.T., A-Z Trail leads right, east, from Zealand Trail 3.7 miles to Avalon Trail, which leads 1.4 miles to U.S. 302. From there, Crawford Path leads 2.9 miles to Mt. Pierce, rejoining A.T. on Presidential Range.) From end of Twinway, continue on Ethan Pond Trail along old railroad grade on side of Whitewall Mountain.

21.5   Lower end of Zeacliff Trail enters from right. A.T. makes gradual curve eastward around end of Whitewall Mountain.

22.3   Reach junction. (Thoreau Falls Trail leads right, passes falls, and continues 5.1 miles to Wilderness Trail, which leads 6.5 miles to Kancamagus Highway. Camping is prohibited at falls.) Trail continues along railroad grade and crosses the North Fork.

22.8   Reach junction. Shoal Pond Trail turns right (leading south 0.8 mile to Shoal Pond and Stillwater Junction in Pemigewasset Wilderness). Trail soon leaves railroad grade, crosses a brook, and continues a gradual ascent.

24.8   Side trail leads left 200 yards, past Ethan Pond, to **Ethan Pond Campsite**. A.T. ascends gradually, reaches height of land, and descends.

25.8   Reach junction. (Willey Range Trail leads left across Kedron Brook and ascends 1.0 mile to Mt. Willey, 2.3 miles to Mt. Field, and farther to A-Z Trail or Avalon Trail.) A.T. bears right, descending on Ethan Pond Trail.

26.1   Kedron Flume Trail descends steeply left (northeast) 1.3 miles to Willey House (food, drink, telephone, bus) on U.S. 302. A.T. descends southeast less steeply.

27.2   Pass Arethusa-Ripley Falls Trail (leads right 0.4 mile to Ripley Falls, 2.5 miles to Arethusa Falls, and 3.8 miles to U.S. 302). A.T. crosses railroad tracks and reaches parking area and hard-surfaced Willey House Station Road. Descend on road.

27.7   Reach U.S. 302, 1.0 mile south of Willey House site, and end of section. To continue on the Trail, cross road, and ascend on Webster Cliff Trail. **Dry River Campground** is 1.5 miles east on U.S. 302 (see New Hampshire Section Three).

Franconia Notch (U.S. 3) to Kinsman Notch (N.H. 112)
New Hampshire Section Five
16.3 Miles

Brief Description of Section

Most of the Trail in this section traverses the northeast-to-southwest Kinsman Ridge through heavily wooded country past several mountain tarns (ponds) and cascades.

From its northern end on U.S. 3 (1,450 feet) in Franconia Notch State Park (see description in Section Four), the Trail climbs northwest on Cascade Brook Trail. At Lonesome Lake, a high mountain tarn on the shoulder of Cannon Mountain, it ascends on the wet and sometimes steep Fishin' Jimmy Trail. Reaching Kinsman Pond, another high tarn, the Trail ascends on the Kinsman Ridge Trail to the northern (4,293 feet) and southern (4,358 feet) peaks of Kinsman Mountain. It descends past Harrington Pond and the cascades of Eliza Brook. Between Eliza Brook and Kinsman Notch (1,870 feet), it follows a wooded ridge.

The change in elevation from Franconia Notch to Kinsman Mountain is considerable. The footway is often wet and rugged.

Water is scarce on the southern part of the ridge, but many waterfalls and cascades are found elsewhere in this section, some on short side trips. The Upper (0.1-mile round trip), Middle (0.7-mile round trip), and Lower (1.2-mile round trip) Kinsman Falls are on the Basin-Cascades Trail near the northern end. At the southern end, in Kinsman Notch, Lost River can be reached on a half-mile side trail leaving the A.T. 0.1 mile north of the notch. Lost River flows into an underground gorge and through a series of cascades and caves.

Side trails in this section offer many possibilities for loop hikes, side trips, and alternate A.T. routes. They are noted in the Trail data, but, for complete information, consult the AMC *White Mountain Guide*. The guide and current Trail information are available from the AMC, Pinkham Notch Visitor Center (see "Important Addresses," page 219).

Lost River

The brook draining the southern part of Kinsman Notch is aptly named Lost River. It disappears below the surface in a narrow, steep-walled glacial gorge. This geologic curiosity and the surrounding area have been preserved by the Society for Protection of New Hampshire Forests as the Lost River Reservation (telephone, cafeteria, souvenirs, no accommodations), a half-mile east of the Trail crossing on N.H. 112. The gorge long ago eroded along a fracture in the granite of Kinsman Notch, later filling with a jumble of large boulders forming many caverns. Lost River cascades through the half-mile subterranean gorge, swirling within immense glacial potholes and flowing over spectacular falls. Trails, boardwalks, and ladders make the caves accessible.

The society also maintains a garden with 300 varieties of native flowers, ferns, and shrubs, an ecology trail, and a museum. The only fee charged is entrance to the gorge.

Road Approaches

Both section ends are accessible from major highways. At the northern end, the A.T. crosses U.S. 3 at Whitehouse Bridge, 5.8 miles north of North Woodstock and 10.2 miles south of Franconia. Park south of the A.T. near New Hampshire State Park Flume Complex, 0.8 mile south of the bridge, and follow the Whitehouse Bridge Trail 1.0 mile to the A.T.

At the southern end, the A.T. crosses N.H. 112 6.2 miles west of North Woodstock, 4.8 miles east of Bungay Corner (junction of N.H. 112 and N.H. 116), and 17.7 miles east of Woodsville. There is a large parking lot with toilet facilities and Trail information just south of the Trail crossing.

Both ends of the section have experienced theft and vandalism. Do not leave valuables in vehicles.

Maps

Map Three (this guide)
AMC Franconia Map
White Mountain National Forest Map (1:250,000)
Franconia Notch State Park Map

The A.T. route might not be current on the following:
USGS 7½-minute topographic quadrangles:
      Lincoln, New Hampshire
      Mt. Moosilauke, New Hampshire
      Franconia, New Hampshire

Shelters and Campsites

This section has one campsite and one shelter, as well as a public campground on U.S. 3 near the northern end of the section.

Lafayette Place Campground: Operated and maintained by New Hampshire Division of Parks in Franconia Notch State Park; at the beginning of the section on a 2.5-mile bike path north of the Trail crossing of U.S. 3; 98 tentsites; fee; limited provisions; showers; telephone; ample water.

Next shelter or campsite on A.T.: north 2.6 miles (Liberty Spring); south 4.8 miles on the A.T., on a 0.1-mile side trail (Kinsman Pond).

Kinsman Pond Campsite: Shelter built and maintained by AMC; 4.8 miles from northern end of section, on 0.1-mile side trail; accommodates 14; also 5 tent platforms; water from pond (should be treated or boiled); better water 1.9 mile north on A.T.

Next shelter or campsite: north 4.8 miles; south 4.0 miles.

Eliza Brook Shelter: Built and maintained by AMC, 8.8 miles from the northern end of section; accommodates 8; water from brook.

Next shelter or campsite: north 4.0 miles; south 9.1 miles (Beaver Brook Shelter).

This section also has one AMC mountain hut, described under "Public Accommodations."

Regulations

The northern mile of the section and the area around Lonesome Lake (including hut) lie in Franconia Notch State Park. Camping and fires are prohibited except at Lafayette Place Campground on U.S. 3.

The rest of the Trail in this section lies within White Mountain National Forest, where camping and fires are restricted to sites 200 feet or more off the Trail.

Supplies and Services

From the Trail crossing of U.S. 3 at the northern end of the section, it is 2.5 miles north to Lafayette Place Campground (limited provisions, showers, telephone), 4.9 miles to Franconia Notch State Park headquarters (aerial tramway, telephone, snacks, souvenirs, bus stop), 10.2 miles to Franconia (ZIP Code 03580, telephone, supermarket, restaurants, laundromat, equipment, bus stop), and 20.0 miles to Littleton (full services, hospital, cobbler, bus stop).

From the Trail crossing of U.S. 3, it is 0.8 mile south to Flume Store (snacks, telephone, souvenirs, bus stop), 5.8 miles to North Woodstock (ZIP Code 03262, telephone, supermarket, restaurants, specialty backpacking store, laundromat), and 6.8 miles to Lincoln (ZIP Code 03251, groceries, laundromat, telephone, outfitter, Linwood Medical Center).

From the Trail crossing of N.H. 112 at the southern end of the section, it is 6.2 miles east to North Woodstock and 7.7 miles to Lincoln (see above). From this crossing, it is 12.0 miles west to Swiftwater (telephone, groceries, restaurant), 15.4 miles to Bath (ZIP Code 03740, telephone, groceries), and 17.7 miles to Woodsville (ZIP Code 03785, telephone, supermarket, restaurant, bus stop).

In an emergency, call any AMC hut or the New Hampshire State Police, (603) 846-5517 or (603) 846-3333.

Public Accommodations

This section has one AMC hut, with dormitory-style lodging and family-style meals (at least one meal must be taken with lodging). Reservations are strongly recommended and may be made at any AMC hut or by calling or writing the Reservations Secretary, Pinkham Notch Visitor Center (see "Important Addresses," page 219).

Lonesome Lake Hut: Leased from the state of New Hampshire and operated by AMC; 2.9 miles from northern end of section; accommodates 44; ample water.

From the Trail crossing at U.S. 3, it is 10.2 miles north to Franconia (motels, cabins), 1.6 miles south to a roadway lined with motels and cabins, and 5.8 miles north to North Woodstock (motels and guest house). From the Trail crossing at N.H. 112, it is 6.2 miles east to North Woodstock.

Trail Description, North to South

Miles	Data

0.0   At the trailhead of Liberty Spring Trail, turn left onto paved bike trail (to reach **Lafayette Place Campground**, turn right, and follow bike trail 2.5 miles). Cross steel bridge over creek. Turn right (west), and pass under U.S. 3 to Cascade Brook Trail. Ascend northwest into woods on old logging road. (Bike trail continues to Whitehouse Trail, which leads 1.0 mile to Flume Complex with parking, meals, snacks, and telephone.) In 0.4 mile, cross Whitehouse Brook on rocks.

1.5   Basin-Cascades Trail descends right 1.5 miles, past Kinsman Falls, to The Basin, a large glacial pothole on U.S. 3. Just beyond this junction, A.T. crosses Cascade Brook on rocks; may be difficult in high water.

2.0   Kinsman Pond Trail diverges left, (ascending 2.3 miles to **Kinsman Pond Campsite**, and 2.4 miles to Kinsman Junction, where it rejoins Trail). A.T. continues upstream parallel to Cascade Brook, becoming rougher.

2.8   Reach junction at edge of Lonesome Lake, where Trail turns left onto Fishin' Jimmy Trail. (Cascade Brook Trail continues straight ahead 0.2 mile to Lonesome Lake Trail, which then leads left to Kinsman Ridge Trail and right to U.S. 3.) A.T. crosses outlet brook of Lonesome Lake and ascends.

2.9   Reach AMC **Lonesome Lake Hut** (no camping allowed). (From hut, Around-Lonesome Lake Trail leads right 0.3 mile to Lonesome Lake Trail, which leads left to Kinsman Ridge Trail or right to U.S. 3.) A.T. continues on Fishin' Jimmy Trail, passing west across lower slopes of Cannonballs, making several ascents and descents and crossing several brooks before ascending steeply and roughly. Eventually, climb slackens.

4.8   Reach Kinsman Junction, where Fishin' Jimmy Trail ends and A.T. continues, ascending on Kinsman Ridge Trail. (Kinsman Pond Trail leads left 0.1 mile to **Kinsman Pond Campsite**, where it is necessary to treat or boil water from pond for drinking. To right, Kinsman Ridge Trail leads over Cannonballs to Cannon Mountain and from there descends to U.S. 3 at aerial-tramway base station.)

5.0   Mt. Kinsman Trail descends right (3.5 miles, past Bald Peak and Kinsman Flume and Profile, in and 1.5 miles more to N.H. 116). A.T. ascends, veering south.

5.4   Reach summit of North Kinsman Mountain (4,293 feet). (Near summit, a short trail leads left, east, to cliff overlooking Kinsman Pond.) Descend south through col (water is sometimes found on right), and then ascend.

6.3   Reach summit of South Kinsman Mountain (4,358 feet). Begin a very rough, exposed descent, requiring considerable extra time.

7.4   Cross small brook. Pass left of Harrington Pond. Descend steeply over wet, rough footway to headwaters of Eliza Brook; cross this brook, and descend along eastern bank past cascades and falls; eventually, enter logging road. Follow it downhill.

8.8   Turn right off road, and cross Eliza Brook. Just beyond, short side trail on right leads to **Eliza Brook Shelter**, with water from brook. Continue, generally southwest. Ascend gradually to pass under powerline, and continue along ridge to col.

9.8   Reach junction. (Reel Brook Trail descends right 4.0 miles to N.H. 116 near Easton.) Trail ascends northern ridge of Mt. Wolf, over several humps.

11.7   Reach East Peak of Mt. Wolf, 3,478 feet; a side trail leads left to outlook on summit. Cross knob on southern ridge of Mt. Wolf (3,360 feet), then descend. Cross small brook.

13.0   Gordon Pond Trail descends left (passes Gordon Pond in 0.3 mile and Gordon Falls in 1.3 miles and reaches N.H. 112 in 4.8 miles). Trail continues along the ridge over several humps with occasional views, eventually climbing steeply by zig-zags to the top of a knob, then beginning a steep descent.

15.6   Dilly Trail descends left 0.8 mile past outlook over Kinsman Notch to Lost River Reservation on N.H. 112. Continue descent.

16.3   Reach N.H. 112 in Kinsman Notch, end of the section. To continue south, cross road, and enter Beaver Brook Trail (see New Hampshire Section Six).

Trail Description, South to North

Miles	Data

0.0   From junction of N.H. 112 and Beaver Brook Trail in Kinsman Notch, cross highway diagonally left, and turn right to follow Kinsman Ridge Trail. Trail soon bears right and ascends steeply.

0.7   Dilly Trail descends right 0.8 mile past outlook over Kinsman Notch to Lost River Reservation on N.H. 112. A.T. continues to climb steeply to the top of a knob, descends steeply to a col, then continues over many humps along the ridge, with occasional views.

3.3   Gordon Pond Trail diverges right (passes Gordon Pond in 0.3 mile and Gordon Falls in 1.3 miles, descending in 4.8 miles to N.H. 112). Trail then begins a climb of Mt. Wolf, crosses a good brook in 0.6 mile, continues over the western summit of Mt. Wolf (3,360 feet), and descends to a sag.

4.6   Side trail leads right (200 feet to outlook on the summit of East Peak of Mt. Wolf, 3,478 feet). Descend along northern ridge.

6.5   Reach junction. (Reel Brook Trail descends left 4.0 miles to N.H. 116 near Easton.) A.T. continues on level ground, and passes under powerline. Descend northeast.

7.5   Reach side trail leading left to **Eliza Brook Shelter** (water available from brook). Just beyond, cross Eliza Brook, turn left, upstream, on old logging road. Turn left again off logging road after approximately 0.3 mile. Trail becomes rough and steep, passing falls and cascades to left in Eliza Brook. Eventually, cross brook near its headwaters, and continue steeply uphill on wet, rough footway.

8.9   Pass right (east) of Harrington Pond. Cross small brook, and climb north. Begin ascent, first moderately, then very steeply and roughly, requiring considerable, extra time. Reach very exposed south knob of South Kinsman, where grade slackens.

10.0   Reach open summit of South Kinsman Mountain (4,358 feet). Descend north through scrub and small evergreens to col (water sometimes found on left), and ascend gradually.

10.9   Reach side trail to good lookout (east) and, 30 yards beyond, summit of North Kinsman Mountain (4,293 feet). Descend north from summit.

11.3   Mt. Kinsman Trail diverges left (descending 3.5 miles past Bald Peak and the Kinsman Flume and Profile, then 1.5 miles to N.H. 116). A.T. continues east, descending gradually.

11.5   Reach Kinsman Junction. (Kinsman Pond Trail leads right 0.1 mile to **Kinsman Pond Campsite**, where it is necessary to treat or boil water from pond for drinking water; 2.4 miles to Cascade Brook Trail to rejoin A.T. Kinsman Ridge Trail, a possible alternate to A.T., turns left, passes over Cannonballs to Cannon Mountain in 3.3 miles, and descends 3.3 additional miles to aerial-tramway base station on U.S. 3. From there, Greenleaf Trail ascends 3.3 miles to summit of Mt. Lafayette, rejoining A.T.) Trail continues ahead on Fishin' Jimmy Trail, descending sometimes steeply. Cross several brooks, then descend more gradually.

13.4   Reach AMC **Lonesome Lake Hut** (camping prohibited). A.T. descends from hut to lake and then east across its outlet. (From hut, Around-Lonesome Lake Trail leads left 0.3 mile to Lonesome Lake Trail, which leads right, east, to U.S. 3 and left, west, to Kinsman Ridge Trail.)

13.5   Reach junction where Fishin' Jimmy Trail ends. (Cascade Brook Trail leads left 0.2 mile to Lonesome Lake Trail, which leads left to Kinsman Ridge Trail or right 1.2 miles to **Lafayette Place Campground**.) A.T. turns right onto Cascade Brook Trail, descending parallel to outlet brook of Lonesome Lake.

14.3   Kinsman Pond Trail enters on right, 2.3 miles from **Kinsman Pond Campsite**. A.T. continues downstream.

14.8   Cross Cascade Brook on rocks; may be difficult. (Just beyond, Basin-Cascades Trail descends left 1.5 miles past Kinsman Falls to The Basin on U.S. 3.) A.T. continues on woods road, crosses Whitehouse Brook on rocks, and continues to U.S. 3, passing under it and reaching a paved bike path.

16.3   Bear left over steel bridge to junction with Liberty Spring Trail. To reach Whitehouse Trail and Flume Complex (parking, meals, snacks), 1.0 mile, bear right on bike path. To continue on Trail, follow Liberty Spring Trail (see New Hampshire Section Four). To reach **Lafayette Place Campground**, follow bike path to left 2.5 miles.

Kinsman Notch (N.H. 112)
to Glencliff (N.H. 25)
New Hampshire Section Six
9.5 Miles

Brief Description of Section

The Trail in this section traverses the massive, bald Mt. Moosilauke (4,802 feet), an area of 30 square miles towering over the southwestern corner of the White Mountains.

From Kinsman Notch (1,870 feet) in the north, the Trail follows the Beaver Brook Trail steeply upward past cascades, takes ladders over cliffs, and ascends to the summit of Mt. Moosilauke. From the summit, the A.T. follows cairns to the Carriage Road, which it follows for a mile, then it takes the Glencliff Trail steeply down the western slope to Glencliff (1,074 feet). This section can usually be hiked in a day, and water is generally abundant.

Use caution when traversing the cliffside section of the Beaver Brook Trail. Mt. Moosilauke is above treeline and subject to the full force of violent storms.

The mountain and its many trails are worth several days' exploration. Side trails are described briefly in this section, but, for complete information, consult the AMC *White Mountain Guide*, available from AMC (see "Important Addresses," page 219). For information on the flora, fauna, geology, and history, as well as trails on the mountain, refer to the DOC *Trail Guide to Mt. Moosilauke*, available from the Dartmouth Outing Club (see page 219).

Mt. Moosilauke

Mt. Moosilauke was a hunting ground for the Pemigewasset Indians, to whom Moosilauke meant "high bald place." In the eighteenth century, European settlers farmed the Moosilauke area. The Indians retreated before the wave of settlement, the region was opened to land grants, and it was not long before much of the virgin forest was cleared for cultivation and timber.

About 1850, agriculture declined, and the mountain became a logging and resort center. Two bridle paths were built to the summit, and, in 1860, a summit hotel, the Prospect House, opened. As the tourist business boomed, the Moosilauke Mountain Road Company completed the five-mile Carriage Road to the summit.

Between 1899 and 1914, paper companies stripped all but the most inaccessible timber from the western side of the mountain. Around 1920, this intensive logging ended, and the U.S. Forest Service purchased most of the land.

The Dartmouth Outing Club (DOC) adopted the Prospect House in 1920, maintaining it as a summer hostel until it burned down in 1942. Its foundation is still visible. The Carriage Road is now used only by hikers. The A.T. follows it for a short distance near the summit.

The mountain is used for recreation and education by thousands of persons each year. Dartmouth College owns the summit and the eastern flanks of the main summit, including the Gorge Brook and upper Baker River drainages; students of the outdoors study its flora, fauna, and geology. The remainder of the massif is part of the White Mountain National Forest.

Road Approaches

Both the northern and southern ends of the section are accessible from major highways. At the northern end, the Trail crosses N.H. 112 (ample parking) 6.2 miles west of North Woodstock, 4.8 miles south of Bungay Corner (junction of N.H. 112 and N.H. 116), and 17.7 miles east of Woodsville (near I-91). At the southern end, the Trail crosses N.H. 25 approximately 0.5 mile north of Glencliff (cars are best parked in Glencliff).

Maps

Map Three (this guide)
AMC Franconia Map
DOC Mt. Moosilauke Map
DOC Trail Map
White Mountain National Forest Map (1:250,000)

The A.T. route might not be current on the following:
USGS 15-minute topographic quadrangle:
    Rumney, New Hampshire
USGS 7½-minute topographic quadrangles:
    Mt. Moosilauke, New Hampshire
    Mt. Kineo, New Hampshire
    Warren, New Hampshire

Shelters and Campsites

This section has two shelters:

Beaver Brook Shelter: Built in 1993 and maintained by DOC, 1.6 miles from northern end of section on a short side trail; accommodates 10; two tent pads; composting toilet; water from brook just beyond shelter on shelter spur.

Next shelter or campsite: north 9.1 miles (Eliza Brook Shelter); south 6.8 miles.

Jeffers Brook Shelter: Built and maintained by DOC; 1.1 miles from southern end of section, 0.1 mile on blue-blazed side trail; accommodates 10; water from brook.

Next shelter or campsite: north 6.8 miles; south 15.8 miles (Hexacuba Shelter).

Regulations

From Kinsman Notch to the Hurricane Trail Junction near Glencliff, the A.T. passes across both White Mountain National Forest (WMNF) and private land. The northern end is part of Lost River Reservation, and the summit of Mt. Moosilauke, from the Ridge Trail Junction to the Carriage Road-Glencliff Trail Junction, is owned by Dartmouth College. WMNF regulations apply throughout the section; namely, camping and fires are permitted only below treeline, at least 200 feet from the Trail, and one-quarter mile from any campsite, hut, cabin, or shelter.

Supplies and Services

From the Trail crossing of N.H. 112 at the northern end of the section, it is 6.2 miles east to North Woodstock (ZIP Code 03262, telephone, supermarket, restaurants, specialty backpacking store, laundromat) and 7.7 miles to Lincoln (ZIP Code 03251, telephone, groceries, outfitter, laundromat, Linwood Medical Center). From this crossing, it is 12.0 miles west to Swiftwater (telephone, groceries, restaurant), 15.4 miles to Bath (ZIP Code 03740, telephone, groceries), and 17.7 miles to Woodsville (ZIP Code 03785, telephone, supermarket, restaurant, bus stop).

At the eastern base of Mt. Moosilauke, accessible from the Trail by the Hurricane Trail (5.1 miles), Carriage Road/Snapper Trail (2.3 miles), Gorge Brook Trail (3.6 miles), or the Ridge Trail (3.5 miles), is Dartmouth College's Moosilauke Ravine Lodge, meals, lodging, telephone, first aid, snacks. Open May 15 to October 15, it is located at the end of a public road, 7.3 miles from Warren.

From the Trail crossing at the southern end, one-half mile north of the center of Glencliff (ZIP Code 03238, telephone), it is 5.0 miles south to Warren (ZIP Code 03279, telephone, groceries).

In an emergency, call the New Hampshire State Police, (603) 846-5517 or (603) 846-3333.

Public Accommodations

From the Trail crossing at N.H. 112, it is 6.2 miles east to North Woodstock (motels, guest house). Bunk rooms and family-style meals are available at the Moosilauke Ravine Lodge (see above); reservations recommended, (603) 764-5858. Public accommodations are not available near the southern end of the section.

Trail Description, North to South

Miles	Data
0.0	From N.H. 112 in Kinsman Notch, Trail heads southwest, where it crosses Beaver Brook on a large bridge with wooden steps and hand rungs. It turns left, ascends, crosses on another bridge, and begins what becomes a very steep, spectacular ascent along the Beaver Brook Cascades. *Trail may be dangerous in wet or icy weather.* Trail eventually leaves cascades, following a tributary, and the grade eases.
1.6	Reach side trail to **Beaver Brook Shelter** on right, with view of Franconia Range. Ascent becomes gradual.

1.9   Reach col between Mt. Blue and Mt. Jim. (Ridge Trail descends left, east, over summit of Mt. Jim, 3.5 miles to Ravine Lodge.) A.T. bears right to ascend around southern side of Mt. Blue. Trail is on ledges at times and at points exposed, with views of Jobildunc Ravine. A half-mile beyond Ridge Trail, pass a spring dripping from a ledge, then 0.1 mile farther, turn sharply right, then left, uphill, slabbing Mt. Blue. Trail climbs, descends to sag, then gains ridge with several viewpoints. Descend, then begin final climb of Moosilauke.

3.4   Reach junction with Benton Trail (leads right 3.1 miles to Tunnel Brook Road, leading north to Benton). A.T. turns left on Benton Trail, continues moderate ascent, passes through treeline, and reaches the exposed north shoulder of Moosilauke. Continue along open ridge; Trail marked by cairns.

3.8   Reach summit-house foundations and summit of Moosilauke (4,802 feet), with one of the finest views in White Mountains, particularly northeast. (Gorge Brook Trail descends sharply left, east, 3.6 miles to Ravine Lodge.) A.T. turns right at summit, descends on the Carriage Road, marked with prominent rock cairns, and soon passes below treeline. Pass over Middle Peak, and pass side trail that leads left 50 feet to view of ravine.

4.8   Reach junction where Trail turns right onto Glencliff Trail. (Carriage Road descends ahead 4.1 miles to Breezy Point, 1.8 miles from N.H. 118 on road passable by automobile. Fifty feet farther on the A.T., a side trail leads left 0.2 mile to South Peak, 4,523 feet.) A.T. steeply descends west on Glencliff Trail, crosses a stream, and continues to descend more moderately.

7.4   Bear left at fork, descend 200 feet, and reach junction at edge of clearing. (Hurricane Trail forks left, passes east over Hurricane Mountain, and reaches Ravine Lodge in 5.1 miles.) A.T. follows right edge of field, crosses brook, and follows left edge of field on cart track. It then passes through an old gate, bears right, then left off the major road onto a smaller track. Cows are often grazing in these fields.

7.8   Pass through stile, turn left onto paved Sanitarium Road, and descend. In 0.3 mile, turn right onto dirt USFS 19. To avoid dangerous crossing of Oliverian Brook, continue straight on Sanitarium Road to its end in Glencliff, turns right on N.H. 25, and follow it 0.5 mile to Trail crossing.

8.2   Cross bridge, and turn left onto Town Line Trail.

8.4   Pass blue-blazed trail on right, which leads 0.1 mile to **Jeffers Brook Shelter**. Trail continues south over several sags and ridges. Eventually, descend to Oliverian Brook and cross on stones (difficult in high water).

9.5   Reach N.H. 25 just north of Glencliff, and turn left. Follow highway 200 yards to end of the section. To continue on Trail, turn right, and ascend southwest into woods (see New Hampshire Section Seven).

Trail Description, South to North

Miles   **Data**

0.0   From N.H. 25, at spot where Trail from south reaches highway just north of Glencliff, proceed northwest 200 yards and turn right (northeast) into woods. (To avoid dangerous crossing of Oliverian Brook, follow N.H. 25 right, southeast, 0.5 mile to Glencliff, turn left on Sanitarium Road, and follow one mile to where A.T. enters from left on North and South roads.) Cross Oliverian Brook, and bear right.

1.1   Blue-blazed trail on left leads 0.1 mile to **Jeffers Brook Shelter**.

1.3   Turn right onto USFS 19. In 0.1 mile, turn left onto paved Sanitarium Road.

1.7   Turn right, away from road, onto Glencliff Trail. Pass through stile, and ascend on lane. In 0.2 mile, cart track joins from left. Follow cart track through gate and along right side of field. Cross brook, then leave track, and keep to left side of second field.

2.1   Turn left, and enter woods. (Hurricane Trail forks right, passes east over Hurricane Mountain, and Ravine Lodge in 5.1 miles.) A.T. crosses brook and continues uphill on old woods road through conifers and hardwoods, passes a stream, and ascends steeply.

4.7 Side trail leads right (0.2 mile to South Peak, 4,523 feet). Fifty feet beyond, reach junction. (Carriage Road descends 4.1 miles right to Breezy Point, approximately 2.5 miles from N.H. 118 by road passable by car.) A.T. turns left and follows Carriage Road north with views west. In 0.3 mile, side trail leads right 50 feet to view. Pass above treeline, and continue along Carriage Road, marked by prominent rock cairns.

5.7 Reach summit of Mt. Moosilauke (4,802 feet), with summit house ruins and one of the finest views in White Mountains, particularly northeast toward the highest peaks in the region. Trail turns 90 degrees left at the summit rock. Immediately beyond, Gorge Brook Trail angles right (descends 3.6 miles to Ravine Lodge). A.T. becomes the Benton Trail, passes to right of summit foundations and along exposed north ridge, marked by large cairns, and descends through treeline.

6.1 Beaver Brook Trail junction. (Benton Trail continues ahead, descending 3.1 miles to Tunnel Brook Road, leading north to Benton.) A.T. turns right and descends moderately, reaches two sags, then climbs to a low ridge with several viewpoints east. Trail descends off ridge, through sag, ascends briefly, then descends moderately, turns sharply right, then immediately left. Trail continues, exposed and on ledges, around Jobildunc Ravine, passes spring on left, then descends.

7.6 Reach col between Mt. Blue and Mt. Jim. (Ridge Trail descends right over summit of Mt. Jim, 3.5 miles to Ravine Lodge.) A.T. descends gradually and then more steeply.

7.9 Spur trail leads left 200 feet to **Beaver Brook Shelter** and view of Franconias. Trail continues to steepen and reaches first of many cascades, descending over wooden steps with hand rungs. It becomes very steep at several points and must be descended carefully (*may be dangerous in wet or icy weather*). Eventually, pass lowest cascade, and descend moderately, cross brook on large bridge, and descend gradually. Trail nears Beaver Pond, turns right, and crosses brook on another large bridge.

9.5 Reach N.H. 112 in Kinsman Notch and end of section. To continue on Trail, cross highway diagonally left, and turn right onto Kinsman Ridge Trail (see New Hampshire Section Five).

Glencliff (N.H. 25) to N.H. 25A
New Hampshire Section Seven
9.8 Miles

Brief Description of Section

The Trail in this section passes through low-country hardwood forests, from Glencliff (1,074 feet) to N.H. 25A (900 feet), across N.H. 25C. This section has two low summits, Mt. Mist (2,220 feet) and Ore Hill (1,866 feet). The A.T. passes Wachipauka Pond. One side trail goes to the summit of Webster Slide Mountain near the northern end. For current information on the Trail in this section, contact the Dartmouth Outing Club (see "Important Addresses," page 219).

Road Approaches

Both ends and the center of the section are accessible from major highways. At the northern end, the Trail crosses N.H. 25 approximately a half-mile northwest of Glencliff. N.H. 25C intersects the center of this section 4 miles west of Warren, and 10 miles east of Piermont. At the southern end, the Trail crosses N.H. 25A (difficult parking at roadside) 1.8 miles east of the Mt. Cube House, 4.3 miles west of Wentworth, and 20.2 miles west of I-93. This crossing is also 10.8 miles east of Orford (on N.H. 10) and 11.2 miles east of Fairlee, Vermont (on I-91).

Maps

Map Four (this guide)
DOC Trail Map

The A.T. route might not be current on the following:
USGS 15-minute topographic quadrangles:
　　　Rumney, New Hampshire
　　　Mt. Cube, New Hampshire
USGS 7½-minute topographic quadrangle:
　　　Warren, New Hampshire

Shelters and Campsites

This section has no campsites; however, the Dartmouth Outing Club planned to build a shelter on the south slope of Ore Hill, one mile north of Atwell Hill Road, sometime in 1998 or 1999.

Regulations

The segment of the Trail between Glencliff (N.H. 25) and the northern summit of Ore Hill (about 0.8 mile south of N.H. 25C) lies within WMNF, where camping and fires are permitted only at sites 200 feet or more from the Trail.

From the northern summit of Ore Hill to N.H. 25A, the Trail passes through Forest Service-protected lands on which camping and fires are prohibited.

Supplies and Services

From the Trail crossing of N.H. 25 at the northern end of the section, approximately half a mile northwest of the center of Glencliff (ZIP Code 03238, telephone), it is 5.0 miles south to Warren (ZIP Code 03279, telephone, restaurant, groceries). Warren is also 4.0 miles east of the Trail crossing at N.H. 25C in the center of the section. From the Trail crossing at the southern end of the section, it is 4.3 miles east to Wentworth (ZIP Code 03282, telephone, restaurant, limited selection of groceries), 10.8 miles west to Orford (ZIP Code 03777, telephone, limited selection of groceries), and 11.2 miles west to Fairlee, Vermont (bus stop).

In an emergency, contact the New Hampshire State Police, (603) 846-5517 or (603) 846-3333.

Public Accommodations

This section has no public accommodations.

Trail Description, North to South

Miles   **Data**

0.0   From N.H. 25 northwest of Glencliff, follow woods road, cross old railroad bed, and then bear left, uphill. Continue on level southeast, then swing southwest, and climb steeply. Pass north of summit of Wyatt Hill, and descend gradually west.

2.0   Reach Wachipauka Pond. A.T. skirts northern and western shores of pond and then ascends west, passing Hairy Root Spring (unreliable in summer). In 0.2 mile, reach saddle between Mt. Mist and Webster Slide Mountain. (Side trail climbs right to summit of Webster Slide Mountain.) Trail climbs south, passing to right of outlook.

2.5   Pass over gentle, wooded summit of Mt. Mist (2,220 feet), and descend gradually south.

5.0   Cross stream (reliable water source). Reach N.H. 25C. Follow it to right, west, for 100 feet. Enter woods on western side of powerline. This is Ore Hill Trail. Ascend; pass WMNF boundary at northern summit of Ore Hill, and continue along ridge.

7.0   Pass side trail to spring (site of proposed Ore Hill Shelter).

8.0   Cross dirt Atwell Hill Road. Continue onto Atwell Hill Trail. Trail descends 0.2 mile, crosses swampy area, and turns left onto old woods road. Turn right off woods road, and descend into swampy area.

9.8   Reach N.H. 25A, south of Upper Baker Pond. Cross highway bridge at right, and follow highway 100 yards to the end of the section. To continue on A.T., turn left onto Mt. Cube Trail (see New Hampshire Section Eight).

Trail Description, South to North

Miles   **Data**

0.0   From Mt. Cube Trail at N.H. 25A, turn right. Cross over highway bridge, and enter woods at left on Atwell Hill Trail, 100 yards east. Pass through swampy area. Turn left onto old woods road. One-half mile from 25A, turn right off woods road, and cross swampy area.

1.8   Cross dirt Atwell Hill Road. Continue straight on Ore Hill Trail. Cross swamp, and ascend gradually.

2.8   Pass side trail on right to spring (site of proposed Ore Hill Shelter). Continue along ridge, cross WMNF boundary at northern summit of Ore Hill, and descend.

4.8   Reach N.H. 25C. Turn right, and pass under powerline. In 100 feet, turn left onto Wachipauka Pond Trail. Cross stream (reliable water source), and ascend northeast.

7.3   Pass over gentle, wooded summit of Mt. Mist (2,220 feet), and descend. Pass outlook on right. Reach saddle between Mt. Mist and Webster Slide Mountain where side trail climbs left to summit of Webster Slide Mountain. A.T. descends east, where it passes Hairy Root Spring (unreliable in summer).

7.8   Reach Wachipauka Pond. Trail skirts western and northern shores of pond, then ascends gradually east. Pass north of summit of Wyatt Hill, and then descend steadily northeast.

9.8   Reach N.H. 25 and end of section, just northwest of Glencliff. To continue on A.T., go left 200 yards on road, and turn right into woods (see New Hampshire Section Six).

N.H. 25A to Lyme-Dorchester Road (Dartmouth Skiway)
New Hampshire Section Eight
16.0 Miles

Brief Description of Section

The Trail in this section crosses two outstanding features—Mt. Cube (2,911 feet) and Smarts Mountain (3,240 feet).

Going south, the Trail enters woods from N.H. 25A, 1.8 miles east of the Mt. Cube House and about 100 yards west of a steel bridge on N.H. 25A. The A.T. ascends gently over mixed terrain, passes several brooks, and crosses a log bridge over Brackett Brook. It rises more steeply on switchbacks to Mt. Cube. A side trail leads left to the northern summit, with views of Mt. Moosilauke and the White Mountains from open ledges. The A.T. ascends to the southern summit, also open, with views of the Connecticut River Valley and the summits of Smarts Mountain and Mt. Ascutney standing alone.

The Trail continues along a ridge and down to Jacobs Brook before ascending Smarts Mountain. It descends on the southern side of the mountain *via* the old Ranger Trail and the Lambert Ridge Trail, with several good views from ledges.

Road Approaches

The northern end of this section is accessible by car on N.H. 25A (difficult parking at roadside) 4.3 miles west of Wentworth and 20.2 miles west of I-93. This crossing is also 10.8 miles east of Orford (N.H. 10) and 11.2 miles east of Fairlee, Vermont (I-91). The southern end is accessible by Lyme-Dorchester Road. Starting at Lyme on N.H. 10, this paved road leads east 3.2 miles to a road fork and the Trail. The Dartmouth Skiway, 0.1 mile beyond on the right fork, has ample parking. The northern fork of this road may be followed as far north as Smarts Ranger Trail Junction (limited parking).

Maps

Map Four (this guide)
DOC Trail Map

The A.T. route might not be current on the following:
USGS 15-minute topographic quadrangle:
    Mt. Cube, New Hampshire

Shelters and Campsites

This section has one shelter, a tentsite, and a cabin:
Hexacuba Shelter: Built and maintained by DOC; on a 0.3-mile side trail, 4.9 miles from northern end of section; accommodates 8; water may be unreliable.
    Next shelter or campsite: north 15.8 miles (Jeffers Brook); south 5.3 miles.
Firewarden's Cabin: Cabin built by N.H. Forest Service, now maintained by DOC; 5.8 miles from southern end of section; accommodates 8; water from Mike Murphy Spring on blue-blazed trail.
    Next shelter or campsite: north 5.3 miles; south 0.1 mile.
Smarts Mountain Tentsite: Maintained by DOC; 5.7 miles from southern end of section on short side trail; water from Mike Murphy Spring.
    Next shelter or campsite: north 0.1 mile; south 6.6 miles (Trapper John Shelter).

Regulations

Camping and fires are prohibited except at Smarts Mountain Tentsite, Firewarden's Cabin, and Hexacuba Shelter, where fires are restricted to fire rings provided there.

Supplies and Services

From the Trail crossing at N.H. 25A at the northern end of the section, it is 4.3 miles east to Wentworth (ZIP Code 03282, restaurant, telephone, limited selection of groceries), 10.8 miles west to Orford (ZIP Code 03777, telephone, limited selection of groceries), and 11.2 miles west to Fairlee, Vermont (bus stop). From the A.T. crossing at the

Dartmouth Skiway at the southern end of the section, it is 1.2 miles west to Lyme Center (ZIP Code 03769) and 3.2 miles west to Lyme [ZIP Code 03768; ATC Regional Office in One Lyme Common Building (see Section Nine); telephone; limited selection of groceries; meals].

In an emergency, contact the New Hampshire State Police, (603) 846-5517 or (603) 846-3333.

Public Accommodations

Several b&bs and a lodge with cottages are located in Lyme, 3.2 miles west of the section's southern end. Other accommodations are located in Fairlee, Vermont and Wentworth, New Hampshire.

Trail Description, North to South

Miles	Data
0.0	From N.H. 25A, 1.8 miles east of Mt. Cube House and next to Upper Baker Pond, enter woods on southern side of road, about 100 yards west of metal highway bridge. Cross small swamp, and ascend on abandoned logging roads. At 0.3 mile, cross a gravel logging road, and ascend.
1.8	Cross log bridge over Brackett Brook, and begin ascending Mt. Cube on switchbacks.
3.3	Reach saddle between North and South Cube summits. (Side trail leaves right to open summit of North Cube.) Trail continues left and climbs to a ledge.
3.5	Reach open south summit of Mt. Cube (2,911 feet) with fine views west. Unnamed side trail (shown on map) leads straight (southwesterly) 1.5 miles to Baker Farm Road, which leads to 25A. A.T. bears left and descends over ledges.
4.9	Cross branch of North Jacobs Brook. Continue 50 feet to side trail leading left, uphill, 0.3 mile to **Hexacuba Shelter**. Trail slabs hillside and descends to cross brook and an old logging road. It then climbs moderately to Eastman Ledges, switches back, and descends.
6.3	Cross logging road and, 0.1 mile beyond, wooden bridge over South Jacobs Brook. Begin ascending ridge up to Smarts Mountain.

10.1   Reach Clark Pond Loop junction. (Side trail leads downhill to
        Lyme-Dorchester Road at Reservoir Pond.)

10.2   Pass **Firewarden's Cabin** on right, now an enclosed shelter
        maintained by DOC. Mike Murphy Spring is 0.1 mile north
        on blue-blazed Daniel Doan Trail (leads 3.5 miles to gravel
        road in Quinttown, four miles from Orfordville). Trail passes
        just east of summit of Smarts Mountain (3,240 feet), with fine
        views from restored fire tower, and continues along ridge.

10.3   Side trail leads left 500 feet to **Smarts Mountain Tentsite**.
        A.T. descends steeply west over ledges, then less steeply
        through spruce forest.

10.7   Turn right off Smarts Mountain Ranger Trail onto Lambert
        Ridge Trail. Descend steeply into swampy col, and ascend
        onto rocky spine of Lambert Ridge.

12.2   Reach northern end of Lambert Ridge. Continue south over
        ledgy ridge, in and out of woods, with good views from
        ledges. Descend into hardwood forest.

14.0   Reach parking lot on Lyme-Dorchester Road. Bear left across
        road bridge, then immediately turn right. In 50 feet, turn right
        again onto old road. Bear left uphill off old road at granite
        A.T. milestone. Cross stream in shallow gorge, then begin
        gradual descent, slabbing northwest side of Winslow Ledge.
        Turn left onto Lyme-Dorchester Road.

16.0   At fork in Lyme-Dorchester Road at Dartmouth Skiway,
        section ends 3.2 miles east of Lyme and 5.0 miles east of East
        Thetford, Vermont. Trail continues straight ahead into woods
        and up Holts Ledge (see New Hampshire Section Nine).

Trail Description, South to North

Miles   **Data**

0.0   At fork in Lyme-Dorchester Road, 3.2 miles east of Lyme and
        5.0 miles east of East Thetford, Vermont, the Trail proceeds
        east on dirt road. Two-hundred yards from start, turn right
        off Lyme-Dorchester Road at overgrown field (blazed post in
        field). Begin gradual ascent, slabbing northwest side of
        Winslow Ledge. Cross a stream, and descend. Bear right onto
        old road at granite A.T. milestone.

2.0   Reach Lyme-Dorchester Road. Bear left across bridge and parking lot, and begin ascent of Lambert Ridge. (Smarts Mountain Ranger Trail leads right from parking lot to summit of Smarts Mountain.) Soon, reach first of numerous ledge outcrops; Trail continues along rocky Lambert Ridge, in and out of woods, with good views.

3.8   Descend Lambert Ridge, cross stream, and begin ascending Smarts Mountain.

5.3   Join Smarts Mountain Ranger Trail, which continues to the summit.

5.7   Side trail leads right 500 feet to **Smarts Mountain Tentsite**. Intermittent spring is just beyond trail junction. A.T. continues east.

5.8   Pass just east of summit of Smarts Mountain (3,240 feet). Smarts Mountain Ranger Trail ends here. Good views from restored firetower at summit. Pass **Firewarden's Cabin**, maintained as shelter by DOC. Mike Murphy Spring is 0.1 mile north of cabin on blue-blazed Daniel Doan Trail (leads 3.5 miles north to gravel road at Quinttown, four miles from Orfordville off N.H. 25A).

5.9   Pass Clark Pond Loop junction. (Blue-blazed trail descends right to Lyme-Dorchester Road.) Continue along ridge and then descend into valley. Eventually, cross wooden bridge over South Jacobs Brook.

9.7   Cross South Jacobs Brook logging road (leads west about 1.5 miles to Quinttown). Trail ascends rocky Eastman Ledges, switches back, descends, and crosses old logging road and brook. Ascend, slabbing hillside.

11.1   Side trail leads right 0.3 mile to **Hexacuba Shelter**. Trail descends 50 feet to branch of North Jacobs Brook, then ascends to ledges southwest of Mt. Cube summit.

12.5   Unnamed side trail joins from left (descends southwesterly 1.5 miles to Baker Farm Road, 1.5 miles from N.H. 25A). Reach South Cube summit (2,911 feet). Bear right across summit. After following ridgecrest short distance descend and make sharp left into woods.

12.7   A.T. leads right from col and descends steeply across switchbacks. (Side trail to open North Cube is straight ahead.)

14.2 Cross log bridge over Brackett Brook, and ascend briefly. Cross gravel logging road, and descend on abandoned logging road.

16.0 Reach N.H. 25A, where section ends. Trail continues right 200 yards along highway and reenters woods on northern side of road (see New Hampshire Section Seven).

Lyme-Dorchester Road
(Dartmouth Skiway) to Connecticut River
(N.H.-Vt. State Line)
New Hampshire Section Nine
18.1 Miles

Brief Description of Section

This section follows the southern end of the White Mountain foothills between Mt. Moosilauke and the Connecticut River. From the Dartmouth Skiway, the Trail passes the crest (about 1,900 feet) and the summit of Holts Ledge (2,100 feet), then goes along the ridge and past the summit of Moose Mountain (2,300 feet).

After passing through Hanover, New Hampshire, home of Dartmouth College (see below), the Trail descends to the Connecticut River (400 feet), the southern end of the New Hampshire A.T. The Trail in this section follows woods roads and footpaths through pastures, fields, and forest. Except for the steep ascents of Holts Ledge and Moose Mountain, the terrain is easy to hike.

This section has three side trails. The Harris Trail begins where the A.T. crosses Goose Pond Road. Follow this road one-half mile west, then a blue-blazed trail 4.1 miles southwest, and rejoin the A.T. between the south summit of Moose Mountain and Three-Mile Road.

The Velvet Rocks Shelter Loop leaves the A.T. at the junction with the Ledyard Spring Trail (spring is approximately 0.2 mile) and leads 0.4 mile to the shelter. Total length of loop is 0.6 mile.

The Trescott Road spur drops 0.6 mile to Trescott Road, 2.3 miles north of Hanover.

The Dartmouth Outing Club office is located on the green in Hanover. For maps and A.T. information for this area, contact the DOC (see "Important Addresses," page 219).

The ATC New England Regional office is located in the village of Lyme, on the southeastern corner of the town common, 3.2 miles west of the intersection of the A.T. with Dorchester Road near the Dartmouth Skiway at the northern end of the section. For Trail information and assistance, visit the office or call (603) 795-4935.

Dartmouth College

Dartmouth College is in the center of the small town of Hanover. On December 13, 1769, King George III of England approved a charter prepared by Governor John Wentworth of New Hampshire, establishing an institution "for the education and instruction of Youth of the Indian Tribes in this Land in reading, writing and all parts of Learning which shall appear necessary and expedient for civilizing and Christianizing Children of Pagans as well as in all liberal Arts and Sciences and also of English Youth and any others." Wentworth decided to name the college after the Earl of Dartmouth, the school's sponsor and benefactor.

The year after the charter was approved, the Rev. Eleazar Wheelock struck off into the New Hampshire wilderness and built a single log hut, the beginning of Dartmouth College. It was there that the first class, all four students, graduated in 1771.

Today, the Ivy League school is primarily a liberal-arts college but also has graduate schools of medicine, engineering, and business. Hikers may want to take advantage of the many cultural opportunities the college offers to the public.

Road Approaches

The northern end of this section is accessible by the Lyme-Dorchester Road. Starting in Lyme (on N.H. 10), this paved road leads 3.2 miles east to the Dartmouth Skiway (ample parking) and the Trail. The Trail crosses Trescott Road, four miles east of Hanover with good parking, and the Goose Pond Road 3.3 miles east of N.H. 10.

At the crossing of the Connecticut River, the Trail is 0.2 mile east of U.S. 5 and I-91 in Vermont. The Trail follows West Wheelock Street for the half-mile between the Connecticut River and N.H. 10 in Hanover (difficult, metered parking), south on N.H. 10 (Main Street) to the next traffic light, where it turns left (east) onto N.H. 120 (Lebanon Street). It then follows N.H. 120 for 0.6 mile to a service station. There, the Trail turns left, leaving Lebanon Street, and skirts the edge of a playing field for a short distance before entering woods. Parking is not permitted in this area, but a Dartmouth College parking lot is available for hikers; stop at the DOC office in Robinson Hall on the green for instructions.

Maps

Map Four (this guide)
DOC Trail Map

The A.T. route might not be current on the following:
USGS 15-minute topographic quadrangles:
    Mt. Cube, New Hampshire
    Mascoma, New Hampshire
USGS 7½-minute topographic quadrangle:
    Hanover, New Hampshire/Vermont

Regulations

Camping and fires are prohibited except at Trapper John, Moose Mountain, and Velvet Rocks shelters.

Please heed carefully the fences and signs near Holts Ledge during the peregrine-falcon nesting season (early spring to midsummer). The falcons, after decades' absence, have been nesting below the ledge since 1987 and must be protected from activity above their nests. This peregrine-reintroduction process is a cooperative program of ATC, DOC, N.H. Audubon, the N.H. Fish and Game Commission, and the U.S. Fish and Wildlife Service.

Shelters and Campsites

This section has three shelters:

Trapper John Shelter: Built and maintained by DOC; 0.9 mile from northern end of section, on 0.2-mile side trail; accommodates 8; ample water.

Next shelter or campsite: north 6.6 miles (Smarts Mountain Tentsite); south 5.9 miles.

Moose Mountain Shelter: Built and maintained by DOC; 6.8 miles from northern end of section, plus 0.5 mile on side trail; accommodates 6; ample water.

Next shelter or campsite: north 5.9 miles; south 9.3 miles.

Velvet Rocks Shelter: Built and maintained by DOC; 2.0 miles from southern end of section on 0.2-mile side trail; accommodates 4; water 0.4 mile east on Velvet Rocks Loop and Ledyard Spring Trail.

Next shelter or campsite: north 9.3 miles; south 7.3 miles (Happy Hill Shelter).

Supplies and Services

From the Trail crossing of Lyme-Dorchester Road at the Dartmouth Skiway at the northern end of the section, it is 1.2 miles west to Lyme Center (ZIP Code 03769) and 3.2 miles to Lyme (ZIP Code 03768, telephone, limited selection of groceries, meals). From the Trail crossing of the Etna-Hanover Center Road, 6.9 miles from the southern end of the section, it is approximately 2.0 miles south to Etna (ZIP Code 03750, limited selection of groceries). The educational and cultural facilities of Dartmouth College, as well as the largest shopping area directly on the Trail in New Hampshire and Vermont, are in Hanover (ZIP Code 03755, telephone, supermarket, specialty backpacking stores, bookstore, restaurants, Dartmouth-Hitchcock Medical Center, bus stop). One mile south of the southern end is Norwich, Vermont, ZIP Code 05055, groceries and meals.

In an emergency, contact the New Hampshire State Police, (603) 846-3333 or (603) 846-5517.

Public Accommodations

Several b&bs and a lodge with cottages are located in Lyme, 3.2 miles west of the northern end of this section.

Accommodations are available near the southern end of the section in Hanover. Norwich, Vermont, has an inn one mile south of the southern end of the section (Vermont Section One). Motels, hotels, and rooming houses near White River Junction, Vermont, and Lebanon, New Hampshire, five miles south of Hanover, provide services over a wide price range.

Trail Description, North to South

Miles   **Data**

0.0   From fork at Lyme-Dorchester Road, Trail ascends gradually southwest into woods.

0.9   Side trail leads to the right 0.2 mile to **Trapper John Shelter** and water. Trail continues to climb gradually, crosses a small intermittent brook, then ascends more steeply along several small ridges.

1.4   Side trail leads left 0.1 mile to Holts Ledge viewpoint and top of Dartmouth Skiway. To protect peregrine-falcon nesting sites, please observe all signs and fencing here. Trail turns right and climbs to height of land on Holts Ledge, then descends, crosses old logging road, and descends to cross beaver-pond dam to road.

3.4   Reach Goose Pond Road (952 feet), bear left 50 feet, then turn right off road into woods, and ascend, at first gradually, then steeply to North Peak of Moose Mountain (2,300 feet). Follow ridgeline and rocky outcroppings of North Peak. Eventually, descend to col between North and South peaks.

6.8   Reach woods road. A.T. continues straight ahead. **Moose Mountain Shelter** is to left 0.5 mile on the Clark Pond Loop Trail.

7.4   Reach South Peak of Moose Mountain (2,290 feet). Descend gradually, with one steep section, to woods road, cross road, and continue descent.

9.0   Cross Mink Brook, and ascend gradually to Three-Mile Road.

9.2   Reach Three-Mile Road. Turn left and then right through small parking lot. Follow trail into woods.

9.7   Cross a woods road (Cory Road). Continue 100 yards, and bear left where old Trail leaves right. Pass through intermittently, open hardwood and pine stands. Eventually, descend across a large field with views to the southwest. Leave field, and descend.

11.7   Cross Etna-Hanover Center Road. Trail passes south of cemetery. Cross two brooks, and climb gradually.

12.4   Bear left onto old road, and follow it about 250 feet, then bear off to road to right. Cross numerous stone walls, and reach old field.

13.1   Cross Trescott Road. Pass through conifer plantation, cross over small knoll, and continue on level section. Cross bridge just south of dam over large beaver pond. Switch back up ledge.

14.1   Make sharp left on old logging road. Ascend, then descend, and bear right, then right again. Begin climbing again, then switch back left, contouring between ledges to ridge. Follow ridge north through clearing near summit of Velvet Rocks.

15.0   Reach Trescott Road Spur Trail on right, which descends 0.6 mile to Trescott Road at a point about 2.3 miles east of Hanover. Continue along ridge over several humps, then descend steeply.

15.6   Reach northern end of **Velvet Rocks Shelter** Loop Trail on right. Ledyard Spring Trail leads right (approximately 0.2 mile to shelter and spring). A.T. bends left through a small notch and continues west.

16.1   Reach southern end of **Velvet Rocks Shelter** Loop Trail on right, 0.2 mile to shelter. Trail continues on crest of ridge then descends and passes a spring (pool on left unreliable). Trail slabs across ridge to southwest, then leaves woods and bears left, following southern edge of playing field.

16.9   Reach N.H. 120 at service station. Turn right, and follow Park Street north about 150 feet to a crosswalk. Cross here, and pass through parking lot of a small bank building, then continue northwest on right side of Lebanon Street. Continue to where Lebanon Street ends (at the light). Turn right on South Main Street, and pass through downtown Hanover.

17.6   Reach the intersection of North Main and East Wheelock streets. Trail turns left (west). (Offices of Dartmouth Outing Club are in Robinson Hall, second building on left, ahead on Main Street.) Descend west on West Wheelock Street.

18.1   Reach western end of bridge over Connecticut River and the New Hampshire/Vermont state line (400 feet above sea level), and end of section. To continue on Trail, follow Vt. 10A west (see Vermont Section One).

Trail Description, South to North

Miles   **Data**

0.0   From western end of bridge over Connecticut River and New Hampshire/Vermont state line (400 feet above sea level), follow hard-surfaced West Wheelock Street east into Hanover.

0.5   Reach intersection of North Main Street and East Wheelock Street. (Offices of Dartmouth Outing Club are in Robinson Hall, second building on left on North Main Street, to the left.) A.T. turns right (south) on South Main Street (N.H. 10), then left at a traffic light at Lebanon Street. Follow Lebanon Street east, then southeast. Just before major intersection, pass through parking lot of bank building.

1.2   Cross Park Street, and turn right. Continue south 100 feet. Reach service station. Turn left, and follow southern edge of playing field until Trail continues into woods. Shortly, bear left (northeast), and slab ridge. Soon, pass spring (pool on right unreliable).

2.0   Reach southern end of **Velvet Rocks Shelter** Loop Trail on left (0.2 mile to shelter). Trail bends right around hill.

2.5   Reach northern end of Velvet Rocks Shelter Loop at junction with Ledyard Spring Trail, both on left (spring about 0.2 mile). Trail turns right (east) and continues over a number of knolls.

3.1   Reach Trescott Road Spur Trail. This trail, former A.T. route, descends 0.6 mile to Trescott Road at a point about 2.3 miles east of Hanover. Trail swings south through clearing near summit of Velvet Rocks, then follows ridge southeast, makes a sharp left turn, slabbing down among ledges. Follow old logging road for some distance.

4.1   Leave logging road. Switch back down through additional ledges. Soon, cross bridge just south of dam over large beaver pond. Continue almost level for some distance, then cross over small knoll, and pass through conifer plantation.

5.0   Cross Trescott Road, and ascend through field. Pass through mature woods over numerous stone walls.

5.7   Bear left onto woods road. Continue 250 feet, then bear right off road. Descend gradually, and cross two brooks. Continue south, then east, with cemetery on left.

6.4   Cross Etna-Hanover Center Road, and ascend hill. Enter a large field, then climb gently across it. Leave this field, and continue gradual ascent through abandoned farmland. Eventually, veer right, joining old trail.

8.4   Cross Cory Road (woods road). Continue, climbing gradually.

8.9 Emerge through small parking lot onto Three-Mile Road. Turn left, then right, reentering woods.

9.1 Cross Mink Brook. Begin gradual ascent. In 0.2 mile, cross woods road; Harris Trail (obscure in places) follows this road left, rejoining A.T. at Goose Pond Road in 4.6 miles. Ascend, sometimes steeply, toward South Peak of Moose Mountain.

10.7 Reach summit of South Peak of Moose Mountain (2,290 feet). Descend to woods road in col between South and North peaks.

11.3 Reach woods road. A.T. continues straight ahead. **Moose Mountain Shelter** is 0.5 mile to the right on the Clark Pond Loop Trail. A.T. follows ridge of Moose Mountain, with occasional views. Descend steeply after North Peak (2,300 feet), then gradually.

14.7 Reach Goose Pond Road (952 feet). Turn left on road, follow 50 feet, then bear right on narrow road through old log landing. Follow road to its end, then cross beaver dam. Bear left in about 100 yards. Begin climbing, first gradually, then steeply. Cross former logging road, then continue climbing steadily, passing over height of land on Holts Ledge.

16.7 Trail turns left at junction. (Side trail leads straight ahead 0.1 mile to Holts Ledge viewpoint and top of Dartmouth Skiway. Please observe all posted precautions in this area to protect nesting peregrine falcons.) Trail descends steeply over several small ridges, crosses intermittent brook, then descends to the left gradually.

17.2 Side trail to the left leads 0.2 mile to **Trapper John Shelter** (water). A.T. descends gradually.

18.1 Reach Lyme-Dorchester Road (880 feet) at fork in road, end of section. Dartmouth Skiway, with ski trails on the northern side of Holts Ledge, is 0.1 mile east. To continue on Trail, cross road, and bear right onto dirt road (see New Hampshire Section Eight).

The Appalachian Trail in Vermont

The Trail in Vermont is more than 146 miles long. The northern part runs east to west, mostly through lowland hardwood country, across wooded hills dotted with fields, pastures, and abandoned roads and farms of an earlier era. The Trail in the southern part of Vermont, from Sherburne Pass to the Massachusetts border, follows the central ridgecrest of the Green Mountains and coincides with the Long Trail for about 104 miles.

Most of the relocations of Trail areas in Vermont that were planned in the 1980s have been completed. Nevertheless, *follow the blazes carefully*.

The terrain of the northern part of the Trail in Vermont, from the Connecticut River Valley west to Sherburne Pass, is a succession of pastures, cleared hills, and patches of timber. It does not follow a continuous ridgecrest but crosses a series of short, but steep and strenuous hills. Stone walls and cellar holes, evidence of former inhabitants, are found frequently. Everywhere are indications of the area's history and its gradual reversion to forest after intensive farming.

Beginning at the Connecticut River, the Trail passes on roads west through the small town of Norwich, Vermont. It ascends Mosley Hill (1,180 feet), passes over the wooded crest of Griggs Mountain (1,570 feet), and descends along Podunk Brook to the White River at West Hartford. It crosses the White River on a highway bridge and passes over Bunker Hill (1,480 feet) on old roads before reaching the abandoned Kings Highway. West of Kings Highway, the Trail passes over Thistle Hill (1,800 feet), then crosses a series of cleared ridges, descends through several valleys, crosses a number of roads, and reaches Vt. 12.

Vt. 12 to Sherburne Pass is the westernmost link in the A.T. chain between the White and Green mountains. It involves considerable exertion in ascending and descending many ridges. From Vt. 12, the route ascends to The Lookout (2,439 feet) and continues west across rugged terrain into Ottauquechee Valley, which is hemmed in by high ridges. The autumn foliage in this section is outstanding. From this valley, the Trail passes Kent Pond and Vt. 100, and into Gifford Woods State Park, which has a virgin hardwood forest. After passing through the park, the Trail rises steeply to its junction with the Long Trail and follows it south to the Massachusetts border.

The Long Trail of Vermont follows the main ridge of the Green Mountains some 268 miles, from the Canadian border to the Massachusetts state line. Like the younger A.T., it is a primitive footpath. It is steep, boggy, and rugged in the tradition of other early New England trails, like those the A.T. follows in the White Mountains of New Hampshire. On the southern part of the Long Trail, the A.T. passes over a number of high summits and through low points in the Green Mountains where major highways cross the range. It winds through wilderness terrain, densely forested with evergreens in higher elevations and northern hardwood trees in lower areas. It also passes a number of scenic mountain lakes. Although not as rough as the route in the White Mountains, the Long Trail terrain is strenuous and rewarding.

From U.S. 4, the Trail climbs south across the Coolidge Range. Short side trails lead to the summits of Pico Peak (3,957 feet) and Killington Peak (4,235 feet). The Trail reaches its highest point in Vermont just below Killington Peak, the second-highest summit in the state (Mt. Mansfield at 4,393 feet is the highest). From the Coolidge Range, the Trail continues south across rolling foothills and crosses a number of roads.

Several relocations between the vicinity of Sherburne Pass and Little Killington Peak were begun in the summer of 1998. The new Trail route follows the Long Trail north from the current "Maine Junction" to Willard Gap. At that point, the Trail will descend southerly to cross U.S. 4 about one mile west of Sherburne Pass. From that point, the Trail will climb gently around the western shoulder of Pico Peak. It will reconnect with the existing A.T. and Long Trail approximately one-half mile south of Pico Camp. Another one-mile relocation leaves the A.T. at Snowden Peak and reconnects with the A.T. at Cooper Lodge. A third relocation will leave the existing A.T. approximately one-half mile south of Cooper Lodge and rejoin the existing Trail on the east flank of Little Killington Peak. See map for depiction of these future routes.

Just south of Vt. 103, the Trail crosses a suspension bridge over Clarendon Gorge. South of Vt. 140, the Trail ascends the ridge of White Rocks Mountain (2,680 feet), passes Little Rock Pond, then descends along Little Black Branch to the Danby-Landgrove Road (USFS 10) at a low point on the Green Mountain crest. Soon after USFS 10, the Trail travels nearly 12 miles through the Green Mountain National Forest's Big Branch and Peru Peak Wildernesses. The Trail then rises to the summit of Baker Peak (2,850 feet), and descends past Griffith Lake. It passes over Peru Peak (3,429 feet) and Styles Peak (3,394 feet) and descends to Mad Tom Notch (2,446 feet).

The Trail steadily climbs Bromley Mountain (3,260 feet), descends and crosses Vt. 11, then climbs to Spruce Peak, and reaches Prospect Rock (2,079 feet). For 2.8 miles, the A.T. passes through the Green Mountain National Forest's Lye Brook Wilderness, a primitive tract of Vermont woodland, reaching Stratton Pond. As it leaves the pond on the western slope of Stratton Mountain, the Trail ascends to the Stratton Lookout Tower near the point where Benton MacKaye may have first conceived the idea of an Appalachian Trail.

The Trail leaves the summit of Stratton Mountain and descends to Arlington-West Wardsboro Road. Alternatively, the Stratton Mountain Trail (the former A.T.) can be followed from Stratton Pond to Arlington-West Wardsboro Road (see maps).

From the Arlington-West Wardsboro Road, the Trail ascends south along a ridge, rising to Glastenbury Mountain (3,748 feet). It continues along a wooded ridge and drops steeply to Vt. 9, but then rises even more steeply to follow a rolling ridge.

The short section of Trail from the Massachusetts-Vermont line to North Adams, Massachusetts, is covered in this guide as a part of Section Nine, for the hiker's convenience. Here the Trail passes over the open rocky ridge of East Mountain, then drops to the Hoosic River and Mass. 2 in North Adams.

Except in the Green Mountain National Forest and one state park, the A.T. runs in a narrow corridor of land largely protected for the Trail. In these corridor sections, camping and fires are permitted only at designated sites.

The Dartmouth Outing Club (DOC) maintains the Trail from the Connecticut River west to Vt. 12. This section is blazed with standard white A.T. blazes in addition to the occasional orange-and-black blazes marking DOC trails.

The responsibility for maintenance of the section from Vt. 12 south to the Massachusetts border lies with the Green Mountain Club (GMC), although parts are maintained by the U.S. Forest Service (USFS).

Additional information on the Trail from Vt. 12 south is available in the *Day Hiker's Guide to Vermont* or *Long Trail Guide*. The latter guide and current information on the A.T. are available from the Appalachian Trail Conference or the Green Mountain Club (see "Important Addresses," page 219). For information on the Trail from Vt. 12 east to the Connecticut River, contact the Dartmouth Outing Club (see page 219).

Green Mountain National Forest

For more than one-half its length in Vermont, in sections from Vt. 140 south to the Mass.-Vt. border, the Trail passes through the Green Mountain National Forest (GMNF). The national forest covers about 250,000 acres, stretching almost 100 miles north from the Massachusetts line. It is not only a recreational resource but provides timber, wildlife, grazing, and water. In each section of this guide, under "Regulations," are instructions for using the forest in that particular area. Camping is permitted in the forest.

In recent years, recreational use of GMNF's backcountry has increased dramatically. In some places, shelters and trails are used by greater numbers of hikers than the local environment can support. Trail erosion, loss of vegetation, water pollution, and disposal of human waste have developed into major concerns. The heavy use around Little Rock Pond is a good example. Here, intense use by hikers and others has damaged the fragile shoreline. Such problems necessitate regulations aimed at reducing the impact camping and hiking have on plant life, soils, and water.

Throughout GMNF, fires at designated sites must be built in the fireplaces provided. Other fires, although ill-advised, may be kindled in the forest. No campfire permits are required. Hikers are encouraged to use portable stoves to reduce the impact on the campsites.

All visitors to GMNF are asked to keep the trailside and overnight sites clean. Some Green Mountain Club sites have facilities for composting food waste. All trash should be carried out.

For further information on policies in GMNF, contact the Supervisor's Office, Green Mountain National Forest (see "Important Addresses," page 219).

Federally Designated Wilderness

The Trail passes through Big Branch and Peru Peak wilderness in Section Six, and in Section Seven through Lye Brook Wilderness. No entry permit is required. However, the regulations concerning the remainder of GMNF also apply here.

Plant Life

Throughout the A.T. in Vermont, cutting or damaging living trees, shrubs, and plants is prohibited. Only downed trees on the ground may be used for fires.

Caretakers

Full-time summer caretakers maintain and supervise a number of backcountry shelters and campsites in the Green Mountains, both within and outside the national forest. At those areas, mentioned in the Trail description, a fee is charged to help defray costs.

State Park

The A.T. also passes through Gifford Woods State Park, which was established to ensure the preservation of certain virgin hardwood forest stands. Camping is permitted within the park at campsites and shelters (see Section Three).

Overnight Facilities

The A.T. hiker has a number of alternatives when planning to spend the night on the Trail in Vermont. Space in Trail shelters fills quickly, so be prepared to tent. South of Sherburne Pass, shelter stays are limited to two consecutive days.

Campsites: A campsite is generally a site with water, toilet facilities, fireplace, and sometimes tent platforms. Several campsites are referred to as "primitive," where, instead of platforms, sites are simply spots cleared for tents. Both platforms and cleared areas allow concentrated use of an area with localized soil compaction. Some campsites have a caretaker and charge a fee.

Shelters: The Trail has a number of Adirondack-style shelters (three walls, open front) that can accommodate four to eight people. Shelters are located near water and have fireplaces and toilet facilities. Camping is permitted in the vicinity of most shelters. At some sites, a caretaker is in residence, and a fee is charged.

Cabins: A cabin is simply a closed shelter. In Vermont, cabins are often called "camps," and are located near water and have privies. At some sites, a caretaker is in residence, and a fee is charged.

Public Accommodations

A wide range of commercial accommodations is available along the public roads the Trail crosses, although sometimes they are some distance from the Trail. Their locations are noted under "Public Accommodations" in each section.

Parking

Because of the possibility of theft and vandalism, travelers are cautioned not to leave cars unattended overnight in remote locations or on the roads noted in the individual sections of this guide. Leaving cars near a home or at a local b&b or other business establishment is recommended, but only if permission can be obtained.

Connecticut River (Norwich)
to White River (Vt. 14 at West Hartford)
Vermont Section One
9.3 Miles

Brief Description of Section

The Trail in this section traverses the partly forested, partly cleared mountains between the Connecticut River and the White River in Vermont. From the Connecticut River bridge (400 feet) at the northern end of the section, the A.T. follows hard-surfaced roads 1.8 miles to Norwich, then follows trails and woods roads. It is a moderate climb around Mosley Hill (Trail elevation 1,180 feet) through white-pine woods, timber, and pastures and along woods roads to DOC Happy Hill Shelter (1,460 feet). Climbing is moderate over the wooded flank (1,570 feet) of Griggs Mountain, followed by a descent through forests to cross Podunk Brook, a brief climb over a low ridge, and a final descent to the White River in West Hartford (400 feet).

Tucker Trail is the only side trail in the section. It can be used as an alternate route to the A.T. between Norwich and Happy Hill Shelter, but it is mostly on roads. For more information on this trail and current information on the A.T. in this section, write the Dartmouth Outing Club (see "Important Addresses," page 219).

Road Approaches

Both the northern and southern ends of this section are accessible from major highways. The northern end of the section (the Connecticut River at Norwich, Vermont, and Hanover, New Hampshire) is reached from the north and south by I-89 and I-91, U.S. 5, and N.H. 10; from the west by U.S. 4 and Vt. 14; and from the east by U.S. 4. Cars can be left in Norwich, where the Trail leaves the paved road.

The southern end of the section, the White River at West Hartford, is reached by Vt. 14, about eight miles west of the junction of I-89 and I-91 in White River Junction, Vermont. Vehicles are usually left at the junction of Tigertown and Podunk roads, 0.6 mile north of the end of the section, although they may be left at the point where the Trail crosses Podunk Road, 1.4 miles from the end of the section.

Maps

Map Five (this guide)
DOC Trail Map

The A.T. route might not be current on the following:
USGS 7½-minute topographic quadrangles:
          Hanover, New Hampshire-Vermont
          Quechee, Vermont

Shelters and Campsites

This section has one shelter:
Happy Hill Shelter: Completed in 1998 and maintained by DOC, 5.3 miles from northern end of section; accommodates 8; water from brook (may be unreliable); also reached from the north by DOC Tucker Trail.
     Next shelter or campsite: north 7.3 miles (Velvet Rocks Shelter); south 8.8 miles (Thistle Hill Shelter).

Regulations

Camping and fires are prohibited, except at Happy Hill Shelter.

Supplies and Services

A half-mile east of the Connecticut River in Hanover, New Hampshire (ZIP Code 03755), are telephones, a supermarket, specialty backpacking stores, a bookstore, restaurants, a bus stop, and Dartmouth-Hitchcock Medical Center. (For more information on Hanover, refer to New Hampshire Section Nine.) Near the northern end of this section, the Trail passes through Norwich (ZIP Code 05055, telephone, groceries, restaurant, hardware store, bank). At the southern end, the Trail passes through West Hartford (ZIP Code 05084, telephone, groceries). Train service is available at White River Junction (five miles south of Hanover); outfitter; hardware store; laundromat; long-term hiker parking.
     In an emergency, contact the Vermont State Police, (802) 442-5421.

Public Accommodations

The center of Hanover, New Hampshire is one-half mile north of the Connecticut River on the A.T., with a broad range of accommodations (see New Hampshire Section Nine). Also near the northern end of the section, the Trail passes through Norwich, Vermont (inn). The southern end has no public accommodations. Motels, hotels, and rooming houses are available in the White River Junction, Vermont, and Lebanon, New Hampshire, areas, 5.0 miles south of the northern end of the section and 8.0 miles east of the southern end of the section, respectively, provide lodging over a wide price range. Additionally, train service is available in White River Junction.

Trail Description, North to South

Miles	Data
0.0	From the western bank of the Connecticut River (N.H.-Vt. state line), ascend on Vt. 10A, and pass under I-91. Reach U.S. 5 North, and follow into Norwich.
1.0	Opposite bandstand (gazebo) in park, turn sharply left onto Elm Street, and gradually descend southwest. Cross Bloody Brook, and ascend. Cross Hopson Road, and ascend more steeply.
1.8	Fifty yards after passing Hickory Ridge Road on left, Trail enters woods on left and follows contour to small stream before climbing steadily.
2.4	Cross powerline opening. About 15 yards south along powerline is a view of Wilder Dam.
3.7	Cross Newton Lane.
5.1	Turn left onto abandoned road, and ascend. (To right, blue-blazed William Tucker Trail descends to upper end of a maintained gravel road, 0.8 mile; descends on road to Bragg Hill Road, 1.3 miles; and continues down Bragg Hill Road and Meadow Brook Road to Main Street, U.S. 5, in Norwich, 3.5 miles.)
5.3	Reach side trail to **Happy Hill Shelter** (0.1 mile to the left). In another 0.1 mile enter overgrown clearing. Bear right, cross small stream, and ascend moderately.
5.8	Cross wooded shoulder of Griggs Mountain (1,570 feet), and descend in woods. In 0.4 mile, bear left in field, and cross

snowmobile trail. Descend along ridge, first gradually, then more steeply. Cross a well-used woods road.

7.0   Cross logging road, and cross East Fork of Podunk Brook. Bear right, and ascend, then contour, cross two logging roads, and descend.

7.9   Cross Podunk Brook and Podunk Road, and climb steeply uphill. Cross over a hardwood ridge, then descend through forests and overgrown pastures.

8.7   Return to Podunk Road, cross road bridge, turn left onto Tigertown Road, and follow under I-89 bridges. At road junction, bear right across railroad tracks.

8.9   Turn left onto Vt. 14, and follow highway south into West Hartford.

9.3   Reach eastern end of West Hartford-Quechee Road at bridge over White River. Turn right, and cross bridge to continue on Trail (see Vermont Section Two).

Trail Description, South to North

Miles   **Data**

0.0   From eastern end of West Hartford-Quechee Road, follow Vt. 14 north from West Hartford Bridge.

0.4   Turn right onto Tigertown Road (marked with a sign). Cross railroad tracks; immediately turn left at junction. Continue under I-89.

0.6   Make sharp right onto Podunk Road, cross bridge, then immediately bear left into woods. Follow Trail steeply uphill through overgrown pastures, then cross a hardwood ridge, and descend.

1.4   Cross Podunk Road and Podunk Brook; ascend, cross a woods road, then begin contouring ridge. Cross a second woods roads, continue level, then descend.

2.3   Bear left, cross East Fork of Podunk Brook and well-used logging road, and ascend steeply. Recross road, and continue up ridge through pine-overgrown pastures. In field, cross snowmobile trail, bear right, and continue ascent.

3.5   Pass over shoulder of Griggs Mountain (1,570 feet).

4.0   Reach side trail to **Happy Hill Shelter** (0.1 mile to right). Descend, and cross seasonal stream. Enter clearing, and bear left on old road.

4.2   Turn right off road into woods. William Tucker Trail descends to gravel road (0.8 mile), which leads downhill to Bragg Hill Road, Meadow Brook Road, and Main Street (U.S. 5) in Norwich (3.5 miles). Trail begins to drop, then climbs gently through hardwood and pine stands.

5.6   Cross Newton Lane.

6.9   Cross powerline. About 15 yards south along powerline is view of Wilder Dam on Connecticut River. Begin descent.

7.5   Join paved Elm Street. Descend steadily. Cross Hopson Road, and descend on easier grades. Cross Bloody Brook, and ascend gradually.

8.3   Turn right onto U.S. 5 in Norwich opposite the park and bandstand. Follow highway south. At traffic light, continue straight on 10-A, pass under I-91 bridges, and descend.

9.3   Reach the western end of Connecticut River bridge and New Hampshire-Vermont border, and end of section. To continue on Trail, cross bridge, and head uphill on West Wheelock Street (see New Hampshire Section Nine).

White River (Vt. 14 at West Hartford) to Vt. 12
Vermont Section Two
12.6 Miles

Brief Description of Section

In this section, the Trail rolls across a patchwork of wooded and cleared hills, ridges, and valleys. The extensive farming that once covered the area is frequently evident. From the White River in West Hartford (400 feet) at the northern end of the section, the Trail ascends over Bunker Hill (1,480 feet). It continues with minor elevation changes and passes over Thistle Hill (1,800 feet), then crosses a number of ridges and valleys and two hard-surfaced roads before reaching Vt. 12 (882 feet).

This section has no side trails, but many woods and abandoned roads intersect the Trail. For current information on the A.T. in this section, contact the Dartmouth Outing Club (see "Important Addresses," page 219).

Road Approaches

Both ends of this section are accessible from major highways. At the northern end, the A.T. crosses Vt. 14 in West Hartford, eight miles west of White River Junction (on I-91) and five miles south of Sharon (on I-89). At the southern end, the Trail crosses Vt. 12, 4.4 miles north of Woodstock.

The Trail also crosses three roads passable by car in the southern half of the section. At 5.5 miles from the southern end of the section, it crosses the dirt Cloudland Road about four miles north of Woodstock. At 3.7 miles from the southern end of the section, it crosses the Pomfret-South Pomfret Road, 1.6 miles north of South Pomfret and 4.6 miles north of Woodstock. At 1.5 miles from the southern end of the section, it crosses the Woodstock Stage Road about one mile north of South Pomfret and four miles north of Woodstock.

Maps

Map Five (this guide)
DOC Trail Map

The A.T. route might not be current on the following:
USGS 7½-minute topographic quadrangles:
    Quechee, Vermont
    Woodstock North, Vermont

Shelters and Campsites

This section has one shelter:
Thistle Hill Shelter: Built in 1995 and maintained by DOC, on a 0.1 mile side trail; 4.8 miles from northern end of section; accommodates 8; water from two nearby streams.

Next shelter or campsite: north 4.0 miles (Happy Hill Shelter); south 11.7 miles (Wintturi Shelter).

Regulations

Camping and fires are prohibited, except at Thistle Hill Shelter.

Supplies and Services

The northern end of the section lies in West Hartford (ZIP Code 05084, telephone, groceries). From the Trail crossing at Vt. 12 at the southern end of the section, it is 4.4 miles south to Woodstock (ZIP Code 05091, bank, doctor, dentist, pharmacy, telephone, supermarket, equipment, laundromat, restaurants, and bus stop).

In an emergency, call the Vermont State Police, (802) 442-5421.

Public Accommodations

The northern end of the section in West Hartford has no public accommodations, but from there it is 8.0 miles southeast to White River Junction, Vermont, and Lebanon, New Hampshire, areas, that have motels, hotels, and rooming houses over a wide price range. The southern end of the section on Vt. 12 is 4.4 miles north of Woodstock (motels, inn).

Trail Description, North to South

Miles   **Data**

0.0 From Vt. 14 in the center of West Hartford, cross White River on 400-foot Quechee-West Hartford Road iron bridge. Pass River Road (runs along western bank of White River). In 0.3 mile, turn right across puncheon up into woods and across swampy area, then climb through open hardwoods.

1.0 Enter hilltop field with outstanding views down the White River Valley. Leave field, descend to cross a small sag, bear right, and climb gently through a red-pine plantation. Cross small woods road; climb through several hilltop pastures.

2.6 Cross woods road, climb to wooded Bunker Hill, descend.

3.3 Cross unpaved Joe Ranger Road. Switch back to open field with views north. Pass through woods, ascend open ridge to the open top of Arms Hill with outstanding views to the south, then descend into mixed woods. After crossing a brook, ascend.

4.8 **Thistle Hill Shelter** is located 0.1 mile to the left on a side trail. Continue ascent.

5.1 Reach top of Thistle Hill. Descend through open woods, crossing several small ridges. Continuing south, cross powerline, and reach open field. Watch for electric fence lines and livestock; this field is used actively. Follow left (southern) edge of field.

7.1 Turn right on unpaved Cloudland Road. In 200 feet, turn left off road, and ascend through overgrown pasture, then open hardwoods. Cross shallow sag, and climb gradually. Reach summit of nameless hill (1,730 feet) at cairn, and descend steadily along edge of an old field.

8.0 Reach blue-blazed spur on left (leads 50 feet uphill to small spring). Beyond spur, follow old town road. In 0.2 mile, pass old four-way junction, and, before long, bear right into an open field before descending steeply through mixed woods.

8.9 Reach paved Pomfret-South Pomfret Road; cross small brook, and ascend into open pasture, then follow old fence row on right. Watch for electric fencing and cows.

9.6 Cross Bartlett Brook, and reach a dirt road. Cross road, then a field. Climb into woods, cross a small ridge, then descend.

10.3   Cross a narrow, dirt road (town highway 38), a small brook and field, then ascend into woods to a notch in Breakneck Hill. Follow contour, then descend, crossing a brook to a woods road. Trail leaves the road to the right into the woods before entering a field. Follow the right (northern) edge of the field (mowed by a local farmer).

11.1   Cross bridge over brook, and reach Woodstock Stage Road. Climb through open hardwoods to the top of Dana Hill. Cross the corner of a hilltop field, then descend steeply through a white-birch grove.

12.6   Reach paved Vt. 12. To continue on Trail, cross road, and pass through A.T. parking lot to bridge over Gulf Stream.

Trail Description, South to North

Miles   **Data**

0.0   From the A.T. parking lot on Vt. 12, 4.4 miles north of Woodstock, cross a small field, and climb steeply, soon passing a white-birch grove. Cross the corner of a hilltop field. Continue east through woods to top of wooded Dana Hill before descending.

1.5   Reach paved Woodstock Stage Road. Cross road and bridge across a brook. Follow left (northern) side of small field, and ascend into woods, crossing another brook and a small notch in Breakneck Hill before descending to another brook.

2.3   Reach a narrow, dirt road (town highway 38). Cross road, and ascend over a small ridge, then descend, first through woods, then diagonally through a field.

3.0   Reach unpaved Bartlett Brook Road. Turn left on road, then right across a small brook. Pass through small, overgrown field, then woods. Cross a stone wall into open pasture, following an old fence row on left. Descend, and cross brook.

3.7   Cross Pomfret-South Pomfret Road, and ascend steeply through mixed woods, then through a hilltop field with views to the south and west. At the edge of the field, turn left, and follow a woods road. Pass old four-way junction, and follow old woods road. Swing around small hill, then ascend east.

4.6   Reach blue-blazed spur on right (leads 50 feet uphill to small spring). Ascend through field. Reach summit of nameless hill (1,730 feet) at cairn. Descend gradually to east through open hardwoods.

5.5   Reach unpaved Cloudland Road. Turn right on road for 200 feet, then turn left off road into field north of red house. Follow right (southern) side of open field (watch for electric fence lines and livestock; this field is used actively), then ascend through woods and under a powerline. Continue northeast, and ascend through woods over several gentle ridges.

7.5   Cross top of wooded Thistle Hill.

7.8   Reach side trail leading right 0.1 mile to **Thistle Hill Shelter**. Descend. Cross small brook, and climb again to the open top of Arms Hill, with fine views to the south. Turn right, and descend open ridge. Pass through woods to open field with views north. Descend on switchbacks.

9.3   Cross unpaved Joe Ranger Road. Ascend up a steep pitch into woods. Climb to wooded Bunker Hill, then descend.

10.0   Cross old town road, and descend through several hilltop pastures. Cross woods road, then descend through a red pine plantation. Cross sag, bearing left, uphill. Reach hilltop field with outstanding views down the White River Valley.

11.6   Leave field, descending steadily through open hardwoods. Cross a swampy area. Cross puncheon, and turn left onto paved Quechee-West Hartford Road. Pass Pomfret Road on western bank of White River, and cross iron bridge (400 feet).

12.6   Reach paved Vt. 14 in village of West Hartford and end of section. Trail continues left (north) on Vt. 14 (see Vermont Section One).

Vt. 12 to Sherburne Pass (U.S. 4)
Vermont Section Three
21.3 Miles

Brief Description of Section

The Trail in this section travels west between two mountain ranges, the White Mountains of New Hampshire and the Green Mountains of Vermont. It follows many ridges, and the terrain is rugged, with steep ascents and descents. The Lookout (2,439 feet), in the northern end of the section, provides a panoramic view.

Vt. 12 marks the northern end of the part of the Appalachian Trail maintained by the Green Mountain Club (GMC).

A portion of the footpath follows old logging roads, which are often rough and overgrown. Virtually the entire section was relocated off old roads in the 1980s. The bulk of the section, north of River Road, is seldom used, except by thru-hikers, providing a greater opportunity for solitude. The Trail also passes through Gifford Woods State Park (see below). Water is readily available in this section.

The junction of the A.T. and the Long Trail is 0.6 mile north of the southern end of this section. The two trails coincide from this point south for 104 miles to the Massachusetts-Vermont state line.

Note: A major relocation in Section Four will result in the junction of the A.T. and the Long Trail being moved north to Willard Gap (see map).

For more information on the Long Trail and the A.T. in this section, refer to GMC's *Long Trail Guide,* available from ATC and GMC (see "Important Addresses," page 219).

Gifford Woods State Park

The Trail passes through Gifford Woods State Park near Vt. 100. This park was created in 1931 to preserve its natural forest, one of the few remaining examples of undisturbed northern hardwoods in New England. Within its 114 acres is a 12-acre plot of virgin forest dominated by sugar maples, Vermont's state tree. In addition, many other species of trees, including an eastern hemlock more than 400 years old, are scattered over the park's remaining acres.

The park is on a major migratory route, and bird watchers gather in spring and fall to study the many species passing through the area.

With 47 campsites, plus overflow facilities and 21 shelters, the park serves as a base camp for day hikes on the A.T. and the Long Trail. There is fishing at Kent Pond, and the spectacular views from Deer Leap are a short hike away.

Road Approaches

Both the northern and southern ends of this section are accessible from major highways. At its northern end, the Trail crosses Vt. 12, 4.4 miles north of Woodstock. At its southern end, it crosses U.S. 4 at Sherburne Pass (ample parking), 10 miles east of Rutland and 3.6 miles west of Sherburne. (This road crossing will move one mile west when the relocations in Section Four are complete.) About two miles from the southern end, the Trail crosses Vt. 100 at the entrance to the Vermont Fish and Wildlife Department public parking area for the Kent Pond boat launch, 0.3 mile north of the intersection of U.S. 4 and Vt. 100.

Four secondary roads also provide access to the Trail—Lookout Farm Road, Chateauguay Road, River Road, and Thundering Brook Road. Lookout Farm Road intersects the A.T. 5.7 miles from Vt. 12. The Chateauguay Road (pronounced Shat-a-gee) approaches to within 0.6 mile of the A.T. at a point 9.2 miles from Vt. 12. To reach the A.T. *via* the Chateauguay Road, proceed 2.2 miles north on hard-surfaced road from Bridgewater Corners at U.S. 4 to Bridgewater Center; continue north on dirt road along the North Branch of the Ottauquechee River to fork at 7.1 miles; follow right fork to house on right at 7.8 miles; continue on foot to Trail junction at 8.4 miles. From the fork, the road may be too wet to be passable by car.

The A.T. reaches River Road 17.7 miles from the northern end of the section. From River Road, the A.T. follows Thundering Brook Road for 0.4 mile, then recrosses the same road (at Kent Pond and Mountain Meadows Lodge) at 18.5 miles. It is approximately 0.3 mile south from Kent Pond to U.S. 4 on Thundering Brook Road.

Maps

Map Five (this guide)
GMC Long Trail Guide

The A.T. route might not be current on the following:
USGS 7½-minute topographic quadrangles:
    Woodstock North, Vermont
    Delectable Mountain, Vermont
    Pico Peak, Vermont

Shelters and Campsites

This section has three shelters:

Wintturi Shelter: Log shelter built in 1994 and maintained by GMC 3.9 miles from the northern end of section; accommodates 8; water from spring 100 yards north of shelter.

Next shelter or campsite: north 11.7 miles (Thistle Hill Shelter); south 9.5 miles.

Stony Brook Shelter: Log shelter built in 1997 and maintained by GMC 13.4 miles from northern end of section; accommodates 6; water from stream 10 yards west.

Next shelter or campsite: north 9.5 miles; south 6.0 miles.

Gifford Woods State Park: At Trail crossing of Vt. 100, 1.9 miles from the southern end; 21 shelters and many campsites (see "Gifford Woods State Park" on page 219); fee charged for overnight use; showers; ample water.

Next shelter or campsite: north 5.7 miles; south 4.4 miles (Pico Camp).

Regulations

Camping and fires are prohibited, except at Wintturi Shelter, Stony Brook Shelter, and Gifford Woods State Park.

Supplies and Services

From the Trail crossing at Vt. 12 at the northern end of the section, it is 4.4 miles south to Woodstock (ZIP Code 05091, telephone, super-market, equipment, laundromat, restaurants, bus stop). From the Trail crossing of Vt. 100 near the southern end of the section, it is 2.3 miles south to Sherburne on U.S. 4 (Killington ZIP Code 05751, restaurants, bus stop, bank, doctor, dentist) and 7.7 miles north to Pittsfield (ZIP Code 05762, telephone, limited selection of groceries, laundromat). The Inn at Long Trail (limited selection of supplies, meals, bus stop) is at the southern terminus of this section on U.S. 4 and will accept and hold parcels marked, "Hold for Appalachian Trail Hiker," if sent *via* United Parcel Service to: Inn at Long Trail, Sherburne Pass, U.S. 4, Killington, VT 05751. From the current (1998) southern end of the section—which will move 1 mile west when the relocations are completed—it is 10 miles west to Rutland (ZIP Code 05701, all services including telephone, supermarket, backpacking store, restaurants, laundromats, airport, train station, Rutland Medical Center, 802-775-7111, bus stop), 1.6 miles east to a store with limited selection of supplies, 3.6 miles east to Sherburne, and 3.6 miles east, then south, *via* the Killington Access Road, to a grocery store and delicatessen.

In an emergency, call the Vermont State Police, (802) 442-5421 (Rutland) or (802) 457-1416 (Woodstock).

Public Accommodations

The northern end of the section on Vt. 12 is 4.4 miles north of Woodstock (motels, inn). Mountain Meadows Lodge is located just south of the A.T. at Kent Pond (on Thundering Brook Road). North of the crossing of Vt. 100 at Kent Pond is an inexpensive lodge offering bed, bath, and breakfast. The Inn at Long Trail (lodging, hiker's special; see "Supplies and Services" for address and more information) is at the southern terminus of the section on U.S. 4 at Sherburne Pass. Many other motels and inns are found to the west along U.S. 4 and in Rutland.

Trail Description, North to South

Miles   **Data**

0.0   From Vt. 12, A.T. parking lot on Barnard Gulf Road (882 feet), cross bridge, then climb through pasture and several fence rows. Enter open field, and climb along its left (southern) side. Near top of field, cross stile over electric fence, and continue ascending into woods. Cross a small ridge and shallow sag, then climb steadily through woods and fields.

1.2   Reach open ridgetop with panoramic views to west (West Bridgewater) and south (to Mt. Ascutney). Make sharp right, and follow open ridge, descending gently into open woods. Cross old town road, and begin a steady climb to the crest of a low ridge, where there is a vista to the south.

3.0   Cross old town road, then climb along northern slope of long ridge, following the contour.

3.9   Reach side trail to **Wintturi Shelter** (0.2 mile right); water from spring 100 yards north of shelter. Begin climbing the center of a long ridge, crossing a woods roads to the height of land on Sawyer Hill.

4.7   Descend from Sawyer Hill, past Don's Rock, to a fine view of the Coolidge Range. Continue a gradual descent along the western side of Pinnacle. In 0.7 mile, turn right onto King Cottage Road, follow it 0.2 mile, then bear left.

5.7   Cross Lookout Farm Road (old town road), and continue along the side of a ridge.

6.4   Reach Lookout Spur Trail. From this junction, the Trail follows the ridge with gradual ups and downs and crosses a woods road at 7.4 miles.

8.2   Reach Lakota Lake lookout. (Lake is below the lookout, with the White Mountains in the distance.) Leave the lookout, and descend through a white-birch stand, then over switchbacks to a reliable brook (8.5 miles) and over a small knoll.

9.2   Cross Locust Creek and Chateauguay Road, then ascend *via* switchbacks over several knolls. From here to north of Stony Brook Shelter, you are in Vermont's Les Newall Wildlife Management Area. Descend, with occasional views to the west, to an unnamed brook, then climb steadily along side of ridge to narrow sag between two ridges. (Note: This sag is known locally as Continental Divide.)

11.2 Cross ridge, passing by a small pond, then begin long, gentle descent, crossing several knolls. At the end of the ridge, descend steeply *via* switchbacks.

13.0 Cross Mink Brook, then Stony Brook.

13.1 Turn right on Stony Brook Road, then left into woods, and climb. (Stony Brook Road, passable by car in season, continues right to Vt. 107.) Reach top of narrow, softwood ridge and fine vista to south over Stony Brook Valley. In 0.2 mile, cross reliable brook, and begin long, gentle ascent.

13.7 Reach side trail to **Stony Brook Shelter** (1,750 feet) 0.1 mile left; water from stream 10 yards west.

14.4 Reach wooded height of land. Descend through shallow saddle, and climb to northern shoulder of Quimby Mountain, then down again, crossing a former logging road.

15.2   Climb to top of unnamed hill (2,600 feet), then descend steeply *via* switchbacks to cross an old woods road. Continue across the top of a broad ridge. Cross a powerline, with limited views to north and south, then climb gently to wooded height of land (2,523 feet). Begin long, gradual descent, crossing numerous intermittent brooks and former logging roads.

16.9   On a bend in a former logging road, reach a vista with splendid views of the Coolidge Range and the Ottauquechee River Valley. In 0.4 mile from vista, bear sharply right off former logging road, and descend through mixed woods.

17.7   Cross unpaved River Road onto Thundering Brook Road (Sherburne town offices are 600 feet to left), cross the Ottauquechee River, and go up a switchback. In 0.4 mile, turn left off road. Begin gentle ascent through open hardwoods and huge boulders, passing over a height of land. Turn right onto old woods road (used as a ski trail in winter), crossing several bridges and passing by a house on left.

18.5   Cross Thundering Brook Road (Mountain Meadows Lodge is 200 feet to left). Cross an open field and swimming area, then return to woods on southern shore of pond. Follow shore across several brooks, then bear left, past waterfall. Cross small footbridge over brook.

19.3   Reach Vt. 100 at Kent Pond boat-launching ramp. Turn right onto Vt. 100 for 300 feet. Bear left off highway onto path that leads to Gifford Woods State Park.

19.4   Continue on gravel road leading to caretaker's house, where open **shelters** and **tentsites** with fireplaces may be rented. Turn left from gravel road onto trail through picnic areas. Rejoin gravel road, and turn right. Continue on gravel road, passing road on left to stone building (toilets and showers). Ascend to camping area, then leave park, and ascend steeply on Trail. Pass Trail register and spur trail on left (leading 20 yards to Ben's Balcony).

20.7   Reach Maine Junction, where the Long Trail enters from right. (On Long Trail to right, it is a short distance to the Deer Loop Trail leading to the rocky overlook above Sherburne Pass, and 1.3 miles to **Tucker-Johnson Shelter**.) Continue straight ahead from junction on combined A.T. and Long Trail, descend steadily southwest for 0.2 mile, then steeply over boulders. *Note:* In 1998, GMC began construction of a major relocation across the Coolidge Range. When it is completed, Maine Junction will move north on the Long Trail to the current Willard Gap. The relocation should open in 1999.

21.3   Reach U.S. 4, just east of the summit of Sherburne Pass (2,150 feet), and end of section. To continue on Trail, enter woods south of highway (see Vermont Section Four).

Trail Description, South to North

Miles   **Data**

0.0   Just east of summit of Sherburne Pass (2,150 feet) on U.S. 4, enter woods on white-blazed trail. Ascend steeply over boulders, then more gradually on rough footway.

0.6   Reach Maine Junction, where A.T. and Long Trail separate. (To left, Long Trail leads a short distance to the Deer Leap Trail leading to the rocky overlook above Sherburne Pass, 1.3 miles to **Tucker-Johnson Shelter**, and then on to Canada.) Bear right on A.T., climb spur, and descend, passing on right a 20-yard side trail to Ben's Balcony (2,100 feet). Descend steeply, then more gradually, on and off a woods road, to the Gifford Woods State Park boundary. Turn left on gravel road opposite tent Platform No. 11. Descend, passing road on right to stone building with toilets and showers. *Note:* In 1998, GMC began construction of a major relocation across the Coolidge Range. When it is completed, Maine Junction will move north on the Long Trail to the current Willard Gap. The relocation should open in 1999.

1.9   Turn left off gravel road (to left is caretaker's house, where **shelters** and **tentsites** with fireplaces may be rented). Pass through picnic area, and turn right to rejoin gravel road. Turn left off road onto path; follow 100 feet to Vt. 100. Turn right onto highway, and follow it south 300 feet.

2.0   Turn left (east) across Vt. 100 to Kent Pond boat-launching ramp entrance. Immediately bear right from road into overgrown meadow. Cross meadow and bridge over Kent Pond inlet brook. Turn left, and follow inlet brook to shore of Kent

Pond. Continue through woods along shore. Reach woods road; follow to open field. Cross field; pass near edge of pond.

2.8 Cross Thundering Brook Road, then follow Thundering Brook Road (used as ski trail in winter) past a house on right and across several bridges. In 0.2 mile, bear left off old woods road, climbing to boulder-strewn height of land before descending gently. Turn right onto unpaved Thundering Brook Road, descend through a switchback, and cross Ottauquechee River.

3.6 Reach intersection with River Road (Sherburne town offices 600 feet to right). Cross road, and ascend *via* switchbacks and former logging roads, crossing several intermittent brooks.

4.4 Reach a vista on a sharp bend in a former logging road, with splendid views of the Coolidge Range and the Ottauquechee River Valley. Continue climbing to wooded height of land (2,523 feet), then begin gradual descent along broad ridge. Cross powerline, with limited views to north and south. Continue along ridge with little change in elevation. Cross a woods road, then begin a steep ascent *via* switchbacks.

6.1 Reach top of unnamed hill (2,600 feet). Descend gradually, cross logging road, then climb to northern shoulder of Quimby Mountain. Cross a small sag,

6.9 Reach crest of unnamed hill (2,618 feet.) Descend, steeply at times, over switchbacks and former logging roads, crossing several intermittent brooks. Slab, then climb, a narrow softwood ridge, reaching a fine vista to the south over the Stony Brook Valley. Begin a steady descent along narrow ridge.

7.6 Reach side trail to **Stony Brook Shelter** (1,750 feet), 0.1 mile to the right; water from stream 10 yards west.

8.2 Turn right onto Stony Brook Road, then sharply left across Stony Brook. (Stony Brook Road continues left to Vt. 107.) From here to near Chateauguay Road, you are in Vermont's Les Newall Wildlife Management Area.

8.3 Cross Mink Brook, and begin climbing steeply over switchbacks to top of narrow ridge. Continue more gentle climb up a broader ridge and across several knolls. Pass a small pond, then slab along northern side of a ridge.

10.1 Reach a narrow sag (known locally as Continental Divide). Descend, crossing a small intermittent brook and numerous logging roads, then climb steadily over a series of small knolls. From the height of land, descend *via* switchbacks through open hardwood forest.

12.1   Cross unpaved Chateauguay Road, then Locust Creek. Ascend over small knoll and down to a reliable brook; ascend steeply *via* switchbacks, then more gradually through a white-birch stand, passing fine southwestern views.

13.1   Reach Lakota Lake lookout. (Lakota Lake is below the lookout, with the White Mountains in the distance.) Follow ridge with gradual ups and downs, crossing a woods road.

14.9   Reach Lookout Spur Trail on left. Continue down the side of ridge.

15.6   Cross Lookout Farm Road (old town road). In 0.1 mile, bear right onto King Cottage Road, follow 0.2 mile, then bear left, and begin gradual ascent along western side of the Pinnacle. Ascend past Don's Rock to a fine view of the Coolidge Range.

16.6   Reach height of land on Sawyer Hill. Descend the center of a long ridge, crossing a woods road.

17.4   Reach side trail to **Wintturi Shelter** (0.2 mile left). Descend along northern slope of long ridge, following the contour.

18.3   Cross old town road (shown on map), and soon reach a vista to the south. Begin a steady descent from a low ridge.

19.4   Cross another old town road, and pass old foundations. Ascend gently into open woods; follow open woods to a sharp left.

20.1   Reach top of open ridge with panoramic views to west (to West Bridgewater) and south (to Mt. Ascutney). Descend steadily through old fields and woods, cross shallow sag and small ridge, and continue descending through woods. Cross stile over electric fence near top of open field. Descend right (southern) side of field, then bear across old pasture and through several fence rows.

21.3   Cross bridge to A.T. parking lot and reach Vt. 12 (Barnard Gulf Road). Cross road to continue north (see Vermont Section Two).

Sherburne Pass (U.S. 4) to Vt. 103

Vermont Section Four
16.9 Miles

Brief Description of Section

The northern part of this section traverses the Coolidge Range of the Green Mountains and the highest elevations crossed by the A.T. in Vermont.

Two short side trails provide access to Pico Peak (3,957 feet) and Killington Peak (4,235 feet). The summit of Killington Peak can also be reached by the Killington Gondola, which leaves from the base lodge at the end of the Killington Access Road off Vt. 100.

Another side trail, Bucklin Trail, leads to Cooper Lodge. Side trails are described briefly in the Trail description; for more information, refer to GMC's *Day Hiker's Guide to Vermont* or *Long Trail Guide*, available from the Green Mountain Club (see "Important Addresses," page 219).

Much of this section is in dense hardwood and evergreen forests. The Trail is often rocky and can become muddy. The southern part of the section descends into foothills, winding through pastures, fields, open woods, and thick second-growth conifers.

Note: In 1998, the Green Mountain Club began work on a major relocation between Maine Junction and Governor Clement Shelter. This relocation will move the Trail to the west of Pico Peak and away from ski-area development. The new crossing of U.S. 4 will be one mile west of Sherburne Pass. The relocation will not change the location of overnight sites. Work will extend into 1999. GMC will post signs notifying hikers of the route changes.

Road Approaches

Both the northern and southern ends of this section are accessible from major east-west highways crossing the Green Mountains. At the northern end, the Trail crosses U.S. 4 (parking by permission only) 10 miles east of Rutland and 3.6 miles west of Sherburne. At the southern end, the Trail crosses Vt. 103 (ample parking) at the Green Mountain

Railroad crossing by Clarendon Gorge 2.2 miles east of U.S. 7, 7.7 miles east of Rutland, and 3.0 miles west of Cuttingsville.

In the southern half of the section, three secondary roads intersect the Trail—Upper Cold River Road, 10.9 miles from the northern end of the section; Cold River Road (Lower Road), 12.5 miles from the northern end; and Lottery Road, 14.8 miles from the northern end. Upper Cold River and Cold River roads connect North Clarendon on U.S. 7, to the west of the A.T., and North Shrewsbury, to the east of the A.T. Lottery Road travels southwest from the Trail to Shrewsbury.

Maps

Map Six (this guide)
GMC Long Trail Guide

The A.T. route might not be current on the following:
USGS 7½-minute topographic quadrangles:
Pico Peak, Vermont
Killington Peak, Vermont
Rutland, Vermont

Shelters and Campsites

This section has four shelters:

Pico Camp: Closed frame cabin built in 1959 and maintained by GMC; 2.5 miles from northern end of section; accommodates 12; water 45 yards north on Trail; 0.4-mile side trail to summit of Pico Peak.

Next shelter or campsite: north 4.4 miles (Gifford Woods State Park); south 2.9 miles.

Cooper Lodge: Built in 1939 by Vermont Forest Service 5.4 miles from northern end of section, now maintained by GMC; closed stone-and-frame cabin; 3 tent platforms; batch-bin composting toilet; fires prohibited; accommodates 16; no fee; water from spring 100 feet south, and also north on Trail; 0.2-mile steep side trail to summit of Killington Peak also joins with the Bucklin Trail.

Next shelter or campsite: north 2.9 miles; south 4.1 miles.

Governor Clement Shelter: Built in 1929 by the family of William H. Field of Mendon, named for Percival W. Clement, governor of Vermont; 7.4 miles from southern end of section; maintained by GMC; stone shelter; accommodates 12; water from stream across road. *Note:*

There have been problems with nonhiker visitors to this shelter. Be cautious with belongings.

Next shelter or campsite: north 4.1 miles; south 6.2 miles.

Clarendon Shelter: Built in 1952 and maintained by GMC; 1.2 miles from southern end of section, on a 0.1-mile side trail; accommodates 8; water from stream 50 feet east.

Next shelter or campsite: north 6.2 miles; south 3.9 miles (Minerva Hinchey Shelter).

Regulations

Camping and fires are prohibited except at designated sites.

Supplies and Services

The Inn at Long Trail (limited selection of supplies, lodging, meals, bus stop) is at the northern terminus of this section and will accept and hold parcels marked, "Hold for Appalachian Trail Hiker," if sent *via* United Parcel Service to: Inn at Long Trail, Sherburne Pass, U.S. 4, Killington, VT 05751. From the northern end of the section, it is 10 miles west to Rutland (ZIP Code 05701, telephone, supermarkets, backpacking stores, restaurants, laundromats, airport, bus stop, train station, Rutland Medical Center, 802-775-7111.) It is 1.6 miles east to a store with limited supplies, 3.6 miles east to Sherburne (Killington ZIP Code 05751, bus stop), and 3.6 miles east, then south *via* the Killington Access Road, to a grocery store and delicatessen.

From the Trail crossing at Vt. 103 at the southern end of the section, it is 1.0 mile west to a small store with limited supplies, and a small camping-supplies store with gas by the pint, 4.2 miles west to North Clarendon (ZIP Code 05759, meals, groceries, bus stop), and 7.7 miles west to Rutland (see above). It is also 3.2 miles east to Cuttingsville (ZIP Code 05738, telephone, groceries, bus stop).

In an emergency, call the Vermont State Police, (802) 442-5421 (Rutland) or (802) 457-1416 (Woodstock).

Public Accommodations

The Inn at Long Trail (lodging, meals, hiker's special with dorm and dinner; see "Supplies and Services" for address and more information) is at the northern terminus of the section on U.S. 4 at Sherburne Pass. Other motels and inns are to the west along U.S. 4 and in Rutland.

From the Trail crossing at Vt. 103 at the southern end of the section, it is 3.0 miles west to lodging, 4.2 miles west to North Clarendon (motels), and 7.7 miles west to Rutland (motels, inns). Rutland and North Clarendon may also be reached to the west from A.T. junctions on Cold River and Upper Cold River roads.

Trail Description, North to South

Miles	Data
0.0	Just east of summit of Sherburne Pass on the south side of U.S. 4 (2,150 feet), enter woods, cross section of old highway, and pass east of ruins of former Long Trail Lodge.
0.8	Pass trail leading right 0.1 mile to upper station of the Little Pico ski lift and the top of the Pico alpine slide. Ascend through hardwoods on northeastern slope of Pico Peak. Pass stream, that disappears into sinkhole on right.
2.1	Reach ski trail with good views to the north. Follow ski trail uphill 300 feet to Pico Junction, and turn left into woods.
2.5	Pass **Pico Camp**. Spring 100 feet north on the A.T. supplies water. (Behind camp, blue-blazed Pico Link Trail climbs steeply 0.4 mile to Pico Peak, 3,957 feet, and summit station of Pico Peak Ski Resort chair lift. In 1997, Killington ski resort began constructing trails to link with Pico Ski area. One of those trails was completed and crosses the A.T. south of Pico Camp.) Continue south; minor elevation changes occur. Pass gully and in 200 feet, a spring.
3.0	Relocation to be installed in 1999: Trail will rejoin existing route from north just south of current site of Pico Camp. Continue south; minor elevation changes occur.
4.3	On west side of Snowden Peak, Trail descends slowly off ridgeline, crosses intermittent brook, then ascends. Reach junction with Bucklin Trail. Turn left, and head uphill to **Cooper Lodge**. (Bucklin Trail descends 3.1 miles west to Wheelerville Road at a point 4.0 miles south of U.S. 4.)
5.4	Reach spring and **Cooper Lodge** (3,900 feet) and then side trail that leads in 0.2 mile to Killington Peak (4,235 feet), second-highest mountain in Vermont. (From summit, Green

Mountains, from Glastenbury Mountain in south to Mt. Mansfield in north, are visible, as well as Taconic and Adirondack ranges in New York and White Mountains in New Hampshire. To southeast is Mt. Ascutney, and to west is Rutland. Killington is part of Coolidge Range, which includes, north to south, Pico Peak, Little Pico, Mendon Peak, Little Killington, Shrewsbury Peak, Smith Peak, Bear Mountain, and Salt Ash Mountain.) A.T. continues south through spruce-fir forest along western slope of Killington. *(Note:* Approximately 0.5 mile south of Cooper Lodge, a relocation was being constructed during 1998. The new route will follow the ridgeline between Killington and Little Killington Peaks, avoiding the Juggernaut ski trail, reconnecting with the existing A.T. at Consultation Point below.) Cross Juggernaut ski trail.

6.4   Shrewsbury Peak Trail leads left (2.0 miles to Shrewsbury Peak and 3.8 miles to dirt road that is 3.0 miles northeast of North Shrewsbury). Cross Juggernaut ski trail again. In 0.3 mile, pass Consultation Point (3,760 feet) east of Little Killington. Descend, at first steeply on rough trail, then more moderately through hardwoods, passing several overgrown logging roads. *Note:* Relocation underway in 1998 (see map). Turn right onto wide logging road.

9.5   Turn right off road, follow trail to **Governor Clement Shelter** (1,860 feet), in overgrown field on right (west). Water is available at large stream east of road. Continue across clearing into woods.

9.6   Turn right onto woods road, and, in 25 feet, turn left off road. Cross Robinson Brook, and ascend. Turn left, slab western bank, and continue. Minor elevation changes.

9.9   Cross stone wall, and ascend in clearing.

10.1   Cross stone wall to left of deer camp, and descend.

10.3   Reach old road, turn sharply left (east), cross Sargent Brook, make sharp right, follow brook downstream.

10.9   Cross Upper Cold River Road on former logging roads. Descend beside Sargent Brook.

11.6   Cross Gould Brook, and descend along left bank, entering wide trail. *Note: This crossing can be hazardous in high water.*

12.5	Turn right to Cold River Road (Lower Road). Cross concrete bridge. Turn left into woods; follow western bank of Northam Brook uphill.
12.7	Leave brook, and soon cross a field.
12.8	Leave field, and turn left onto Keiffer Road.
12.9	Turn right off road, and ascend beside stone wall.
14.0	Reach ridgecrest.
14.3	Pass Hermit Spring (unreliable) on right.
14.6	Enter pasture.
14.8	Cross unpaved Lottery Road (passable by car), and ascend through another pasture into a grove of sugar maples. Be sure to close farm gates at the road crossing.
15.2	Reach airport beacon on top of Beacon Hill (1,760 feet). Trail drops steeply.
15.7	Cross brook, and reach old town road (Crown Point Military Road, built during the French and Indian Wars). (Turn left, and descend 0.1 mile to **Clarendon Shelter**.) To continue south, cross town road, climb gently to rock promontory, then descend through steep gorge. Pass under powerline, then through woods; cross a stile through an open field.
16.9	Cross stile, and reach Vt. 103 (869 feet) at railroad crossing. To continue on Trail, cross Vt. 103 and railroad tracks, and descend to Clarendon Gorge (see Vermont Section Five).

Trail Description, South to North

Miles	Data
0.0	Cross Vt. 103 (869 feet) and Green Mountain Railroad tracks. Cross two stiles, an open field, and powerline right-of-way. Climb through steep notch onto rock promontory, then descend gently.
1.2	Reach old town road (Crown Point Military Road, built during the French and Indian Wars). (To reach **Clarendon Shelter**, turn right, and descend 0.1 mile.) To continue north, cross road, and ascend through open hardwoods.
1.7	Reach airplane beacon on top of Beacon Hill (1,760 feet). Descend through grove of sugar maples and across pasture.
2.1	Cross unpaved Lottery Road; be sure to close farm gates. Pass through another pasture into woods.

2.6   Pass Hermit Spring (unreliable) on left. Climb, pass over ridgecrest, and descend.

3.8   Cross small brook.

4.1   Turn left onto unpaved Keiffer Road. Bearing left on road, enter field to right.

4.3   After crossing field, reenter woods, and reach western bank of Northam Brook. Follow brook to left.

4.4   Reach Lower Cold River Road. Follow road to right, cross concrete bridge, then bear left, and follow old road.

4.9   Enter woods road. Follow left bank of river upstream.

5.3   Cross Gould Brook. *Note: This crossing can be hazardous in high water.* Ascend hogback between two streams. Follow Sargent Brook upstream.

6.0   Cross Upper Cold River Road. Continue, paralleling brook.

6.6   Enter logging road with bridge to left. Make sharp left across bridge, and, 200 feet beyond, make sharp right off road; ascend into woods.

6.8   Cross stone wall.

7.0   Enter clearing, and descend to stone wall.

7.3   Follow western bank, turn right, cross Robinson Brook, and turn right onto woods road.

7.4   Turn left off woods road, and continue across clearing to **Governor Clement Shelter** (1,860 feet) in overgrown field on left (west). Water is located at stream 200 feet east. *(Note: Relocation to be constructed in 1999. See map.)* Continue 125 feet to woods road, and turn left. In 0.3 mile, turn left from logging road onto trail. Climb steadily northeast through hardwoods and into spruce forest. Ascend steeply over rough trail. Eventually reach Consultation Point (3,760 feet). *[Note: Relocation begun in 1998. From Consultation Point, the Trail will ascend the shoulder of Little Killington Peak, avoiding the Juggernaut ski trail then follow the broad ridgeline (west of the current A.T.) to a point approximately 0.5 mile south of Cooper Lodge.]* Descend slightly along eastern slope of Little Killington. Cross Juggernaut ski trail.

10.5   Shrewsbury Peak Trail leads right (2.0 miles to Shrewsbury Peak, and 3.8 miles to dirt road, which is 3.0 miles northeast of North Shrewsbury). Cross Juggernaut ski trail again, and ascend gently through evergreen forest along southern and western slopes of Killington Peak.

11.5   Relocation underway in 1998. Reach Spur Trail to Killington Peak. Killington Peak, 4,235 feet in 0.2 mile. (From summit, Green Mountains from Glastenbury Mountain to Mt. Mansfield are visible, as well as Adirondack and Taconic ranges in New York, and White Mountains in New Hampshire. To southeast is Mt. Ascutney; to west is Rutland. Killington is part of Coolidge Range, which includes, north to south, Pico Peak, Little Pico, Mendon Peak, Little Killington, Shrewsbury Peak, Smith Peak, Bear Mountain, and Salt Ash Mountain). Then reach Cooper Lodge and, 1/4-mile below it, the Bucklin Trail. Trail follows Bucklin Trail, then turns right and descends, crossing a small, intermittent brook. It then climbs gradually, reconnecting with the old A.T. west of Snowden Peak. (Bucklin Trail descends west 3.2 miles to Wheelerville Road, at a point 4.0 miles south of U.S. 4). Pass spring, and cross to eastern flank of Pico Peak.

13.9   Relocation to be opened in 1999. Trail will bear to western side of Pico Peak and cross U.S. 4 one mile west of Sherburne Pass Description below will be obsolete.

14.4   In 1997, Killington ski resort began constructing trails to link with Pico ski area. One of those trails crosses the A.T. south of Pico Camp. Pass **Pico Camp**. Spring 100 feet north on Trail provides water. (Behind camp, Pico Link climbs steeply 0.4 mile to Pico Peak, 3,957 feet. Summit station of Pico Peak Ski Resort chair lift is here.) From Pico Camp, continue north.

14.8   Reach Pico Junction. Follow ski trail downhill 300 feet. Turn right into woods. Trail zigzags down northeastern slope, passing brook that disappears into sinkhole on left.

16.1   Pass trail leading left 0.1 mile to upper station of Little Pico ski lift and top of Pico alpine slide. Descend to Sherburne Pass.

16.9   Reach end of section at U.S. 4, just east of summit of Sherburne Pass (2,150 feet). To continue on Trail, cross highway into woods (see Vermont Section Three).

Vt. 103 to Danby-Landgrove Road
(USFS 10)
Vermont Section Five
14.4 Miles

Brief Description of Section

In the northern part of this section, between Vt. 103 (869 feet) and Vt. 140 (approximately 1,280 feet), the Trail passes through open woods and fields. Adjacent to Vt. 103, the Trail crosses Clarendon Gorge, cut by the Mill River. In the southern part of the section, the Trail passes across White Rocks Mountain and by Little Rock Pond (1,854 feet) in a hardwood forest. Between Little Rock Pond and the Danby-Landgrove Road (approximately 1,500 feet), at the southern end of the section, the Trail follows the left bank of the Little Black Branch. Between Greenwall Shelter and USFS 10 (Danby-Landgrove), the Long Trail/A.T. passes through the White Rocks National Recreation Area.

This section has three side trails. The Homer Stone Brook Trail provides access to the A.T. at Little Rock Pond from South Wallingford on U.S. 7. The Green Mountain Trail leads 5.1 miles from Little Rock Pond to USFS 10 (Danby-Landgrove Road), 100 yards west of the Long Trail/A.T., crossing the summit of Green Mountain. The Keewaydin Trail provides access to White Rocks Mountain from USFS White Rocks Picnic Area on USFS 52.

For information on these trails and the area, refer to GMC's *Day Hiker's Guide To Vermont* and the *Long Trail Guide*. Both guides and current Trail information are available from the Green Mountain Club (see "Important Addresses," page 219).

Note: In 1998, GMC began construction of a relocation between a point one-half mile south of Minerva Hinchey Shelter and a point one-half mile south of Greenwall Shelter. This relocation was to open in the fall of 1998.

Road Approaches

The northern end of this section is on Vt. 103, a major east-west highway crossing the Green Mountains 2.2 miles east of U.S. 7, 7.7 miles east of Rutland (*via* U.S. 7), and 3.0 miles west of Cuttingsville.

The southern end of the section is accessible by car at the Danby-Landgrove Road 0.6 mile east of the Big Branch Picnic Area, 3.5 miles east of Danby on U.S. 7, and 10.3 miles west of North Landgrove. The road, not maintained during winter, is paved from the Trail crossing west to Danby, but is gravel east to North Landgrove.

Vt. 140 intersects the Trail 5.3 miles from the northern end of the section. This point is 2.1 miles east of the White Rocks Picnic Area, 3.5 miles east of U.S. 7 in Wallingford, and 3.0 miles west of East Wallingford (junction of Vt. 155 and Vt. 103).

Maps

Map Six (this guide)
Long Trail Guide

The A.T. route might not be current on the following:
USGS 15-minute topographic quadrangle:
    Wallingford, Vermont
USGS 7½-minute topographic quadrangle:
    Rutland, Vermont

Shelters and Campsites

This section has four shelters and one campsite. Shelters between Vt. 140 and the Massachusetts-Vermont line are maintained jointly by USFS and GMC. GMC stations a caretaker at some shelters from mid-May through October; fee is charged.

Minerva Hinchey Shelter: Frame, open-front structure built in 1969 by GMC; 2.7 miles from northern end of section; accommodates 18; on short side trail; water from spring, 150 feet south.

Next shelter or campsite: north 3.9 miles (Clarendon Shelter); south 4.5 miles.

Greenwall Shelter: Built in 1962 by USFS; 7.2 miles from the northern end of section; accommodates 8; 600 feet northeast on side trail is a spring (may fail in dry seasons).

Next shelter or campsite: north 4.5 miles; south 4.7 miles.

Little Rock Pond Shelter: Built in 1962 by USFS; 2.5 miles from the southern end of the section; accommodates 8; moldering privy; caretaker in residence; fee; spring 0.3 mile south on A.T.

Next shelter or campsite: north 4.7 miles; south 0.5 mile.

Little Rock Pond Campsite: 2.0 miles from southern end of section; tent platforms only; batch-bin composting toilet; caretaker in residence; fee; water from spring 0.1 mile north on A.T.

Next shelter or campsite: north 0.5 mile; south 0.2 mile.

Lula Tye Shelter: Built in 1962 by USFS; named for the corresponding secretary of the GMC from 1926 to 1955; on short side trail 1.8 miles from southern end of section; accommodates 8; caretaker in residence; fee; water from spring 0.3 mile north on A.T.

Next shelter or campsite: north 0.2 mile; south 3.1 miles (Big Branch Shelter).

Regulations

Camping and fires are restricted to shelters and designated campsites, except as noted below.

Camping within 0.5 mile of Little Rock Pond is limited to the following designated sites: Little Rock Pond Shelter, Little Rock Pond Tenting Area, and Lula Tye Shelter.

The southern half of the section, from Greenwall Shelter to Danby-Landgrove Road, lies within Green Mountain National Forest (GMNF). Throughout GMNF, dispersed camping is allowed at least 200 feet from water and 100 feet from any trail; fires must be built in the fireplaces provided. No campfire permits are required.

Cutting or damaging living trees, shrubs, and plants is prohibited. Only dead material on the ground may be used for fires. All trash must be carried out.

Supplies and Services

From the Trail crossing at Vt. 103 at the northern end of the section, it is 0.5 mile west to a dairy bar; 1.0 mile west to a small store with limited groceries, a telephone, and a small camping-supplies store with white gas sold by the pint; 4.2 miles west to North Clarendon (ZIP Code 05759, groceries, bus stop); and 7.7 miles west to Rutland (ZIP Code 05701, telephone, supermarkets, backpacking stores, restaurants, laundromats, airport, bus stop, Rutland Medical Center, 802-775-7111). From this crossing, it is also 3.0 miles east to Cuttingsville (ZIP Code 05738, telephone, groceries, bus stop).

From the Trail crossing at Vt. 140, it is 3.5 miles west to Wallingford (ZIP Code 05773, telephone, groceries, meals, bus stop) and 3.0 miles east to East Wallingford and the junction of Vt. 155 (ZIP Code 05742, telephone, groceries).

From the Trail crossing of the Danby-Landgrove Road, it is 3.5 miles west to Danby (ZIP Code 05739, telephone, groceries, bus stop).

In an emergency, contact the Vermont State Police, (802) 442-5421.

Public Accommodations

From the A.T. crossing at Vt. 103 at the northern end, it is 3.0 miles west to accommodations, 4.2 miles west to North Clarendon (motels), and 7.7 miles west to Rutland (motels, inns). From the crossing at Vt. 140, it is 3.5 miles west to Wallingford (motel). From the A.T. crossing of the Danby-Landgrove Road, it is 3.5 miles west to Danby (motels).

Trail Description, North to South

Miles   **Data**

0.0   Where Vt. 103 (869 feet) crosses Green Mountain Railroad tracks, 2.1 miles east of U.S. 7, Trail descends south to Clarendon Gorge.

0.1   At the head of Clarendon Gorge, cross suspension bridge over Mill River (bridge is dedicated to memory of Robert Brugmann). Climb south up ridge, pass two lookouts, and follow ridgecrest.

2.1   Reach Spring Lake Clearing (1,620 feet). (Controlled burns are used here as a management tool to retain vistas and provide a clearing for wildlife.) Reenter woods, and climb ridge. Descend to clearing.

2.7   Spur trail leads left 200 feet to **Minerva Hinchey Shelter.** Spring is 150 feet south. Cross clearing. Enter woods, and pass under powerline. (*Note:* South of the powerline a 1998 relocation climbs over Bear Hill west of the existing Trail. GMC will post trail signs to inform hikers of changes to the route, which will make the next four entries obsolete.) One-third mile from shelter, turn right onto road, and, after 100 yards, turn left onto trail. Ascend south through hardwoods, and cross brook.

3.7   Pass over summit ridge of Button Hill (approximately 2,010 feet). Descend western side of Button Hill. Turn right onto farm road that passes through open area. Turn left at ruins. Pass to right of site of Long Trail/A.T. Buffum Lodge, destroyed by fire in 1966. Nearby brook provides water. One-half mile beyond, turn left onto gravel road, passable by car, and descend.

5.3   Reach Vt. 140. Turn left on highway, make immediate right onto trail over Roaring Brook. Ascend, passing west of minor peak. Cross grass-grown road, and continue south through woods and pastures.

6.3   Cross gravel Sugar Hill Road. (To right, road descends 3.7 miles to Wallingford; to left, 3.1 miles to East Wallingford.) Trail continues straight on dirt road, passable by car, for about 0.4 mile to house (no parking at end of road), then descends. Cross brook, then boundary line of Green Mountain National Forest. Ascend through fields. Reach end of pasture. Continue on woods road.

7.2   Reach **Greenwall Shelter** on left. Spring, which may fail in dry seasons, is 600 feet northeast. Ascend west, climbing northern side of White Rocks Mountain.

7.4   1998 relocation over Bear Mountain will rejoin the existing route here.

7.7   Keewaydin Trail leads 1.2 miles to White Rocks Picnic Area. Note: At this point the relocation rejoins the current A.T.

8.0   Spur trail descends steeply to right, 0.2 mile to White Rocks Cliff (view). A.T. ascends to ridge of White Rocks Mountain. Pass side trail leading 100 yards right, to spring. Pass through spruce woods just west of summit of White Rocks Mountain (2,680 feet). Descend steadily along ridge through hardwoods. Eventually, in brook valley, cross overgrown South Wallingford-Wallingford Pond Road.

11.0   Cross Homer Stone Brook. Pass through clearing. Continue southwest with little change in elevation.

11.9   Side trail leads 100 feet left (east) to **Little Rock Pond Shelter.** Water is available 0.4 mile south on Trail.

12.0   Reach Homer Stone Brook Trail (descends right, west, 2.5 miles to South Wallingford and U.S. 7). Just beyond, reach the northern end and outlet of Little Rock Pond. The Green Mountain Trail turns to the right. (It follows the northern and western shores of the pond, reaches the summit of Green Mountain, 2,500 feet, in 1.0 mile, and continues 4.1 miles to USFS 10, 100 yards west of Long Trail/A.T.) Trail takes left fork here, skirting along eastern shore of pond. In 0.3 mile, pass spring that supplies water for Little Rock Pond Shelter, Lula Tye Shelter, and Little Rock Pond Campsite.

12.4 Reach spur trail leading left (east) 100 feet to **Little Rock Pond Tenting Area**; 250 feet beyond, reach southern end of Little Rock Pond at junction with Little Rock Pond Loop Trail (skirts western side of pond and connects with Green Mountain Trail, that intersects the A.T. at northern end of pond).

12.6 Path leads left 100 feet uphill to **Lula Tye Shelter**. Water is 0.3 mile north on Trail, from the same spring that supplies Little Rock Pond Shelter and campsite. Descend gradually through hardwoods and along brook. Cross Little Black Branch, and recross it in 0.2 mile where Trail turns right onto old logging road.

14.4 Reach Danby-Landgrove Road (USFS 10), just west of bridge over Black Branch (1,500 feet), 3.5 miles west of Danby and U.S. 7, and end of section. To continue on Trail, turn left (east) over bridge, and continue 300 yards before bearing right onto Trail (see Vermont Section Six).

Trail Description, South to North

Miles   **Data**

0.0 From Danby-Landgrove Road (USFS 10), just west of bridge over Black Branch (1,500 feet), enter woods on old logging road. Cross Little Black Branch, and recross it in 0.2 mile.

1.8 Path leads right 100 feet (east) uphill to **Lula Tye Shelter**. Water from spring is located 0.3 mile north on Trail.

2.0 Reach southern end of Little Rock Pond at junction with Little Rock Pond Loop Trail (skirts western side of pond and rejoins A.T. *via* Green Mountain Trail at the northern end of the pond at mile 2.4). Skirt eastern shore of pond. In 250 feet, reach spur trail leading right (east) 100 feet to **Little Rock Pond Tenting Area**. In 0.1 mile, pass spring.

2.4 At northern end of Little Rock Pond, Green Mountain Trail leaves left. (It follows northern and western shores of pond, reaches Green Mountain summit, 2,500 feet, in 1.0 mile, and continues 4.1 miles to USFS 10, 100 yards west of Long Trail/A.T.) In a few yards, Homer Stone Brook Trail leaves left. (It descends west 2.5 miles to South Wallingford and U.S. 7.)

2.5   Path leads 100 feet east to **Little Rock Pond Shelter**. Water is 0.4 mile south on Trail from same spring that supplies Lula Tye Shelter. Continue northeast with little change in elevation. Pass through clearing.

3.4   Cross Homer Stone Brook and, 0.2 mile beyond, overgrown South Wallingford-Wallingford Pond Road. Climb steadily along ridge of White Rocks Mountain, eventually passing just west of the summit (2,680 feet). Pass side trail leading to spring, 100 yards left.

6.4   Spur trail descends very steeply left 0.2 mile, to viewpoint at brink of White Rocks Cliff. Trail bears east.

6.7   Keewaydin Trail leaves left (descends 0.8 mile to USFS White Rocks Picnic Area).

7.0   1998 relocation over Bear Mountain begins here and rejoins the existing A.T. just south of Minerva Hinchey Shelter. The new route should open in fall 1998.

7.2   Reach **Greenwall Shelter**. Spring, which may fail in dry seasons, is 600 feet to northeast. In 0.1 mile, Trail enters pasture, curves left, and passes Green Mountain National Forest boundary line. Reach farmhouse (no parking at end of road) after crossing brook, and follow narrow road, passable by car.

8.1   Cross gravel Sugar Hill Road. (To left, west, road descends 3.7 miles to Wallingford; to right, 3.1 miles to East Wallingford.) Continue north through woods and pastures, and cross grass-grown road. Pass west of a minor summit, and descend.

9.1   Cross Roaring Brook, and immediately reach Wallingford Gulf Road, Vt. 140. Turn left on highway, then immediately right (north) up gravel road (passable by car). In 0.5 mile, turn right (north) uphill, onto old farm road. Pass to left of site of Long Trail/A.T. Buffum Lodge, destroyed by fire in 1966. Nearby brook provides water. At ruins in large clearing, take right fork, and ascend overgrown slope. Enter woods, and climb steeply.

10.7   Reach summit ridge of Button Hill (2,010 feet). Cross brook, and descend north through hardwoods. Turn right onto road and, after 100 yards, turn left onto trail. *(At this point relocation reconnects with existing A.T.)* Pass under powerline.

11.7   Spur trail leads right 200 feet to **Minerva Hinchey Shelter**. Spring is 150 feet south. Ascend hill behind camp.

12.3   After descent, reach Spring Lake Clearing (1,620 feet), with views of Coolidge Range to northeast and Taconic Range in New York to west. (Controlled burns are used here as a management tool to retain vistas and provide a clearing for wildlife.) Reenter woods where powerline emerges, and follow ridge north. Reach lookout. Drop steeply north, passing another lookout.

14.3   Reach Mill River at head of Clarendon Gorge. Cross high suspension bridge over gorge. Ascend briefly.

14.4   Cross Green Mountain Railroad tracks, and reach Rutland-Bellows Falls Highway, Vt. 103, at end of section (869 feet). To continue, follow Vt. 103 briefly east (right), then turn left onto old town road (see Vermont Section Four).

Danby-Landgrove Road (USFS 10) to Vt. 11 and 30

Vermont Section Six
17.3 Miles

Brief Description of Section

The Trail in this section closely follows the crest of the Green Mountains through hardwood and spruce forests. From the Danby-Landgrove Road (1,500 feet) in the north to Vt. 11 and 30 (1,840 feet) in the south, the Trail passes over four summits: Baker Peak (2,850 feet), Peru Peak (3,429 feet), Styles Peak (3,394 feet), and Bromley Mountain (3,260 feet). It also passes scenic Griffith Lake, that has one shelter and a campsite. This section is in the Green Mountain National Forest (GMNF). Between USFS 10 (Danby-Landgrove) and Griffith Lake, the Trail passes through the Big Branch Wilderness; between Griffith Lake and USFS 21 (Mad Tom Notch), the Peru Peak Wilderness.

This section has three side trails. The Lake Trail provides access to Griffith Lake from U.S. 7. The Baker Peak Trail, coinciding with the Lake Trail from their beginning at U.S. 7, meets the A.T. just south of the summit of Baker Peak. The third trail, the Old Job Trail, the original A.T./L.T. route in the area, is used as a lowland alternative between Big Branch Bridge and Griffith Lake, covering a distance of 5.3 miles. Leaving the A.T. just south of the Big Branch Bridge, this trail follows Big Branch, then Lake Brook upstream, passes Old Job Shelter, and rejoins the A.T. at Griffith Lake. For complete information on these side trails and the area, refer to GMC's *Day Hiker's Guide to Vermont* and *Long Trail Guide*. Both guides and Trail information are available from the Green Mountain Club (see "Important Addresses," page 219).

Road Approaches

The northern end of the section is accessible by car on the Danby-Landgrove Road, 0.6 mile east of the Big Branch Picnic Area, 3.5 miles east of Danby on U.S. 7, and 10.3 miles west of North Landgrove. The road, not maintained in winter, is paved from the Trail crossing west to Danby, but is gravel east to North Landgrove.

The southern end of the section is on Vt. 11 and 30, a major highway that crosses the Green Mountains, 5.5 miles east of Manchester Center on U.S. 7 and 4.4 miles west of Peru.

Gravel USFS 21 intersects the Trail 12.0 miles from the northern end of the section. From this point, it is 2.5 miles east to GMNF Hapgood Pond Recreation Area and 4.3 miles east to Peru on Vt. 11.

Maps

Map Seven (this guide)
Long Trail Guide

The A.T. route might not be current on the following:
USGS 15-minute topographic quadrangles:
　　　　Wallingford, Vermont
　　　　Londonderry, Vermont

Shelters and Campsites

The four shelters, and two tentsites in this section are maintained jointly by GMC and USFS. GMC stations a caretaker in summer at Peru Peak Shelter and at the campsite on Griffith Lake to help hikers and supervise shelters and camping in the vicinity of the pond (see "Regulations"). At these sites, a fee is charged to defray costs.

Big Branch Shelter: Built in 1963 by USFS; 1.3 miles from northern end of section; accommodates 8; water from Big Branch.

Next shelter or campsite: north 3.1 miles (Lula Tye Shelter); south 0.2 mile to 1.0-mile side trail.

Old Job Shelter: Built in 1935 by CCC; 1.5 miles from northern end of section on one-mile side trail; accommodates 8; water from Lake Brook.

Next shelter or campsite: north 0.2 mile on A.T.; south 1.5 miles.

Lost Pond Shelter: Gift of Louis Stare, Jr.; built in 1965 on Cape Cod, dismantled, transported to present site, and assembled; 3.0 miles from northern end of section; accommodates 8; water from brook in ravine below shelter.

Next shelter or campsite: north 1.5 miles; south 4.1 miles.

Griffith Lake Tenting Area: A number of designated sites with tent platforms; 7.1 miles from northern end of section; caretaker in residence; fee; water from Peru Peak Shelter.

Next shelter or campsite: north 4.1 miles; south 0.5 mile.

Peru Peak Shelter: Built in 1935 by CCC; 7.6 miles from northern end of section; accommodates 10; caretaker in residence; fee; water from adjacent brook.

Next shelter or campsite: north 8.9 miles; south 8.9 miles.

Bromley Tenting Area: Two tent platforms with toilet; 0.8 mile from southern end of section.

Next shelter or campsite: north 2.8 miles; south 3.5 miles (Spruce Peak Shelter).

Regulations

This section lies within Green Mountain National Forest (GMNF). Camping is restricted to shelters and designated campsites or dispersed camping at least 200 feet from any water and 100 feet from the Trail. Fires at designated sites must be built in the fireplaces provided; campfire permits are not required. Only downed wood may be used for fires. Cutting or damaging living trees, shrubs, and plants is prohibited. All trash must be carried out.

Camping within 0.5 mile of Griffith Lake is limited to the following designated sites: Griffith Lake Tenting Area and Peru Peak Shelter.

Supplies and Services

From the Trail crossing at Danby-Landgrove Road, it is 3.5 miles west to Danby on U.S. 7 (ZIP Code 05739, lodging, telephone, groceries, restaurant, bus stop). Otter Creek Campground is one mile north of Danby on U.S. 7. From the Trail crossing of USFS 21, it is 2.5 miles east to USFS Hapgood Pond Recreation Area (camping) and 4.3 miles east to Peru on Vt. 11 (ZIP Code 05152, telephone, groceries). From the Trail crossing of Vt. 11 and 30, it is 5.5 miles west to Manchester Center (ZIP Code 05255, telephone, supermarket, equipment, restaurants, laundromat, bus stop) and 4.4 miles east to Peru (see above).

In an emergency, contact the Vermont State Police, (802) 442-5421.

Public Accommodations

From the Trail crossing at Danby-Landgrove Road, it is 3.5 miles west to Danby. From the Trail crossing of Vt. 11 and 30, it is 5.5 miles west to Manchester Center (motels, hostel). Inns, motels, and tourist homes are located on Vt. 11 between Manchester Center and Peru, not far from the Trail crossing.

Trail Description, North to South

Miles	Data

0.0   Section begins on Danby-Landgrove Road (USFS 10), 3.5 miles east of Danby and U.S. 7. Cross bridge over Black Branch, and ascend southeast on road. At 0.2 mile from start, just beyond wide turnout on right, bear right onto Trail. (At this point, it is 10.4 miles east to Landgrove and, from there, 2.5 miles to Vt. 11.) Soon enter Big Branch Wilderness, continue east on ridge, and descend to northern bank of Big Branch (water).

1.3   Reach **Big Branch Shelter**. Ascend along northern side of river, passing stone foundation of old water wheel. Cross suspension bridge over Big Branch, and follow southern bank upstream.

1.5   Reach junction with Old Job Trail. (Old Job Trail continues straight ahead, passes **Old Job Shelter** in 1.0 mile, then climbs along Lake Brook, rejoining A.T. at Griffith Lake in 5.3 miles. Old Job Trail is often used as an alternate to A.T. between Big Branch and Griffith Lake.) At this junction, A.T. bears to right uphill. In 0.1 mile, bear right onto woods road, and ascend steadily. Bear right onto wide, woods road.

3.0   Spur trail leads right to **Lost Pond Shelter**, with water from Stare Brook in ravine below shelter; 0.1 mile beyond shelter, turn right onto wide, fire road, follow for 100 yards, and turn left onto trail in woods. Ascend south gradually, then moderately. Eventually, reach northern end of ridge. Just before Trail breaks out onto ledge, bad-weather bypass trail leads left.

5.0   Reach summit of Baker Peak (2,850 feet). From summit, A.T. coincides with Baker Peak Trail in steep descent over open rocks. Pass southern end of summit; bypass trail on left.

5.1   Reach junction. (Baker Peak Trail descends straight, southwest 1.0 mile to Lake Trail, which leads 2.5 miles farther to U.S. 7.) A.T. bears left and continues descent of Baker Peak. Cross two woods roads, and ascend.

6.8   Lake Trail descends right, west (3.5 miles to public road, that leads right 0.5 mile to U.S. 7, 2.0 miles south of Danby). A.T. descends straight ahead through small cleft and leaves Big Branch Wilderness.

6.9   Reach northern end of Griffith Lake. Old Job Trail enters from left. Continue south on bog bridging along eastern side of lake.

7.1   Pass to left of **Griffith Lake Tenting Area**. In 0.1 mile, cross Lake Brook, then another stream, and follow winding trail through evergreen forest.

7.6   Reach **Peru Peak Shelter**; water available from adjacent brook. Ascend east, and enter Peru Peak Wilderness.

8.9   Reach wooded summit of Peru Peak (3,429 feet). (Short side trail leads left to lookout.) Pass south over several knobs, then climb steeply.

10.6   Reach summit of Styles Peak (3,394 feet). Follow ridge southwest 0.5 mile, then drop steeply south to southeast.

✗ 12.0   Leave Peru Peak Wilderness and reach Mad Tom Notch
↓   Road (USFS 21). Water usually available from pump. Cross gravel USFS 21 at height of land in Mad Tom Notch (2,446 feet). (From notch, it is 2.5 miles east to **Hapgood Pond**, a USFS camping area, and 4.3 miles east to Vt. 11.) From road, ascend south to ridge through hardwoods and spruce.

14.0   Pass over northern summit of Bromley Mountain (3,120 feet). Descend into col, then climb steeply toward Bromley.

14.5   Reach main Bromley Mountain summit (3,260 feet). (To left 100 feet is summit station of Big Bromley chair lift and observation tower.) Trail descends on wide ski trail (westernmost of several trails leaving mountain). At 0.2 mile from summit, bear right (important turn) into woods on trail. Descend steadily, and sometimes steeply.

15.2   Make sharp right near small brook on left. Descend gradually. Reach Bromley Brook.

16.5   Pass trail leading left 50 feet to **Bromley Tenting Area**. Just beyond, cross bridge over Bromley Brook. Continue on wide trail, descending gradually, pass under powerline, and cross bridge. Turn right onto gravel road.

17.3   Pass through parking lot. Cross Vt. 11 and 30 (1,840 feet) at end of section. To continue on Trail, climb highway bank into hardwoods. (See Vermont Section Seven.)

Trail Description, South to North

Miles   **Data**

0.0   From Vt. 11 and 30 (1,840 feet), 5.5 miles east of Manchester Center and 4.4 miles west of Peru, follow gravel road northwest 0.2 mile, then turn left onto Trail into woods. Cross bridge over brook, pass under powerline, and ascend gradually.

0.8   Cross bridge over Bromley Brook. Just beyond, spur trail leads right 50 feet to **Bromley Tenting Area**. A.T. climbs steadily northeast.

2.1   Near small brook (last reliable water for 7.6 miles), make sharp left, and begin steady and, in some places, steep ascent of Bromley Mountain. Near summit, enter wide novice ski trail, and follow left uphill.

2.8   Reach summit of Bromley Mountain (3,260 feet). (To right 100 feet is summit station of Big Bromley chair lift and observation tower.) Continue along western edge of clearing, make sharp left just beyond end of chair lift, pass to left of several outbuildings, leaving northern side of open summit, and then descend steeply into col. Pass over northern summit of Bromley Mountain (3,120 feet), and follow ridge north.

5.2   Cross gravel USFS 21 at height of land in Mad Tom Notch (2,446 feet). (From notch, it is 2.5 miles east to **Hapgood Pond**, USFS camping area, and 4.3 miles to Vt. 11.) Water is usually available from pump at USFS 21. Enter Peru Peak Wilderness and ascend steeply to ridge of Styles Peak.

6.7   Reach summit of Styles Peak (3,394 feet), with view east and south toward Bromley. Drop steeply north. Continue north over several knobs.

8.4   Reach wooded summit of Peru Peak (3,429 feet). (Short side trail leads right to lookout.) Make zigzag descent.

9.7   Exit Peru Peak Wilderness, and reach **Peru Peak Shelter.** Water is available from adjacent brook. Proceed west, cross several streams, and then, at woods road, turn right. Reach Griffith Lake, and follow eastern shore.

10.2   Pass to right of **Griffith Lake Tenting Area** on bog bridging.

10.4   Old Job Trail descends right (northeast) along Lake Brook. (It passes **Old Job Shelter** in 4.3 miles and then swings west to rejoin A.T. at Big Branch in 5.3 miles. It is an alternative to A.T. between Griffith Lake and Big Branch.) A.T. continues straight ahead (north) and enters Big Branch Wilderness.

10.5   Lake Trail bears left and descends west 3.5 miles to public road, that leads north, right, 0.5 mile to U.S. 7, 2.0 miles south of Danby. A.T. follows ridge north, descends, crosses two woods roads, and begins ascent of Baker Peak.

12.2   Reach junction with Baker Peak Trail (that descends left, southwest, 1.0 mile to Lake Trail, that leads 2.5 miles farther to U.S. 7). A.T. and Baker Peak Trail bear right and coincide for final rocky scramble to summit of Baker Peak. (Bad-weather bypass trail is on right and is recommended in windy or slippery conditions.)

12.3   Reach summit of Baker Peak (2,850 feet). Leave summit, reenter woods, and pass northern end of bypass trail on right. Pass over northern end of ridge, and begin descent. Eventually, turn right onto wide fire road, and follow it for 100 yards. Turn left into woods on old woods road.

14.3   Spur trail leads left to **Lost Pond Shelter;** water available from Stare Brook in ravine below shelter. A.T. continues north along woods road. In 0.5 mile, bear left onto narrow woods road, descending steadily.

15.8   Reach Big Branch and northern terminus of Old Job Trail entering from right (leads to **Old Job Shelter** in 1.0 mile). Bear left along Big Branch. Cross suspension bridge over Big Branch. Bear left on road down northern side of river, passing stone foundation of old water wheel.

16.0   Reach **Big Branch Shelter;** water available from stream. Continue downstream, then ascend ridge to north of Big Branch, leaving Big Branch Wilderness. Reach Danby-Landgrove Road (USFS 10). (Landgrove is 10.4 miles east, right, and Vt. 11 is 2.5 miles farther.) Bear left on road.

17.3   Cross bridge over Big Black Branch, and reach end of section. (At this point, it is 3.5 miles west to Danby on U.S. 7.) To continue on Trail, turn right (north) into woods on former logging road (see Vermont Section Five).

Vt. 11 and 30 (Manchester-Peru Highway) to Arlington-West Wardsboro Road
Vermont Section Seven
17.5 Miles

Brief Description of Section

The most notable features in this section are Stratton Pond (2,555 feet) on the western slope of Stratton Mountain and the summit itself. Stratton Pond is the most visited site on the Vermont A.T., and overuse has had serious impacts on the pond's fragile shoreline. To keep damage to a minimum and allow areas to be rehabilitated, GMC stations caretakers at the pond's shelter sites to supervise their use. Please cooperate with them to preserve the beauty of the pond.

Between Vt. 11 and 30 (1,840 feet) in the north and the Arlington-West Wardsboro Road (2,340 feet) in the south, the Trail passes over Spruce Peak (2,060 feet), Prospect Rock (2,079 feet), and Stratton Mountain (3,936 feet). For 2.8 miles in the middle of the section, the Trail passes through Lye Brook Wilderness, a 14,300-acre tract of primitive Vermont woodland.

This section has four side trails. The Lye Brook Trail provides access from Manchester on Vt. 11 to the A.T. at Stratton Pond. The Branch Pond Trail provides access to the Lye Brook Trail at Bourn Pond from the Arlington-West Wardsboro Road, 2.2 miles west of the Trail crossing at its southern end. The Stratton Pond Trail provides an alternate route from the Arlington-West Wardsboro Road to Stratton Pond. The North Shore Trail is a short loop around Stratton Pond.

For complete information on the side trails and the area, refer to GMC's *Day Hiker's Guide to Vermont* and the *Long Trail Guide*. Both guides and Trail information are available from the Green Mountain Club (see "Important Addresses," page 219).

Stratton of the Past

In the mid-nineteenth century, Stratton Mountain was a prosperous farming community. The area has since reverted to woodland, but cellar holes, apple trees, and lilac bushes are reminders that people once lived in this remote part of the Green Mountains.

Arlington-West Wardsboro Road (formerly the Stratton Turnpike, locally known as the Kelley Stand Road) was once used for travel between Boston and the spas at Saratoga Springs, New York. West of the A.T. crossing is Kelley Stand, a former stage stop for travelers with a picnic site.

Road Approaches

The northern end of this section is on Vt. 11 and 30, a major highway crossing the Green Mountains, 5.5 miles east of Manchester Center on U.S. 7 and 4.4 miles west of Peru.

At the southern end of the section, parking is available 0.1 mile north of the section boundary, where the Trail leaves Arlington-West Wardsboro Road. Much of the road east to West Wardsboro is paved, but west to Arlington it is narrow gravel road. The road is not maintained in winter or in/spring mud season (mid-May usually) from the Trail crossing to Arlington.

Maps

Map Seven (this guide)
Long Trail Guide

The A.T. route might not be current on the following:
USGS 15-minute topographic quadrangle:
    Londonderry, Vermont
USGS 7½-minute topographic quadrangles:
    Manchester, Vermont
    Sunderland, Vermont

Shelters and Campsites

Shelters in this section are maintained jointly by USFS and GMC. This section has three shelters and one tentsite, all on side trails. GMC stations caretakers at the shelters and campsites around Stratton Pond to help hikers and supervise camping and shelter use (see "Regulations"). At those sites, a small fee is charged to help defray costs.

Spruce Peak Shelter: Log shelter; 0.1 mile on side trail, 2.7 miles from northern end of section; constructed in 1983 by the Brattleboro section of GMC, USFS, and a work crew from the Rutland Community Correctional Center; accommodates 16; batch-bin composting toilet; spring 100 feet south at end of a spur trail.

Next shelter or campsite: north 3.5 miles (Bromley Tentsite); south 3.1 miles (William B. Douglas).

William B. Douglas Shelter: Built in 1956 by GMC; 5.8 miles from northern end of section; 0.5 mile south off A.T. on Branch Pond Trail; accommodates 10; spring 50 feet south.

Next shelter: north 3.1 miles (Spruce Peak); 4.6 miles (Stratton Pond).

North Shore Tenting Area: 7.1 miles from southern end of section, 0.5 mile west off A.T. on North Shore Trail; 3 tent platforms; batch-bin composting toilet; caretaker in residence; fee charged; water from Stratton View Spring 0.1 mile west.

Vondell Shelter: Built in 1967 by International Paper Company; 7.0 miles from southern end of section; 0.2 mile west of A.T. on Lye Brook Trail; accommodates 8; caretaker in residence; fee; water available 0.1 mile east at Bigelow Spring.

Next shelter or campsite: north 4.6 miles (Douglas Shelter); south 10.6 miles (Story Spring Shelter).

Stratton Pond has a number of designated camping sites maintained and supervised by a GMC caretaker; fee charged.

Regulations

The Trail from Prospect Rock to Winhall River, 2.8 miles of the route in the middle of the section, is in GMNF's Lye Brook Wilderness. Camping and fires are regulated in the GMNF. Camping in the wilderness is restricted to designated campsites and shelters or dispersed to sites 200 feet from water and 100 feet from any trail. Throughout GMNF, fires at designated sites must be built in the fireplaces provided. Campfire permits are not required.

Cutting or damaging living trees, shrubs, and plants is prohibited. Only downed wood on the ground may be used for fires. All trash must be carried out.

Camping within 0.5 mile of Stratton Pond is limited to the following designated sites: North Shore Tenting Area and Vondell Shelter. Camping is not allowed on Stratton Mountain.

Supplies and Services

From the Trail crossing of Vt. 11 and 30, it is 5.5 miles west to Manchester Center (ZIP Code 05255, telephone, supermarket, backpacking equipment, restaurants, laundromats, bus stop) and 4.4 miles east to Peru (ZIP Code 05152, telephone, groceries). From the crossing of the Arlington-West Wardsboro Road, it is 13.2 miles west to Arlington (ZIP Code 05250, telephone, groceries, bus stop) and 8.0 miles east to West Wardsboro (ZIP Code 05360, telephone, groceries).

In an emergency, contact the Vermont State Police, (802) 442-5421.

Public Accommodations

From the Trail crossing of Vt. 11 and 30, it is 5.5 miles west to Manchester Center and motels and a hostel. Inns, motels, and tourist homes are on the highway between Manchester Center and Peru, not far from the Trail crossing. From the Trail crossing of the Arlington-West Wardsboro Road, it is 13.2 miles west to Arlington and inns.

Trail Description, North to South

Miles	Data
0.0	From parking area on Vt. 11 and 30, 5.5 miles east of Manchester Center and 4.4 miles west of Peru, cross road. Climb highway bank, and continue through hardwoods and a boulder field. In 0.4 mile, cross stream, overgrown old Vt. 11 and 30, and a powerline right-of-way. Cross another stream, and ascend steeply, passing two vistas, and reach ridgetop. Gradually descend narrow ridge through hardwoods. Cross a woods road and another powerline right-of-way, and ascend.
2.3	Reach side trail leading right 400 feet to Spruce Peak (2,060 feet). Bear left, and continue with minor elevation changes.
2.7	Reach spur trail leading 0.1 mile west to **Spruce Peak Shelter**, with spring 100 feet south of the shelter. Trail crosses small stream in gully, bears sharp left, and ascends toward ridge. It reaches a high point in 0.6 mile and continues, at first roughly level, then descending gradually after a small stream.

4.8   Reach Old Rootville Road. (Road descends west, right, 1.5 miles to maintained road, which leads 0.7 mile to Vt. 11 and 30, 2.0 miles east of Manchester Center.) Directly across the road, blue-blazed spur trail descends west 150 feet to Prospect Rock (2,079 feet), with fine views. Trail turns left and follows road. In 0.9 mile, bear right on smaller road.

5.8   Reach end of dirt road at end of clearing. Make sharp right, and cross bridge. One hundred feet beyond, reach Lye Brook Wilderness boundary and Branch Pond Trail bearing right. (Former A.T., now Branch Pond Trail, leads right to **William B. Douglas Shelter** in 0.5 mile, to **North Bourn Pond Tenting Area** in 3.5 miles; to junction with Lye Brook Trail and **South Bourn Pond Shelter** in 4.1 miles; and to A.T. at Stratton Pond, *via* Lye Brook Trail, in 6.5 miles.) From junction, head east, on or beside old road. In 0.2 mile, bear left off road, then continue to southeast with minor elevation changes. Eventually, enter Winhall River Valley.

8.6   Turn right onto old woods road, and cross footbridge over Winhall River. Trail leaves Lye Brook Wilderness. One hundred feet beyond, make sharp right off road, pass over low knoll into wet area, and ascend northern slope of nameless ridge. In 0.4 mile, reach high point on northern slope; gradually descend south. Cross small stream, and ascend to ridge. Continue with minor elevation changes for some distance, then descend.

10.4 Reach northeastern corner of Stratton Pond. (North Shore Trail leads right 0.5 mile to **North Shore Tenting Area.**)

10.5 Turn left at Stratton Pond Trail Junction. (To right, Lye Brook Trail on southern shore of pond leads 0.2 mile to **Vondell Shelter.**) Climb slightly.

10.6 Stratton Pond Trail leaves right (leads 3.7 miles to Arlington-West Wardsboro Road). Trail continues past spring and beaver pond and descends to brook. Ascend gradually.

11.7 Cross gravel road. In 0.5 mile, cross a brook, and begin a switchbacking ascent of Stratton Mountain, passing a good vista to west and a spring.

13.7 Reach summit of Stratton Mountain (3,936 feet). (Firetower on summit provides unobstructed view of surrounding mountains and countryside. Somerset Reservoir and Mt. Pisgah are to south, Glastenbury Mountain is southwest, and

Taconics, including Mt. Equinox, highest peak of this range, lie to the west. Ascutney Mountain is to northeast, and Mt. Monadnock to southeast. To north are Stratton's North Peak and upper station of Stratton chair lift, reached by an 0.8-mile spur trail.) GMC caretaker may be in residence to assist hikers. Leave summit, heading south, and pass spring.

14.4   Bear right where old, maintained Long Trail/A.T. route continues down ridge. Descend by a series of switchbacks, passing two vistas and the col between Little Stratton and Stratton mountains.

16.0   Cross gravel road, and continue over flat terrain, passing cellar holes and well of old farmstead. Cross woods road, and descend gradually, passing east and south of beaver pond. Follow fairly level route to site of old logging camp (parking area) on north side of Arlington-West Wardsboro Road (Kelley Stand Road). Turn right on this road.

17.5   Cross East Branch of Deerfield River. Reach end of section 200 feet beyond. To continue on Trail, turn left into woods (see Vermont Section Eight).

Trail Description, South to North

Miles   **Data**

0.0   From point 200 feet west of East Branch of Deerfield River, Trail follows Arlington-West Wardsboro Road (Kelley Stand Road) east across bridge over river. Turn left into site of old logging camp where limited parking is available. Enter woods, and follow fairly level route, passing beaver pond. Ascend gradually. Cross woods road; pass cellar holes and well of old farmstead.

1.5   Cross gravel road, and gradually ascend southwestern ridge of Stratton Mountain. Trail follows bench below summit of Little Stratton Mountain to a col between Little Stratton and Stratton mountains. Ascend *via* series of switchbacks, passing two vistas.

3.1   Bear left where old Long Trail/A.T. route comes in from right. Pass spring, and continue ascent.

3.8   Reach summit of Stratton Mountain (3,936 feet). (Firetower on summit provides unobstructed view of surrounding mountains and countryside, and to the northeast, the White Mountains of New Hampshire are visible for the first time for northbound A.T. hikers. Somerset Reservoir and Mt. Pisgah are to south, Glastenbury Mountain is southwest, and Taconics, including Mt. Equinox, the highest peak of this range, lie to west. Ascutney Mountain is northeast and Mt. Monadnock is southeast. To north are Stratton's North Peak and upper station of Stratton chair lift, reached by an 0.8-mile spur trail.) GMC caretaker may be in residence to assist hikers. Wide trail straight ahead follows ridge to northern summit. A.T. bears west (left) just beyond tower. Descend *via* series of switchbacks; pass spring and good view to west. Eventually cross brook, and descend gradually.

5.8   Cross gravel road, and continue gradual descent. Reach woods road, and follow for 0.1 mile. Ascend over small knoll and across brook. Pass a beaver pond.

6.9   Stratton Pond Trail leads to left 3.7 miles to Arlington-West Wardsboro Road. Descend slightly.

7.0   Reach Stratton Pond Junction. A.T. turns right. Ahead, Lye Brook Trail along southern shore of pond leads to a spring in 0.1 mile and **Vondell Shelter** in 0.2 mile. (Beyond Vondell Shelter, Lye Brook Trail is alternate route; leads in 2.2 miles to **South Bourn Pond Shelter** and then, *via* Branch Pond Trail, to **North Bourne Pond Tenting Area** in 2.8 miles; to **William B. Douglas Shelter** in 6.0 miles and back to A.T. in 6.5 miles.)

7.1   Reach northeastern corner of Stratton Pond at trail junction. (North Shore Trail leads to left, continuing around pond to **North Shore Tenting Area** in 0.5 mile and junction with Lye Brook Trail at Stratton Pond outlet in 0.7 mile.) Ascend north from pond, then continue, with minor elevation changes, over two ridges. Descend into Winhall River Valley.

8.9   Make sharp left onto woods road. In 100 feet, cross footbridge over Winhall River. Trail enters Lye Brook Wilderness. Turn left off old woods road, and follow river upstream. Ascend away from river; at top of rise, turn sharply right. Continue with minor elevation changes through several wet areas. Eventually, bear right onto old road. Trend west on, or beside, woods road.

11.7   Pass Lye Brook Wilderness Boundary, and reach trail junction. A.T. turns right. (Branch Pond Trail goes left, south, to **William B. Douglas Shelter** in 0.5 mile, junction with Lye Brook Trail at South Bourn Pond Shelter in 4.1 miles, and A.T. at Stratton Pond, *via* Lye Brook Trail, in 6.5 miles.) Continue 100 feet; cross brook, and turn left onto well-used dirt road. In 0.1 mile, gravel Old Rootville Road enters from right. Follow road west.

12.7   Reach junction. Trail turns sharply right up stone steps, leaving road. (Straight ahead, Old Rootville Road continues 1.5 miles to maintained road, that leads 0.7 mile to Vt. 11 and 30, 2.0 miles east of Manchester Center. To left, blue spur trail descends 150 feet to Prospect Rock, 2,079 feet, with fine views.) Ascend away from dirt road, crossing a small stream. Continue to high point on western flank of ridge, and descend. Turn sharply right, and cross small stream in gully. Continue with minor elevation changes.

14.8   Reach spur trail leading 0.1 mile west (left) to **Spruce Peak Shelter**. Spring is 100 feet south of shelter.

15.2   Bear right. Pass side trail leading left 400 feet to Spruce Peak (2,060 feet). Descend north. Cross small brook and under powerline. Descend, then climb narrow ridge. Descend steeply, then more gradually. Cross a stream and under another powerline. Cross Vt. 11 and 30.

17.5   Reach Vt. 11 and 30 and entrance to parking area, where section ends. To continue on A.T., pass through parking area and onto gravel road (see Vermont Section Six).

Arlington-West Wardsboro Road to Bennington-Brattleboro Highway (Vt. 9)
Vermont Section Eight
22.6 Miles

Brief Description of Section

From both ends of this section, the Trail ascends to and follows a rolling ridge through a wilderness of hardwoods and evergreens to the summit of Glastenbury Mountain (3,748 feet), in the center of the section. The summit is completely covered with tall spruce. The unused firetower at the top, that should be climbed with care, provides a sweeping view of the area.

Between Story Spring Shelter and South Alder Brook, the Trail passes through an area of beaver activity, where the footway may be quite wet. Nonetheless, in dry weather, water may be in short supply along the ridges.

One side trail, the West Ridge Trail, can be used as an alternate route to the A.T. between Goddard Shelter and Vt. 9. It follows a prominent ridge west of the A.T. and is described briefly in the north-to-south Trail description. For complete information on this trail and more information on the area, refer to GMC's *Day Hiker's Guide to Vermont* and the *Long Trail Guide*. Both are available from the Green Mountain Club (see "Important Addresses," page 219).

Road Approaches

At its northern end, the Trail in this section crosses the Arlington-West Wardsboro Road 200 feet west of the East Branch of the Deerfield River. This point is 2.2 miles east of the trailhead of Branch Pond Trail, 4.8 miles east of Kelley Stand, 13.2 miles east of Arlington on U.S. 7, 4.0 miles west of Stratton, and 8.0 miles west of West Wardsboro on Vt. 100. The road is paved for most of its distance east to West Wardsboro but is narrow, graveled road to East Arlington. It is not maintained in winter and spring mud season (mid-May, usually). Arlington-West Wardsboro Road has ample parking near the east branch of Deerfield River.

The southern end of the section on Vt. 9, the Bennington-Brattleboro Highway (ample parking), a major highway crossing the Green Mountains, is 5.1 miles east of Bennington, 2.8 miles west of Woodford, and 4.8 miles west of Woodford State Park. Roadside theft and vandalism have occurred frequently at this crossing. Do not leave valuables in vehicles.

Maps

Map Eight (this guide)
Long Trail Guide

The A.T. route might not be current on the following:
USGS 15-minute topographic quadrangle:
    Londonderry, Vermont
USGS 7½-minute topographic quadrangles:
    Sunderland, Vermont
    Woodford, Vermont

Shelters and Campsites

This section has five shelters, all jointly maintained by USFS and GMC:

Story Spring Shelter: Built in 1963 by GMC; 3.6 miles from northern end of section; accommodates 8; spring 150 feet north on A.T.

Next shelter: north 10.6 miles (Vondell Shelter); south 4.6 miles.

Caughnawaga Shelter: Built in 1931 by Camp Najerog; 8.2 miles from northern end of section; bunks accommodate 4; water from brook 30 feet in front of shelter.

Kid Gore Shelter: Built in 1971 by GMC and Camp Najerog alumni; also 8.2 miles from northern end of section, on 0.1-mile side trail; accommodates 8.

Next shelter or campsite: north 4.6 miles; south 4.3 miles.

Goddard Shelter: Log lean-to built in 1985 by GMC and USFS; 12.5 miles from northern end of section; accommodates 12; spring 40 feet east on Trail.

Next shelter or campsite: north 4.3 miles; south 8.5 miles.

Melville Nauheim Shelter: Built in 1977 by GMC; 1.6 miles from southern end of section; bunks accommodate 8; water available from stream where side trail leaves A.T.

Next shelter or campsite: north 8.5 miles; south 5.9 miles (Congdon Shelter).

Regulations

This entire section passes through Green Mountain National Forest. Camping is not allowed near Hell Hollow Brook. Elsewhere, camp at least 200 feet from water and 100 feet from trails. Fires at designated sites must be built in the fireplaces provided. Elsewhere, use camping stoves. Cutting or damaging living trees and plants is prohibited. Only downed wood may be used for fires. All trash must be carried out.

Supplies and Services

From the crossing of the Arlington-West Wardsboro Road, it is 13.2 miles west to Arlington (ZIP Code 05250, telephone, groceries, bus stop) and 8.0 miles east to West Wardsboro (ZIP Code 05360, telephone, groceries). From the Trail crossing of Vt. 9, the Bennington-Brattleboro Highway, it is 3.9 miles west to a store (groceries) and 5.1 miles west to Bennington business district (ZIP Code 05201, telephone, supermarkets, backpacking equipment, restaurants, laundromat, cobbler, bus stop).

In an emergency, call the Vermont State Police, (802) 442-5421.

Public Accommodations

From the Trail crossing of the Arlington-West Wardsboro Road, it is 13.2 miles west to Arlington (inns). From the Trail crossing at Vt. 9, it is 2.4 miles west to a motel and 5.1 miles west to Bennington (wide range of accommodations). Two motels are east of the Trail crossing in Woodford.

Trail Description, North to South

Miles   **Data**

0.0   On Arlington-West Wardsboro Road, 200 feet west of East Branch of Deerfield River, turn south off road. Descend to brook crossing. Climb to ridge above East Branch of Deerfield River. Follow ridge, with little change in elevation, and reach woods road. Follow woods road to clearing with views of Little Stratton Mountain. Bearing southwest across clearing, follow another woods road.

0.9   Cross Black Brook to woods road, and ascend low knoll, crossing over its broad top. Descend to cross series of beaver ponds.

1.9   Cross USFS 71 (limited parking). Ascend gradually, passing through former logging area.

3.6   Reach **Story Spring Shelter** on left. Bear sharply right opposite shelter, and descend. Pass beaver swamps, and bear left.

4.5   Cross two adjacent branches of South Alder Brook. Bear left 250 feet beyond second brook, opposite old beaver pond, and ascend southwest. Cross shoulder of ridge. Descend, then ascend. Make sharp right below summit of nameless peak (3,412 feet), descend steeply south, and cross several small streams.

8.2   Reach Glen Haven and **Caughnawaga Shelter** on right. Water is available from brook 30 feet in front of shelter. Just beyond, side trail leads left 0.1 mile to **Kid Gore Shelter**. A.T. climbs to ridge, passes Big Rock, and then continues along this long ridge, bearing generally southwest.

12.2 Reach spruce-covered summit of Glastenbury Mountain (3,748 feet). (Abandoned firetower, renovated by USFS, is an observation deck. From tower, one can see Berkshires to south, Taconics to west, Equinox and Stratton mountains to north, and Somerset Reservoir, Mt. Pisgah, and Haystack Mountain to east. *Note:* Camping is not permitted on the summit.) Descend south from summit.

12.5 Reach **Goddard Shelter** with spring, 40 feet east, on A.T. This is last reliable water source until Hell Hollow Brook, 6.7 miles south on A.T. (Blue-blazed West Ridge Trail leaves A.T. at this point and leads 7.8 miles southwest along ridge, with no water on southern half, to Bald Mountain Trail, that Bald Mountain Trail can be followed east and south 2.6 miles to Vt. 9, 1.2 miles west of Trail crossing of Vt. 9, or west 3.5 miles to Bennington.) A.T. descends very steeply east from shelter, then flattens out and follows a ridge for nearly a mile. Trail reaches a large rectangular boulder near the summit of nameless peak (3,150 feet), then descends steadily south, crosses two woods roads, reaches a sag, and ascends.

15.0   Reach Glastenbury Lookout. Ascend south along ridge. Trail swings off ridge, then climbs steeply up western side of ridge. Pass just west of summit of nameless peak (3,331 feet), and descend steadily southwest.

16.8   Pass Little Pond Lookout (3,060 feet), and continue southwest along narrow ridge. Reach summit of Little Pond Mountain (3,100 feet), and continue southward on ridge.

18.2   Reach summit of Porcupine Ridge (2,815 feet). Descend steadily southwest. Pass through balsam and spruce swamp on puncheon.

19.4   Cross bridge over Hell Hollow Brook. (Camping along brook is prohibited.) Cross twin brooks, and ascend southwest. Reach high point east of summit of Maple Hill, and swing right, southwest.

20.5   Cross under powerline, where the line reaches its highest point on southern side of Maple Hill (2,620 feet). (From here can be seen Bennington and Mt. Anthony to west and Mt. Snow, Haystack Mountain, and the northern end of the Hoosac Range to the east.) Descend southward.

21.0   Cross brook. Just beyond, trail leads left 300 feet to **Melville Nauheim Shelter.** A.T. descends gradually southwest, crossing two woods roads.

21.9   Pass through fissure of Split Rock. Pass lookout, and descend steeply, switchbacking, to City Stream, and follow it upstream (left) briefly. Cross stream on William A. MacArthur Memorial Bridge.

22.6   Reach Bennington-Brattleboro Highway, Vt. 9 (1,360 feet) and end of section. To continue on Trail, cross road (see Vermont Section Nine).

Trail Description, South to North

Miles   Data

0.0   On Bennington-Brattleboro Highway, Vt. 9, (1,360 feet), 5.1 miles east of Bennington and 2.8 miles west of Woodford, Trail heads east into woods and crosses City Stream on William A. MacArthur Memorial Bridge. Follow north bank briefly downstream before bearing uphill for a steep, switchbacking climb.

0.7   Pass through fissure of Split Rock. Climb gradually, and cross two woods roads.

1.6   Side trail leads right 300 feet to **Melville Nauheim Shelter.** A.T. ascends north, crossing brook.

2.1   Cross under powerline, where the line reaches its highest point on the southern side of Maple Hill. From this point, 2,620 feet, can be seen Bennington and Mt. Anthony to the west and Mt. Snow, Haystack Mountain, and northern end of the Hoosac Range to the east. Trail reaches high point east of wooded summit of Maple Hill, then descends and crosses twin brooks.

3.2   Cross bridge over Hell Hollow Brook. This is last reliable water until **Glastenbury Shelter.** (Camping along brook is prohibited.) Trail passes through balsam and spruce swamp on puncheon, then climbs steadily northeast.

4.4   Reach summit of Porcupine Ridge (2,815 feet). Follow ridge northeast to lookout. Continue on ridge, descending somewhat, then climb to summit of Little Pond Mountain (3,100 feet). Descend briefly, then continue along narrow ridge.

5.8   Pass Little Pond Lookout (3,060 feet). Continue northeast along ridge. Then, climb steadily toward unnamed peak (3,331 feet), passing just west of summit. Descend steeply northwest along western side of ridge. Grade becomes moderate, and Trail swings back onto the ridge.

7.6   Reach Glastenbury Lookout and connecting ridge to Bald Mountain. Descend north to sag. Cross two old woods roads, and climb steadily. Gain ridge near large rectangular boulder (3,150 feet), and follow ridge for nearly a mile before a moderate, then very steep, ascent.

10.1   Reach **Goddard Shelter**, with spring 40 feet east on the A.T. (Blue-blazed West Ridge Trail leaves A.T. at this point and leads 7.8 miles southwest along ridge, with no water on southern half, to Bald Mountain Trail, that may be followed east and south 2.6 miles to Vt. 9, or west 3.5 miles to Bennington.) From shelter, climb north.

10.4   Reach summit of Glastenbury Mountain (3,748 feet). The abandoned firetower was renovated by USFS as an observation deck. From the tower the Berkshires can be seen to the south, Taconics to the west, Equinox and Stratton mountains to the north, and Somerset Reservoir, Mt. Pisgah (Mt. Snow), and Haystack Mountain to the east. No camping is permitted on summit. From summit, A.T. descends gently north on a long ridge, eventually turning left (north) at a large boulder and descending more steeply, passing south end of shelter loop (below).

14.2   In Glen Haven, a side trail leads right 0.1 mile to **Kid Gore Shelter**. Two hundred fifty feet beyond is **Caughnawaga Shelter**. From shelter, Trail turns sharply right and proceeds 0.4 mile over several ups and downs to a brook, then climbs steeply to an unnamed summit (3,412 feet). Trail then descends gradually northeast and bears right opposite old beaver pond.

18.1   Cross two adjacent branches of South Alder Brook, and begin short, steep ascent.

19.0   Reach **Story Spring Shelter**. Spring is beside Trail, 150 feet north of shelter.

20.7   Cross gravel road, USFS 71. Ascend a low knoll, and descend to woods road.

21.7   Cross Black Brook. Follow woods road to clearing on ridge west of East Branch of Deerfield River, with fine views of Stratton Mountain. Continue along ridge, cross brook, and ascend.

22.6   Reach Arlington-West Wardsboro Road and end of section. Turn right (east) to continue on Trail. (See Vermont Section Seven.)

Bennington-Brattleboro Highway (Vt. 9) to Mass. 2 (North Adams)
Vermont Section Nine
18.1 Miles

Brief Description of Section

This section covers the Trail from Vt. 9 (approximately 1,360 feet) to Mass. 2 (approximately 630 feet). It includes part of the Appalachian Trail in Massachusetts, in addition to the southernmost part of the Trail in Vermont.

The Trail route in the Vermont part of this section passes through rolling hardwood terrain, at elevations ranging from 2,000 to 3,000 feet, but also passes along ridgelines. On the ridge, the route traverses Harmon Hill (2,325 feet) and a nameless ridge (summit is 3,025 feet). In Massachusetts, the A.T. traverses East Mountain (2,340 feet). The Trail also follows logging roads, often passing through lowland hardwood forests. The 965-foot climb from Vt. 9 to Harmon Hill is the steepest of the section.

This section has two side trails, noted in the Trail data. The Broad Brook Trail provides access to the A.T. near Seth Warner Shelter and Primitive Camping Area from White Oaks Road in Williamstown, Massachusetts (difficult stream crossings in high water). Pine Cobble Trail provides access to the A.T. on East Mountain from Mass. 2 in Williamstown. For hikers wishing to pass through Williamstown, Pine Cobble Trail is an alternate route.

For further information on these trails and the A.T. in this section, refer to the *Long Trail Guide,* available from ATC and GMC (see "Important Addresses," page 219). For descriptions of the Pine Cobble Trail and the A.T. south of this section, refer to the *Appalachian Trail Guide to Massachusetts–Connecticut*, available from ATC.

Road Approaches

Both the northern and southern ends of this section are accessible from major highways. The northern end (ample parking) is on Vt. 9, the Bennington-Brattleboro Highway, a major highway crossing the Green

Mountains. The Trailhead is 5.1 miles east of Bennington, 2.8 miles west of Woodford, and 4.8 miles west of Woodford State Park. The southern end of this section is on Mass. 2 at the A.T. footbridge over the Hoosic River, opposite Phelps Avenue, at a point 2.9 miles east of the Williamstown business area, and 2.5 miles west of the center of North Adams. Cars may be parked with permission and at owner's risk at Scarafoni's Ford dealership on Mass. 2, 0.8 mile east of the Trail crossing.

Maps

Map Eight (this guide)
Long Trail Guide
Williams College Outing Club Guide Book
Map One accompanying *Appalachian Trail Guide to Massachusetts–Connecticut.*

The A.T. route might not be current on the following:
USGS 15-minute topographic quadrangle:
  Bennington, Vermont
USGS 7½-minute topographic quadrangles:
  Woodford, Vermont
  Bennington, Vermont
  Stamford, Vermont
  Pownal, Vermont
  Williamstown, Massachusetts

Shelters and Campsites

Two shelters and two campsites with tentsites and toilet facilities in this section are maintained jointly by USFS and GMC.

Congdon Shelter: Shelter built in 1967 by GMC; 4.3 miles from northern end of section; accommodates 8; tentsites on ridge behind camp; water available from nearby brook.

Next shelter or campsite: north 5.9 miles (Melville Nauheim Shelter), south 7.2 miles.

Seth Warner Shelter: Built in 1965 by trainees under Manpower Development Act; 6.6 miles from southern end of section; accommodates 8; water from brook 350 feet west (may fail in dry seasons).

Seth Warner Primitive Camping Area: 200 feet south of Seth Warner Shelter on side trail; tentsites and toilet facilities.

Next shelter or campsite: north 7.2 miles; south 5.3 miles.

Sherman Brook Primitive Campsite: 1.3 miles from the southern end of the section, 0.1 mile west on blue-blazed loop trail; water at spring, southern end of loop trail; tentsites.

Next shelter or campsite: north 5.3 miles; south 4.8 miles (Wilbur Clearing Shelter).

Regulations

Although parts of this section pass through Green Mountain National Forest (GMNF), most of the A.T. is in the state-owned Stamford Meadows Wildlife Management Area. In accordance with Vermont law and GMC/landowner agreements, camping and fires are permitted only at designated sites, even on GMNF and Vermont state lands.

Supplies and Services

From the A.T. crossing of Vt. 9, the Bennington-Brattleboro Highway, it is 3.9 miles west to a grocery store and 5.1 miles west to the Bennington business district (ZIP Code 05201, telephone, groceries, supermarkets, backpacking equipment, restaurants, laundromat, cobbler, bus stop). Less than a mile east of the Trail crossing of Mass. 2 are facilities (telephone, supermarket, fast food, laundromat, hiking equipment). It is 1.0 mile to the YMCA (showers, pool) and 2.5 miles east to the center of the North Adams business district (ZIP Code 01247, cobbler, bus stop). Telephones, restaurants, and a supermarket are west of the Trail crossing. It is 2.9 miles west to the Williamstown business district (ZIP Code 01267, bus stop and all other services except cobbler).

In an emergency, call the Vermont State Police, (802) 442-5421, or the Massachusetts State Police, (413) 743-4700.

Public Accommodations

From the Trail crossing at Vt. 9, it is 2.4 miles west to a motel and 5.1 miles west to Bennington with a wide range of accommodations. Two motels are east of the Trail crossing. In Williamstown, west of the Trail crossing at Mass. 2, are a number of motels.

Trail Description, North to South

Miles   **Data**

0.0   From Bennington-Brattleboro Highway, Vt. 9, (1,360 feet), A.T. climbs steeply west on rock steps. After 0.6 mile, bear southwest, and climb more gradually, eventually reaching clearing.

1.8   Reach open summit of Harmon Hill (2,325 feet). Descend south, cross small brook, pass over low ridge and wide woods road, and descend. Skirt former beaver pond, and descend east.

4.3   Reach **Congdon Shelter** on left. Water is available from nearby brook. Descend east to Stamford Stream, follow it south (right) upstream. Climb away from stream, cross logging road, and gain ridge, then descend to crossing of Sucker Pond outlet brook. Ascend south gradually. Cross woods road. (Right, it is 0.2 mile to Sucker Pond, a public water supply with no swimming or camping allowed; left, 5.9 miles to Vt. 9.)

6.3   Side trail leads 0.1 mile west to Sucker Pond. Climb south.

7.3   Reach northwest summit (2,840 feet) of Consultation Peak. Veer southeast, then south, over several minor knobs.

8.5   Cross Roaring Branch at base of beaver dam. Skirt right side of old beaver pond, and ascend, reaching northern summit of nameless ridge (2,900 feet).

9.4   Pass under north powerline, then reach southern summit (3,025 feet) of nameless ridge. Descend steadily, passing lookout with views.

11.2   Cross Mill Road. (It is 4.0 miles west to the Barber Pond Road and 6.4 miles to Pownal Center and U.S. 7 on nearly impassable roadway. It is 4.2 miles east to Stamford on Vt. 8 and Vt. 100, on road passable by car under favorable conditions.) Pass under powerline shortly beyond County Road.

11.5   Blue-blazed side trail leads right, west, 0.2 mile to **Seth Warner Shelter**. Brook 350 feet to the west has water, except in dry seasons. **Seth Warner Primitive Camping Area** is 200 feet south on side trail.

11.7   Cross narrow, dirt road. (Broad Brook Trail initially follows this road to right, then descends west 4.0 miles to White Oaks Road, 3.0 miles north of Williamstown.) Continue generally south along eastern side of ridge, crossing three former logging roads and two small streams; eventually descend to a more significant brook, then ascend gradually.

14.3   Reach Massachusetts-Vermont state line. (This is southern terminus of Long Trail.) A.T. continues south, and soon leaves woods.

15.1   Reach Eph's Lookout (2,254 feet). Descend south along ridge.

15.7   On rocky knoll, blue-blazed Pine Cobble Trail descends right (0.2 mile to Pine Cobble, 1,894 feet, and 1.9 miles farther to Cole Avenue in Williamstown). Trail makes sharp left, passes to left of marshy pond, and descends steeply and circuitously around an old rock slide, bypassed by bad-weather trail.

16.1   Turn right onto old woods road. In 0.1 mile, reach northern end of campsite loop (see below). Reach old bridge abutments on Sherman Brook. Ascend gradually, away from brook.

16.8   Reach Pete's Spring. Side trail leads right 0.1 mile to **Sherman Brook Primitive Campsite.** Ascend away from brook, then drop steeply to follow Sherman Brook.

17.8   Leave Sherman Brook. Enter private road, and soon enter driveway leading 50 feet to Massachusetts Avenue, that Trail follows to right.

18.1   Turn left, and cross footbridge over railroad tracks and Hoosic River to reach Mass. 2 and end of section. To continue on A.T., proceed straight ahead (south) on Phelps Avenue.

Trail Description, South to North

Miles   Data

0.0   In North Adams, Mass., on Mass. 2, opposite Phelps Avenue, proceed north, crossing footbridge over Hoosic River and railroad tracks. Turn right (east) onto Massachusetts Avenue. Just before reaching stone bridge, turn left up driveway, and, after 50 feet, turn west onto private road. Soon, leave this road, and head north into woods.

0.3　Reach small reservoir on Sherman Brook, and follow brook upstream. In 0.4 mile, make short, steep ascent away from brook, then descend.

1.3　Reach Pete's Spring (side trail leads 0.1 mile left to **Sherman Brook Primitive Campsite**); continue descent. Meet Sherman Brook at old bridge abutments. Bear northwest, and ascend, passing northern end of campsite loop; soon reach old woods road, and follow for some distance.

2.0　Swing west. Bad-weather loop trail leads right. Trail climbs steeply and circuitously around old rock slide (views), rejoins loop trail, and skirts bog.

2.4　Reach high point of open, rocky ridge. (Blue-blazed Pine Cobble Trail descends left 0.2 mile to Pine Cobble, 1,894 feet, and 1.9 miles farther to Cole Avenue in Williamstown.) A.T. bears right, ascending along ridge.

3.0　Near the end of open area, reach Eph's Lookout (2,254 feet, named for Ephraim Williams, founder of Williams College). Just beyond, enter woods.

3.8　Cross Massachusetts-Vermont state line. (This is the southern terminus of Long Trail, maintained by GMC. A.T. and Long Trail coincide to beyond Sherburne Pass on U.S. 4.) A.T. descends gradually northeast from state line. In 0.4 mile, cross brook. Climb to eastern side of low ridge. Follow old woods road for some distance, then bear left; regain ridge with limited views. Cross three former logging roads and two small streams.

6.4　Cross narrow dirt road. (Broad Brook Trail at first follows road to left, then descends west 4.0 miles to White Oaks Road, 3.0 miles north of Williamstown.) A.T. continues north.

6.6　Blue-blazed side trail leads left 0.2 mile west to **Seth Warner Shelter**, with brook (350 feet west) that provides water, except in dry seasons. **Seth Warner Primitive Camping Area** is 200 feet to the south on a side trail. A.T. continues northeast.

6.9　Cross Mill Road after passing under powerline. (Under favorable conditions, this road is passable by car to the east. It is 4.0 miles west to Barber Pond Road and 6.4 miles west to Pownal Center and U.S. 7. It is 4.2 miles east to Stamford on Vt. 8 and Vt. 100.) Climb steadily northeast, pass lookout, and reach summit of nameless ridge (3,025 feet). Follow ridge north.

8.7　Pass under powerline and then over northern summit of the nameless ridge (2,900 feet). Descend, sometimes steeply, to north; follow along left side of old beaver pond.

9.6　Cross Roaring Branch at base of beaver dam. Pass over several minor knobs.

10.8　Reach Consultation Peak (2,840 feet). Descend.

11.8　Side trail leads 0.1 mile west to Sucker Pond (public water supply; no swimming or camping allowed). Cross woods road (to left, it is 0.2 mile to Sucker Pond; to right, it is 5.9 miles to Vt. 9). Descend gradually, heading generally north, to Sucker Pond's outlet brook. Ascend ridge, and cross logging road, then descend to Stamford Stream, and follow down, eventually bearing left and ascending.

13.8　Reach **Congdon Shelter**, with water available from nearby brook. Ascend ridge behind cabin, skirting area of former beaver activity. Gain low ridge, and cross a wide woods road and, after a level stretch, cross a small brook, and ascend again.

16.3　Reach open summit of Harmon Hill (2,325 feet). To north are Bald and Glastenbury mountains. Veer east across clearing, enter woods, and descend. Soon bear right, and drop very steeply on rock steps.

18.1　Reach Bennington-Brattleboro Highway (Vt. 9) and end of the section. To continue on Trail, cross road into woods (see Vermont Section Eight).

Important Addresses

Appalachian Mountain Club
Pinkham Notch Visitor Center
Box 298
Gorham, NH 03581-0298
(603) 466-2727

Appalachian Mountain Club
5 Joy Street
Boston, MA 02108
(617) 523-0636

Appalachian Trail Conference
P.O. Box 807
Harpers Ferry, WV 25425
(304) 535-6331

Appalachian Trail Conference
New England Regional Office
18 on the Common, Unit 7
P.O. Box 312
Lyme, NH 03768-0312
(603) 795-4935

Dartmouth Outing Club
Robinson Hall, Box 9
Hanover, NH 03755
(603) 646-2428

Green Mountain Club
Rural Route 1, Box 650
Vermont 100
Waterbury Center, VT 05677
(802) 244-7037

Green Mountain National Forest
231 North Main Street
Rutland, VT 05701
(802) 747-6700

White Mountain National Forest
719 North Main Street
Laconia, NH 03246
(603) 528-8721

Emergency Numbers

AMC Pinkham Notch
Visitor Center
(603) 466-2721

Massachusetts State Police
(413) 743-4700

New Hampshire State Police
(603) 846-5517
(603) 846-3333

Vermont State Police
(802) 875-2112
(802) 773-9101

Map Sales

USGS Earth Science
Information Center
(703) 648-6892
(202) 208-4047

Summary of Distances

51.0	Mt. Washington	260.0
52.4	**Lakes of the Clouds Hut**	258.6
56.4	Mt. Pierce (Mt. Clinton)	254.6
57.2	**Mizpah Spring Hut, Nauman Tentsite**	253.8
58.9	Mt. Jackson	252.1
60.3	Mt. Webster	250.7
63.6	Crawford Notch State Park, U.S. 302, **Dry River Campground**	247.4
66.5	**Ethan Pond Campsite** side trail	244.5
71.3	**Zealand Falls Hut**	239.7
72.5	Zeacliff side trail	238.5
75.5	Mt. Guyot, **Guyot Campsite** side trail	235.5
77.5	South Twin Mountain	233.5
78.3	**Galehead Hut**	232.7
80.5	**13 Falls Tentsite** side trail	230.5
81.0	**Garfield Ridge Campsite** side trail	230.0
84.9	Mt. Lafayette, **Greenleaf Hut** side trail	226.1
85.9	Mt. Lincoln	225.1
86.6	Little Haystack Mountain, **Lafayette Place Campground** side trail	224.4
88.7	**Liberty Spring Tentsite**	222.3
91.3	Franconia Notch State Park, U.S. 3	219.7
94.2	**Lonesome Lake Hut**	216.8
96.1	**Kinsman Pond Campsite** side trail	214.9
96.7	North Kinsman Mountain	214.3
97.6	South Kinsman Mountain	213.4
100.1	**Eliza Brook Shelter** side trail	210.9
103.0	East Peak, Mt. Wolf	208.0
107.6	Kinsman Notch, N.H. 112	203.4
109.2	**Beaver Brook Shelter** side trail	201.8
111.4	Mt. Moosilauke	199.6
116.0	**Jeffers Brook Shelter** side trail	195.0
117.1	N.H. 25, Glencliff	193.9
119.1	Wachipauka Pond	191.9
119.6	Mt. Mist	191.4
122.1	N.H. 25C	188.9
125.1	Atwell Hill Road	185.9
126.9	N.H. 25A	184.1
131.8	**Hexacuba Shelter** side trail	179.2
137.1	**Firewarden's Cabin**	173.9

137.2	**Smarts Mountain Tentsite** side trail	173.8
137.6	Lambert Ridge Trail	173.4
142.9	Lyme-Dorchester Road fork, Dartmouth Skiway	168.1
143.8	**Trapper John Shelter** side trail	167.2
144.3	Holts Ledge side trail	166.7
146.3	Goose Pond Road	164.7
149.7	**Moose Mountain Shelter** side trail	161.3
154.6	Etna-Hanover Center Road	156.4
156.0	Trescott Road	155.0
158.5	**Velvet Rocks Shelter** side trail (west end)	152.5
160.5	Dartmouth College, Hanover, N.H.	150.5
161.0	Connecticut River, N.H.-Vt. Line	150.0
166.3	**Happy Hill Shelter**	144.7
169.7	Tigertown Road at Podunk Road, I-89	141.3
169.9	Vt. 14, West Hartford, Vt.	141.1
170.3	White River Bridge	140.7
173.6	Joe Ranger Road	137.4
175.1	**Thistle Hill Shelter** side trail	135.9
177.4	Cloudland Road	133.6
179.2	Pomfret-South Pomfret Road	131.8
181.4	Woodstock Stage Road	129.6
182.9	Vt. 12	128.1
186.8	**Wintturi Shelter** side trail	124.2
191.1	Lakota Lake Lookout	119.9
192.1	Locust Creek and Chateauguay Road	118.9
196.3	**Stony Brook Shelter** side trail	114.7
201.4	Thundering Brook Road (north Trailhead)	109.6
202.2	Vt. 100, Gifford Woods State Park	108.8
203.6	Junction with Long Trail, Tucker-Johnson Shelter	107.4
204.2	U.S. 4, Sherburne Pass	106.8
206.7	**Pico Camp**	104.3
209.6	**Cooper Lodge**, Killington Peak Trail	101.4
213.7	**Governor Clement Shelter**	97.3
215.1	Upper Cold River Road	95.9
216.7	Cold River Road (Lower Road)	94.3
219.0	Lottery Road	92.0
219.4	Beacon Hill	91.6
219.9	**Clarendon Shelter** side trail	91.1
221.1	Vt. 103	89.9

221.2	Clarendon Gorge, Mill River Bridge	89.8
223.8	**Minerva Hinchey Shelter** side trail	87.2
226.4	Vt. 140	84.6
227.4	Sugar Hill Road	83.6
228.3	**Greenwall Shelter**	82.7
229.1	Trail to White Rocks Cliff	81.9
233.0	**Little Rock Pond Shelter**	78.0
233.1	Homer Stone Brook Trail	77.9
233.5	**Little Rock Pond Tenting Area**	77.5
233.7	**Luia Tye Shelter**	77.3
235.5	Danby-Landgrove Road	75.5
236.8	**Big Branch Shelter**	74.2
237.0	Old Job Trail (north end) to **Old Job Shelter**	74.0
238.5	**Lost Pond Shelter**	72.5
240.5	Baker Peak	70.5
242.4	Griffith Lake (northern end)	68.6
242.6	**Griffith Lake Tenting Area**	68.4
243.1	**Peru Peak Shelter**	67.9
244.4	Peru Peak	66.6
246.1	Styles Peak	64.9
247.5	Mad Tom Notch, USFS 21	63.5
249.5	Bromley Mountain (main summit)	61.5
252.0	**Bromley Tenting Area**	59.0
252.8	Vt. 11 & 30	58.2
255.1	Spruce Peak side trail	55.9
255.5	**Spruce Peak Shelter** side trail	55.5
257.6	Old Rootville Road, Prospect Rock side trail	53.4
258.6	**William B. Douglas Shelter** side trail	52.4
261.4	Winhall River footbridge	49.6
263.2	Stratton Pond, North Shore Trail to **North Shore Tenting Area**	47.8
263.3	**Vondell Shelter** side trail	47.7
266.5	Stratton Mountain	44.5
268.8	Arlington-West Wardsboro Road	42.2
270.3	East Branch of the Deerfield River	40.7
273.9	**Story Spring Shelter**	37.1
278.5	**Caughnawaga & Kid Gore Shelters**	32.5
282.8	**Goddard Shelter**	28.2
285.3	Glastenbury Lookout	25.7
287.1	Little Pond Mountain	23.9

Acknowledgments

Special thanks go to former field editor Jim Barnes of Norwich, Vt., ATC Regional Representative Kevin Peterson, Assistant Regional Representative J. T. Horn, and David Hardy of the Green Mountain Club.

Thanks also go to the Appalachian Mountain Club; Earl Jette, Chuck Wooster, Kevin Stone, Teri Balser, Ann Schrot and Jim DeCarlo of the Dartmouth Outing Club; Brian T. Fitzgerald of the Green Mountain Club; Peter Richardson and Ed Janeway, for providing badly needed information and advice on the Trail; Fred Kacprzynski of the White Mountain National Forest; and Nort Philips of the Manchester District of the Green Mountain National Forest.

Acknowledgment should be made to the Maine Appalachian Trail Club for permission to use in revised form the material for the Mahoosuc Range in Maine from *Appalachian Trail Guide to Maine*.

Index

AppalachianTrail Conference
P.O. Box 807
(799 Washington Street)
Harpers Ferry, West Virginia 25425

(304) 535-6331
1-888-AT STORE (publications orders only)
<www.atconf.org>

Open 9 a.m. – 5 p.m. weekdays all year
(except Christmas, New Years Day)
Weekends & holidays, 9 a.m. – 4 p.m.
mid-May through October

Memberships
Individual – $25
Family – $30
A.T. Maintaining-Club Members – $18
Senior Citizens (65+) – $18
Full-time Students – $18

Appalachian Mountain Club
5 Joy Street
Boston, Massachusetts 02108

(617) 523-0636
<www.outdoors.org>

Memberships
Individual — $40
Family — $65
Senior (69+) — $25
Junior (<23) — $25

The Green Mountain Club
Rural Route 1, Box 650
(Route 100)
Waterbury, Vermont 05677

(802) 244-7037
<gmc@sover.net>

<www.greenmountainclub.org>

Memberships
Individual — $27
Family — $35
Sponsor — $45
Defender — $70
Protector — $100
Nonprofit or Youth Group — $30